*A quiet residential street in Rome belies the hectic pace of the modern city.*

# CULTURE SHOCK!

## Rome
### At your Door

Frances Gendlin

**Graphic Arts Center Publishing Company**
Portland, Oregon

**In the same series**

| | | | |
|---|---|---|---|
| Australia | Hong Kong | Philippines | London at Your Door |
| Bolivia | India | Singapore | Paris at Your Door |
| Borneo | Indonesia | South Africa | |
| Britain | Ireland | Spain | A Globe-Trotter's Guide |
| Burma | Israel | Sri Lanka | A Parent's Guide |
| California | Italy | Sweden | A Student's Guide |
| Canada | Japan | Switzerland | A Traveller's Medical Guide |
| Chile | Korea | Syria | A Wife's Guide |
| China | Laos | Taiwan | Living and Working Abroad |
| Cuba | Malaysia | Thailand | Working Holidays Abroad |
| Czech | Mauritius | Turkey | |
| Republic | Mexico | UAE | |
| Denmark | Morocco | USA | |
| Egypt | Nepal | USA—The | |
| France | Netherlands | South | |
| Germany | Norway | Vietnam | |
| Greece | Pakistan | | |

Illustrations by TRIGG

© 1997 Frances Gendlin
Reprinted 1998

This book is published by special
arrangement with Times Editions Pte Ltd
Times Centre, 1 New Industrial Road, Singapore 536196
International Standard Book Number 1-55868-306-2
Library of Congress Catalog Number 96-77241
Graphic Arts Center Publishing Company
P.O. Box 10306 • Portland, Oregon 97296-0306 • (503) 226-2402

Printed in Singapore

# CONTENTS

# ACKNOWLEDGEMENTS

This book could not have been written without the participation of my colleagues both in the United States and Rome. That the information is so varied is certainly owing to their suggestions, and the book is more complete for their kind participation. This is not to say that any mistakes are theirs; they are mine alone. All guide books, no matter how current, suffer from outdated information, and for a city that used to claim it never changed, Rome is making up for lost time. Although perhaps eternal, Rome is like any modern city – moving on. Thus, although materials were current at publication, it shouldn't be surprising to find some information already changed.

Andrea Cetta devoted much time and consideration, working diligently on all aspects of the material, checking information, proofreading, and making valuable suggestions throughout. Anna Maria Cetta patiently chauffeured me through terrorising traffic to all corners of the city, commented on the first draft, and made useful suggestions as well. Maureen B. Fant, Sally Silvers and Lorena Leopizzi reviewed parts of the manuscript, making constructive comments. My appreciation and gratitude go to all and especially to Yolanda Bernadini and Phebe Archer, who read and checked the final drafts.

Thanks to Katherine Vossen and Steve Wilson for encouraging my love of Rome; to Luca Setti, Riccardo Wallach, Fiorella Simoni and Luigi Balis-Crema, Antonello and Rossella Cetta, Paola Mori, Brad Bloomer, Patricia Alagna, and Allan Jacobs for conversations about life in the Eternal City; to Rabbi Abramo Piattelli for information on the Jewish community and to Michael De Nola for introducing me to his family. And to my own family for their encouragement and support.

# INTRODUCTION

*While stands the Colosseum, Rome shall stand; when falls the Colosseum, Rome shall fall; and when Rome falls, the world*
— St. Bede, 8th century

## ROME—EXPECTATIONS AND REALITY

The first guidebook to Rome was published more than a thousand years ago. The *Einsiedeln Itinerary*, named for the Swiss monastery in which it was found, dates from the 9th century; along with detailing eleven holy walks around the city for sojourning pilgrims, showing routes from St. Peter's to other cathedrals, it describes many facets of Rome that must have been indispensable to a new arrival, from information about the city's gates and towers to the location of public latrines. This and other early guides, known collectively as *Mirabilia Urbis Romae (Marvels of Rome)* were copied and reissued throughout the late Middle Ages, continuing for centuries to acclimatise new sojourners to a city and culture that had already been evolving for a thousand years, a city that took some getting used to, even then.

By the time of these early guides, religious pilgrims had been making the journey to Rome for many hundreds of years: the first official basilica of St. Peter's was begun in AD 324, after Constantine's conversion to Christianity, and it was built over the spot where the remains of the martyred St. Peter had been buried by early Christians more than two hundred years before. Constantine's conversion officially opened Rome to Christianity and thus to the religious travellers who have been swelling the population of the city ever since. Some holy years have seen upwards of a million pilgrims in Rome, but every year hundreds of thousands continue to come, some briefly and others to stay longer, to renew their spiritual contact with the Church, by now almost two thousand years old.

## ROME: THE PLACE TO BE

Non-religious pilgrims have also sojourned here, if not to pay homage to the Church, at least to experience in a secular way what had once been the *caput mundi*, the capital of the world, and to inspire their arts amid its spectacular beauty and seductive Mediterranean charm. Shelley wrote *Prometheus Unbound* seated in the Baths of Caracalla, painter Ingres was the director of the French Academy in Rome, and Lord Byron wrote parts of *Childe Harold's Pilgrimage* after visiting the Colosseum at night; it was he, in fact, who translated St. Bede's statement above into English from the Latin. Goethe lived in Via del Corso, and Keats in a house on the edge of the Spanish Steps: both quarters are now museums. Rome has inspired composers as well, such as Hector Berlioz who wrote *Roman Carnival* and Franz Liszt, the *Fountains of Villa D'Este*. The list could go on. But it was the poet Robert Browning who summed it up: "Everyone soon or late comes round by Rome."

Even before the advent of Christianity, the long period of the Imperial *Pax Romana* saw an influx of commercial and diplomatic traffic into the city, creating industries and vast import/export markets by land and sea, but above all, courting power. Imperial Rome, the *caput mundi*, encompassed all the Mediterranean lands and extended to the Danube to the north. The Empire prospered: bridges were built, roads were extended, and lodgings and services to host the people coming to gain favour of one sort or another became a staple of Rome's commercial life. About a million people lived in Rome; no other capital in the world would be so complex and extensive for more than another thousand years. Rome was the place to be.

## MODERN ROME

If today this is not exactly true, Rome still remains a presence on the international scene, although quite changed: a world capital steeped in its glorious past, somewhat confused in its present, and moving fitfully toward its future, as it must. If its international importance is somewhat dimmed, it nonetheless remains a significant destination for modern-day religious pilgrims, artists, scholars, and this century's multinational traders. Thousands of foreigners are making Rome their home, whether working, studying, writing, painting, or just enjoying the Roman way of life. Rome is the seat of the United Nations Food and Agriculture Organization, major banks have commercial branches here, multinational firms have offices, and there are hundreds of international enterprises, large and small. The American Academy and the British School welcome their countries' scholars each year, university students come for their semesters abroad, and clerics of all nationalities work and study at the Vatican for months at a time.

I too have been a sojourner in Rome off and on for years, and anecdotes about my first extended stay are by now part of the saga of my life. Being an organised person and having tried before my departure to make sure every detail was arranged correctly, I thought when I arrived in Rome I would be able to start directly on my work.

*The modern and the ancient stand side by side in many Roman districts.*

But I soon discovered that my residence hotel that had advertised "direct dial" for its telephones required dialling zero to get the outside line, something I hadn't considered when planning how to access my E-mail; I couldn't get it to work. Over the next few days I called the E-mail carrier, the communications software and computer companies as well: their interest was limited, their suggestions few. I tried the Italian phone company and the E-mail support lines, leaving messages and waiting for people to call back. Some did, some didn't, and some offered enthusiastic advice directly opposite to that of the person before. Some said that it was impossible with my computer, others suggested I call someone else, but right now he'd be out to lunch, and when I finally reached him he wasn't the right person at all.

My Italian, adequate in most situations, was strained in discussing details of modems and bauds. Finally, after several days and only because I persisted, not letting anyone hang up until I had at least been told someone else to call, I learned the code sequence needed to bypass the Italian dial signal and the procedure for getting the outside line. Had I not persisted in this and in several other instances where my planning was inadequate, I would not have succeeded in the work I came to do. Nor would I have decided to write this book to help other people coming to Rome get acclimatised to the city more quickly than I — and many others before me — had done.

Tourist guides generally put forth Rome's ever-fascinating history, and they list the most interesting sights, the best restaurants and most comfortable hotels. They try to present the material in an eye-catching manner the others don't, and they each offer an approach of their own. All, however, have one thing in common: they are designed for people visiting for a short while and then moving on, not those who are coming to stay.

This book, different in approach, starts where tourism ends, and it is designed to offer specific advice and assistance about daily life in Rome for those coming to stay awhile, including examples of a representative variety of needed services and shops. Whether the *permanenza* is for a month or two or a year or two, the type of information needed for a successful, enjoyable stay will be deeper and more detailed than that of tourist guides. Where and how to look for appropriate housing, how to manage finances, how to stay healthy and where to get fit, and indeed how best to access the Internet, buy a computer, find temporary offices, or even a children's school or the best hamburger, are but a few examples of information found here that should help you become a part of this complicated yet marvellous city. Getting used to any new city takes time, but Rome, so traditional in attitude, yet coping with so many modern changes, may take more time — and ingenuity — than one may suspect.

Much of your success will depend on your expectations as to what life should be like in Rome. As you will quickly see, life here is a balancing act, and Romans excel in *l'arte d'arrangiarsi*, the art of figuring out how best to make do. A newcomer's preconceived ideas may not always materialise into fact, and it's best to arrive with few expectations that life in Rome is more-or-less like that at home, except for the language. It isn't. Every culture has its own characteristics and attitudes; each city has its particular approach to life. Start from scratch and take Rome as it is: love its beauty, enjoy its agreeable differences, adapt to its peculiarities, cope with its difficulties, and simply try to live life *alla romana*. It's a pleasure few foreigners get to have, and it will be a pleasure if you let it be so. Romans themselves remember what Rome once was, despair of what it is becoming, and take for granted its eternal charm. Some foreigners have lived here so long they have taken on Roman attitudes, for Rome, like any large capital city, can often be wearing; yet others manage somehow to keep a sense of balance throughout their stay and appreciate the adventure that is Rome. But suggesting that you simply try to live like a Roman is probably misleading, for very little about life in Rome is simple at all.

Imagine living in a city whose founding was April 21, 753 BC. In America the Declaration of Independence wouldn't be signed for another two thousand years, and by that time many ruins of ancient Rome were being uncovered and some already restored. Imagine living in a city founded a thousand years before clocks were invented, and even more than that, before the Norman Conquest. Such is Rome, a city whose two thousand years of history are evident on almost every street, yet whose modern inhabitants seem to have their feet planted firmly in the 20th century — but the 19th and the 18th centuries as well.

## WHEN IN ROME ...

*"Paese che vai, usanza che trovi,"* is Italian for "When in Rome, do as the Romans do." Yet it's much easier said than done. Ask three Romans chatting at a *caffè* how to find a place you're looking for and you might get several decisive yet different answers, leaving the group still deciding after you've gone on your way. It isn't that Romans don't know their city or how it works, for they do, within their own particular spheres. It's that in Rome all the spheres, large and small, are changing, and it takes some manoeuvring to figure out how to do whatever it is that is needed, and it might well be hard to explain or find. And, in truth, if you get answers at all these days, you might get two different responses from the same person — whether in a business, shop or government office — on two different days. Or none at all.

The residents, of course, with a particularly Roman kind of fatalism, take all of this for granted, and after a while, you should too. Not everything runs smoothly, to say the least. People work on high-tech computers in ancient *palazzi* now turned into modern offices, but the turn-of-the-century elevator may not be reliable. They wait for modern public transportation next to some of the most ancient ruins in town, but the buses are crowded and sometimes don't stop. They dine on sites where perhaps Julius Caesar did too, although the tourists have now discovered them, and on weekends they drive out into the countryside on roads 1500 years old, repaved many times over, but not much wider.

So don't be surprised if you're almost late to hear a lecture on advanced communications technology only to find you're the first one there and not even the lecturer has arrived. Don't be surprised to see a group of young Romans laughing and lingering over dinner at a cafe in the ancient Campo de'Fiori, and then to realise that at any given moment, more than half of them are talking into their cellular phones. But don't you be late for a meeting, and don't you get up in the middle of a meeting to make a phone call somewhere else. It won't make you look good.

*Anche l'occhio vuole la sua parte,* is a saying meaning 'appearances count.' This is nothing new to Rome. In terms of the physical, women of ancient Rome were buried with their finest jewellery, and even today the art of looking good, *fare bella figura,* is important in indicating that all is well. Even more important, though, the appearance that life is proceeding smoothly and that all tasks will be done on time is what is important to convey, despite all evidence to the contrary, and this is the true 20th century spectacle, the Roman equivalent of 'the show must go on.'

## THE ETERNAL CITY

Clinging fiercely to this rather uneasy equilibrium, Romans used to describe their city as eternally unchanging: *"Roma non cambia mai,"* they said, but no longer, for they now say that all is changing, and of course, for the worse. Having survived since World War II by plying *l'arte d'arrangiarsi,* Romans now seem uncertain as to how this should manifest itself. And it is certainly true that Italy seems in flux. *Tangentopoli,* the kickback scandal that overturned the traditional political structure in the early 1990s, ousted government officials from the top down to local levels, and Italy has not yet produced a stable, unified government. *Mani pulite,* the 'clean hands' operation, is trying valiantly to sort out exactly who did what, but although some two thousand people have been charged with corruption — including several former prime ministers — only about three hundred have been tried, and it is said that just one person is actually in jail. Italians understand the need for constitutional and political reform, a new start, but agreement on procedures and goals has yet to be reached. Yet the government is promulgating modernised laws, making efforts to simplify the bureaucracy, trying to adhere to austerity budgets and reduce the national debt, and by means of privatisation, slowly reducing its dominant role in the economy.

Adding urban issues to the mix, Rome is striving to maintain its ancient and agreeable Mediterranean traditions, yet forced in the doing to adapt to the 20th century. Rome has formally instituted several new revitalisation projects — *Roma per te* (Rome For You), *Roma per Roma* (Rome for Rome) and *Centopiazze* (One hundred piazzas) — designed to restore the city's beauty, improve its infrastructure, enhance its services and ultimately modernise the quality of life. Streets are being repaved and piazzas restored. Permits are now required to drive into the medieval Centro Storico, and although traffic and parking remain difficult, they are improving. Experiments continue with pedestrian zones in the tourist parts of the city, including the central piazzas, and where pollution has eaten into the ancient ruins and monuments, they are being restored. The repairs to major traffic arteries will certainly help in the long run, although they are causing some short-term traffic disruptions.

A Great Jubilee planned for the year 2000 will bring added construction to parts of the city for the next few years. To make Rome better suited to handle the thirty million pilgrims expected to mark the beginning of the third millennium of Christianity, there is planned a new subway stop near the Vatican, a refurbishing of the Vatican's own railroad station, an underpass across the Tiber, a new pedestrian zone, and a much-needed multilevel parking lot. Public transportation is to be improved and extended, the Colosseum is being repaired, the Campidoglio is being worked on, the four major basilicas are being restored. Preparations also include the cleaning of museums and other churches throughout the city, adding hotel rooms and enhancing telephone service. All these efforts, although creating some temporary disorder, will be of lasting benefit to Rome. Even now, improvements to the bus lines are taking place, buildings seem cleaner, the city seems less polluted, and in another few years all this should be more evident.

In the meantime it's easy to understand that Romans might not be sure how to get to a particular street, although they probably knew the week before. Rome is changing. In terms of telephone numbers, for example, the numbers in this book were current as of publication date. In most guides this would be a brief disclaimer, but here it is important, for it is only one indication of Rome in the process of change. Telephone numbers are being standardised at eight digits from the traditional six or seven, so they may not be the same as when you called a week before. One woman expressed frustration that her friends hadn't been calling her, only to find that her number had been changed without notification to her. In fact, if here you see a telephone number of six or seven digits, valid at time of printing, note that soon it too will change.

Laws too are changing, and even those affected don't always know what is current: the requirements for prescriptions at pharmacies, for example, previously lax, are now tightening, and some medicines are no longer available over the counter that were a few months ago. The cover charge in restaurants has been abolished; some eating establishments bring bread only upon request, others charge separately for it, and many just absorb it into the price of the meal. Yet the changes are significant in that they form part of a modernisation of the societal outlook: in 1996, for example, a law was finally enacted that recognised rape as a crime against a person and punishable as such, and not just against some vague morality. Other laws change, but may not be noticed: since 1975 smoking has been banned in Italian museums, libraries and hospital corridors, and since 1980 on airline flights. In 1996 smoking was banned in all public buildings, except restaurants and bars, but people continue to smoke and few object.

## GOING WITH THE FLOW

Just take Rome in stride and adapt to its rhythm. Shops open around 9:30 am and stay open until 1:00 pm or 1:30 pm, when a three-hour standstill shuts commerce down. Except for the shops that are open 'nonstop.' Stores open up again in the late afternoon and close early evening, perhaps 7:30 pm or 8:00 pm. Except for government offices which close at 2:00 pm and don't reopen at all, except that a few of them do. Groceries close Thursday afternoons in winter and Saturday afternoon in summer; markets are open only in the morning and fish markets two days a week. Other shops stay closed Monday mornings, unless it summer, when they too close Saturday afternoon. Unless it's August when much of everything is closed anyway.

A few shops here and there are beginning to open on Sunday, but so far only a few. And banks? Most banks are open weekdays until 1:30 pm and then again for about two hours sometime later in the day, unless it's Thursday before a weekend holiday, when they take a long weekend break. Most official functions use the 24-hour international clock, although people in conversation do not. Thus, a train might leave at 17:40 or a television program might begin 20:35. Also, Daylight Savings Time may not start or end with dates that coincide with your country, so time differences will fluctuate depending on the date.

And then there are the strikes. One-day strikes just to call attention to a problem are common, and although they can cripple transportation including international air travel for a day or so, or leave the financial centres closed, they are announced in advance, so people can make do. Contributing to all this, the Romans themselves wouldn't consider standing in line when there's a crowd; they push forward, instinctively knowing somehow when it is their turn.

All of this requires *pazienza*, and if Romans have mastered it, so can you. The current watchwords in Rome are *fai da te*, or 'do it yourself.' Figuring out what you need, figuring out how to get it, and then pursuing every course until success is in your grasp, is the key long-term residents have found to successful living in Rome.

Patience pays off, for Rome, paradoxical city that it is, remains a splendid place to live. The sunlight of Rome has a dreamy southern quality that tempers its faults, and it is the same sunlight that warmed the Forum of the Caesars. Here is perhaps the only major city in the world where you can experience in your daily life the continuity of time moving ever forward in its cycles. Here cool, comfortable apartments are housed in restored medieval palazzi and the freshest of food is sold in markets hundreds of years old. A hidden trattoria with a beaded curtain for a door can surprise you with the quality of its food, all *fatto a mano*, prepared in house. Good water can still be drunk from spigots in the streets, and unusual aromatic breads are baked according to traditions and in ovens centuries old.

Rome the Eternal enters one's life at every step, yet technological conveniences are not lacking, and they make living among 2000 layers of history easier than one would think possible; conversely, these layers of history in everyday life make the pace of modern living more agreeable. Today's life is still lived outdoors in the same ancient piazzas as generations before, and the Mediterranean atti-

Photo: K. Griffiths and A. Lister

*The piazza has always been at the centre of Roman street life.*

tude toward life can warm the soul. Here the extended family —
parents, siblings, children, uncles, cousins, in-laws, cousins of in-laws
— is still the focus of people's lives and people retain forever friend-
ships formed in school days. Ties are long and deep, yet there is
always room at the table for a new friend to join in.

If, however, it takes some time to become a real part of the
*tessuto sociale*, the fabric of Rome, it is partly because as everywhere else, people are busy with their own agendas and their own
way of exercising the *arte d'arrangiarsi*. But it is more than that:
over the ages the city has seen regimes and conquerors come and
go, and Popes who change the city plan only to have the next one
change it again. As former Prime Minister Giulio Andreotti is
quoted as saying, "The history of the city through the centuries,
with its endless string of events, which contains everything and
the reverse of everything, makes it difficult to shock or surprise a
Roman."

Through all its changes, its people have survived, carrying
on. If some people seem brusque on first acquaintance, it is only

because they have seen it all, including the hordes of tourists who have taken over their town, of which they will at first think you're a part. But if you let it be known that you are here to stay — at least for a time — and if you are game to try out your Italian, proficient or not, they will go out of their way to be friendly. When I first approached shopkeepers in Rome, saying I was planning to list their services in a new guide to Rome, I was surprised to be asked coldly, several times, how much they would have to pay. After I explained that there would be no fee, the mood changed and I got all the information I could use, as the now-friendly conversations went on at length.

Yet if Romans are friendly and encouraging it doesn't mean, in the complexities of their culture, that you should address new acquaintances with the familiar *tu*. Some — especially younger people — call everyone *tu*, yet others are offended if you get familiar too soon. Pay attention to each situation and especially in business dealings, use last names until you're given some indication that it's time to open up. In shops or restaurants, you will be addressed formally, and you should respond the same way. You won't hear strangers casually saying *Ciao* to each other; it's *buon giorno* for hello, and *arrivederci* — or the even more formal *arrivederla* — for goodbye. Women of any age may be surprised to be addressed as *signora*, married or not. The lack of instant familiarity connotes not unfriendliness, but respect.

## SAFETY IN ROME

In fact, people should understand that Rome is a surprisingly non-violent city. Because of the reputation of Italian men as making unwarranted sexual advances to women, it may be difficult at first for women to understand that Rome may be safer than their own city at home. Apart from the occasional pickpocket, especially in the tourist areas, or a late-night mugging near Stazione Termini, there is little true violence in Rome, and, with care, just about any neighbourhood is safe enough to traverse. Roman men, notorious for their amorous heckling of women, actually do only that; if they're ignored or made to understand they're not wanted, generally — admittedly after some annoying persistence on their part — they'll go away.

Nonetheless, normal precautions are important, as they are at home. Don't carry your keys and your address together, don't carry a lot of extra cash or credit cards, and don't flaunt expensive jewellery. Know where you're going and take the most public route to get there. Fortunately, crimes in Rome are generally against property and not against persons themselves; unfortunately modern conditions require vigilance. Even the gangs of little children that frequent the tourist areas do no more than steal a wallet or purse, if they can. Do not let yourself be distracted by one child while another is picking your pocket. Keep conscious hold of your purse on the most crowded of buses or metros in the tourist centre, and do not keep a wallet in a back pocket.

Adhering to the above, I never had any real problem, not at any time of day nor in any neighbourhood. Using my research as an excuse to wander unannounced in every corner of the city, I had many pleasant adventures traversing unknown streets, trying unusual pasta combinations in trattorias I might never find again, discovering fountains, courtyards and alleyways no tourist guides describe.

Pity the poor visitor who sees the obvious sights in the tourist guide, walks the standard routes, and then moves on, never grasping what is truly eternal about Rome. I think that in my wanderings I have begun to make a dent, and now you have the opportunity to start out on this same journey of discovery: you'll find it well worth the effort. *In bocca al lupo* — good luck. And *benvenuti a Roma* — welcome to Rome.

# Chapter One

# THE CITY

## ROME'S LIVING HISTORY

Rome is one of the great cities of the world. While it may no longer be the *caput mundi*, evidence that it once was the capital of the world is in every street, on every corner, in every alley. Just look around. There's more first class art visible in Rome than in any other city, from the Bernini fountains in the squares Romans walk through every day on their way to work, to the Sistine Chapel that tourists line up to see almost every day of the year, There's more history on view than in any other major city, from ruins of marble pillars from Imperial Rome lying serenely undisturbed next to a major bus hub, to the medieval city gates, still the best entrances into modern Rome, and even to the everyday streets themselves, some — such as Via Appia and Via Cassia — dating back more than fifteen hundred years. Yet Rome is by no means a museum. Its ancient monuments and streets are nestled into its modern daily life, and its daily life is continually enlightened by its illustrious past.

# ROMAN GEOGRAPHY

It seems strange that Rome lies on about the same latitude as New York, for its climate is distinctly different, distinctly Mediterranean. Life is lived outdoors for most of the year, at the piazza cafe, under the trattoria umbrella, during the late afternoon stroll, the *passeggiata*. Summers are hot, but there's often a seasonal breeze, the *ponentino*, that does its best to mitigate the stifling heat. Winters are cool and damp, not excessively cold, but that season's wind, the *tramontana*, can make it feel so. There are no skyscrapers in central Rome, and no building in the centre is higher than the dome of St. Peter's. But it's a hilly city — founded on the famous seven, and now encompassing more than twenty. It's also a city of layers, and although on a first visit much of its charm seems readily on view, so much more is hidden that it would take years of adventurous exploration to fathom it. Its more than three million inhabitants don't bother: they bustle through their daily lives, skirting the artifacts, ignoring the art, drinking their coffee and chatting in ancient piazzas, understanding the city only because it is their own. For a newcomer, this would be a waste, for coming to know Rome, step by step, *passo passo*, should be one of the pleasures of the stay.

Although Rome may seem the antithesis of city planning, it should at least become slightly understandable by following its history: knowing which areas were formed in ancient, medieval or recent times, which streets were cut through others and when, why the names of some streets change in the middle, why some houses have numbers inconsistent with those on either side. And why, even if it seems incomprehensible, the city — from its ancient core to its modern suburbs — remains as liveable as other world capitals, more modern and specifically planned.

One reason Rome remains so liveable is that the city has never become industrialised; only the third largest industrial city in Italy, none of its industries are in the city centre, the largest being to the east at Tiburtina, to the south at Magliana and Laurentina, and further at the towns of Pomezia and Latina. Generally, the major Italian-owned industries are headquartered to the north. Instead modern Rome remains a draw for tourists, scholars and students, the political and bureaucratic centre, and the holy destination for tens of thousands of pilgrims each year.

It is these three aspects of modern Rome — tourism, bureaucracy, religion — that demonstrate its history, on view in every street. Ancient Rome was clustered around the Forum, whose ruins can be visited near the river. The commerce and administration of medieval Rome centred in the narrow streets of the Centro Storico, as it does today. And religious Rome, historically centred around St. Peter's and what is now the Vatican, made an even more indelible mark on the development of the entire city.

## THE RELIGIOUS INFLUENCE

If the city can be thought of as having three periods, the ancient, papal and modern, then much of today's city's plan still bears the evident legacy of papal, baroque Rome. Then it was evolving into a city of holy destinations and the means to get to them. Think of the Popes coming from St. Peter's to their basilicas, San Giovanni in Laterano or Santa Maria Maggiore, and imagine the concourses needed to allow their progression. Then you will understand the straight streets such as Via Merulana, leading directly from one basilica to the other, or Via Giulia designed under Pope Julius II to bring him from the Tiber into the heart of Rome; think of the *palazzi* built by the wealthy to be near these processional streets. Think too of the thousands of pilgrims coming for Holy Years and absolution of sins, and the principal gates of ingress needed to process them. Then you will understand the Porta del Popolo, for example, the entry into Rome from the North, and the streets Pope Sixtus V planned to link the city gates. And last, think of the services needed by these pilgrims — the inns, stables, public baths,

TOURISM    BUREAUCRACY    RELIGION

markets — and you will understand the development of the areas adjacent to the gates, and in fact the development of the Rome one sees today.

## THE TIBER

The city is built toward the mouth of the meandering 396-kilometre Tiber, which from ancient until recent times controlled the daily life of what had been a basically Mediterranean port city.

Only 30 kilometres from the ancient port of Ostia, life revolved around this river that winds leisurely through the city, mostly to good commercial effect, but sometimes the city was inundated and its commerce interrupted: in 1598 some 1500 people died from the flood. On some building walls near the river you can see marble depictions of how high the water reached during the periodic floods. High enough and often enough that embankments were built at the end of the last century, stopping the flooding and allowing the city to grow cohesively, but distancing the river finally from everyday occupation. As the city expanded and more people moved away from the low-lying areas, the river played a less important role and today, polluted and distanced from the

27

populace, swimming is prohibited and fishing is discouraged. Yet this may be changing: water pollution is monitored, sewage dumping is banned and purification plants are in operation.

Rome had by the end of the last century existed for two millennia, contracting and expanding until it finally almost burst after 1870, when it became the capital of the newly united Italy. Although pilgrims had always been a staple of the Roman scene, the unification brought a new wave of immigration from the rest of Italy. A *gran febbre* of construction was begun, a fever that changed the character of the entire city. Neighbourhoods were created out of nowhere, buildings quickly erected where previously there had only been green fields. Job seekers of all sorts found employment, and they stayed and mingled to become the Romans of today. The city, even then a hodge-podge of ancient and medieval streets and dwellings, became more so, as hastily constructed neighbourhoods and roads intermingled with ancient, narrow streets, as new layers were added to the old, as more arteries were carved through those straight Papal concourses, by now ancient in themselves.

If Rome and Italy prospered, the city and its swelling population did not, and in the 1930s, Mussolini embarked on a deliberate plan to restore the glory of Rome. This, unfortunately, included destroying some of that very glory in the process. Construction of the wide modern boulevards — Via dei Fori Imperiali and Via della Conciliazione, as well as the central Piazza Venezia — while creating major new arteries through the city, dispossessed thousands of Romans of their longtime homes, destroying beautiful ancient squares and famous old churches as well. Even some of the Roman Forum itself was buried forever under the modernisation designed to glorify the city's past. Fascist architecture — dramatic monolithic square structures with oversized windows and doors — dominated, especially at the Foro Italico, at the University of Rome, and in EUR, a 'new Rome' begun by Mussolini to showcase an unrealised World's Fair, but largely a pleasant office and residential district today.

Now the important arteries, ancient, medieval and recent, lead to the Piazza Venezia; major streets from all directions converge there, skirting the 1885 marble monument to Vittorio Emanuele II, sometimes disparagingly called the 'wedding cake' or 'typewriter.' **Via del Corso** comes from Piazza del Popolo to the North; **Corso Vittorio Emanuele II** from the west toward the Vatican, turning into **Via del Plebiscito**; **Via dei Fori Imperiali** from the south past the Colosseum; and the westerly **Via Nazionale** from Piazza della Repubblica and Stazione Termini. No matter where you live, no matter what means of transportation you choose, these arteries will bring you directly to the heart of Rome.

# ESTABLISHING CRITERIA FOR YOUR NEIGHBOURHOOD

Choosing an area of the city to live in requires careful planning. Of course the criteria will fit the purpose and duration of your visit and your own particular style. If, for example, you are doing three months' research at a particular library, you may wish to be within walking distance. If you seek quiet, a 15-minute Metro ride to a comparatively peaceful part of the city should be considered; in fact, proximity to public transportation should always be taken into account. For families, access to schools and parks will come into play. Thus, establishing your own criteria for the right neighbourhood comes first.

Before you begin though, remember that life in Rome — as in any large city — is a balancing act and that Romans excel in *l'arte d'arrangiarsi*, the art of figuring out how best to make do. If the city sometimes seems to be held together only by sheer determination, and if Romans fight the traffic, complain about the constant noise, lament the rising prices and declining services, and head out of town every weekend they can, they still wouldn't live any other place. Life in Rome will work best if you realise that occasional compromise is a fact of life, and that it's easier just to shrug off less important issues and insist only on those that count. In the long run, a dose of the Roman fatalism will help.

Once you've determined your priorities, finding the right neighbourhood shouldn't be difficult; in one way or another, any can be appropriate. Any area that you find appealing to look at, to walk through, to visit more than once, should be considered. Not much in Rome is hidden: there are few 'bad' neighbourhoods (around the Stazione Termini comes to mind), but if you happen to enter one, you'll realise it immediately. Each quarter — each street — has its own characteristics and quirks, its conveniences and annoyances. Some are expensive and plush, others crowded and lively; some are residential and peaceful, a few seemingly never sleep. Romans live in all of them — in every street, alley, and corner — from verdant, peaceful **Parioli** to the tourist-crowded **Centro Storico,** in large walled-in gardened villas and in small cramped apartments above that area's shops.

As in any crowded, traffic-burdened city, Romans consider it a priority to be near a park or other open space. Large green parks dot the city maps, and many smaller ones provide a shady refuge on a summer day. Villa Borghese and Villa Ada are easily accessible to much of the city east of the Tiber; to the west, the Gianicolo and Villa Sciarra can be reached from Trastevere and Monteverde, as can Villa Pamphili, Rome's largest park. Monte Mario is to the northwest.

## High on the Hills
In this regard, too, the hills are important, cool respites and strategic positions from ancient times. The Palatine, Rome's oldest inhabited hill, was home to kings, emperors and popes for more than a thousand years. Even now, trying to mitigate the stifling summer heat, many people who can afford it live on hills, in the

most elegant neighbourhoods, where the air is relatively cool and fresh. The original seven hills, of course, were (reading clockwise) Quirinale, Viminale, Esquilino, Celio, Palatino, l'Aventino and Campidoglio. Now within the city confines there are some twenty hills, among them Monteverde, the Gianicolo, and Monte Mario (the highest in the city) to the west, and east of the river, Monte Parioli and Pinciano, Monte Antenne, and even Monte Testaccio, the ancient artificial hill made of pot shards. Some, such as l'Aventino, are still, two millennia later, among the most sought after residential parts of Rome.

## Considering Transport

Yet getting to these hills or to any part of town requires thinking about transport. Even for Romans, who seem born attached to their cars, being near public transportation is a must, for traffic is intense and parking in many areas difficult. If you are near the Metro, you are connected to central Rome. From EUR at the south to the Vatican, from Piazza di Spagna to Tuscolana, from Trastevere to Nomentana — much of Rome is no more than a short subway ride away. Buses run to all areas; with a monthly pass assuring transfer from one to the other, all of Rome is accessible. Look at the Bus/Metro map to see which buses and metros go to the neighbourhood you are considering; look to see if more than one bus goes there, for a variety of directions for transport is optimal. In the centre you won't need a car for everyday use.

Some popular residential areas do require a car, and this then requires a major decision: whether you want to take on the stress of daily driving into Rome. If you are coming for a few months, you can rent a car for the few weekends you'd like to explore the countryside. If you're going to stay a year or two, you will have to decide whether you want a car, which, although creating other problems, will broaden your possibilities for residence and lifestyle. The development of new condominium complexes

around Via Cassia to the north has made the northern areas attractive to Romans and expatriates alike. The areas around **Tomba di Nerone**, **Giustiniana**, and **Olgiata** all sport many of the conveniences of downtown Rome — shops, hospitals, markets — and they are near several of the international schools making them popular for young families. Olgiata even has its own golf club and a mini-mall.

These spread out areas have a distinctly suburban feel, with larger homes, quieter streets, greener areas. Near to the city's ring road, if you have a car you can get around the city easily and use the services and commercial centres on the periphery. But in truth, to live here you must have a car, and most of the newer apartment complexes have protected parking facilities. Yet, the Cassia leading into the centre itself is still, after 1500 years, a narrow road with congested traffic, making a daily commute, no matter how short in miles, long in time. And, once you're home in the suburbs, you probably won't want to get into your car in the evening to head back into the city for an evening out. Nor will your friends who live in the city centre want to fight the traffic to come and see you very often. Nonetheless, these northern areas are developing quickly, providing an agreeable suburban lifestyle.

In the same situation to the south is **Casal Palocco**, near
Fiumicino and more convenient to EUR and the industries centred to the south. A newly planned suburb of two-storey gardened
villas, swimming pools and tennis courts, and a shopping centre,
it feels like any modern housing development. Suburban type services are fairly close, and some of the international schools are
nearby. Yet this area also requires a car: the COTRAL buses shuttle residents through heavy traffic to EUR, and from there the
metro provides access to the city centre.

Cars are also necessary for living in some of the newly popular areas closer in: **Monte Mario** is a large, cool, and airy residential district at the northwest edge of the city, with modern apartments and private villas, and is an upcoming area. **Vigna Clara**,
**Fleming,** and **Colli della Farnesina**, all now considered a part of
the urban centre, are residential and welcoming, offering blocks
of spacious condominiums with leafy trees and gardens, some with
swimming pools or even tennis courts. They are also close to the
international schools. Although being closer in than the suburbs,
bus rides into the centre during rush hours can seem intermina-
ble, and having a car is important. Two areas closer in, **Parioli
and Pinciano**, are especially coveted, for they offer the attractions of the city centre and proximity to major parks, yet with
their gardened villas and quieter streets, they retain the feel of
quiet remove so attractive in the more suburban areas, but it's
important to have a car.

The neighbourhoods closer in — **The Centro Storico, Prati,
Trastevere, Ludovisi, Salario, Colosseo, Esquilino** — although
noisier, more polluted, and more crowded, are the heart of Rome.
Walking about the city centre day after day is the way to understand
Rome, for it is a city to discover almost by chance — the hidden
alley, the unexpected fountain. In the centre is where you'll find
Romans living as their ancestors did, and here is where you'll be best
able to take part yourself. And getting where you're going in just ten

minutes by walking or on public transit is a not-insignificant advantage. Restaurants to be explored in every hidden corner, the cobblestoned and picturesque streets to be traversed more than once, the new friends you'll greet as you head to the daily market — all will help make life in Rome a pleasant adventure.

Whatever neighbourhood you're considering, look at it, wander around, and observe the life there. Are there inviting bars, shops, groceries and a market within walking distance? How would your child get to school? Would you be able to go out for a pizza or to see a film without having to use public transportation or a car? How's the traffic and the noise? Are there major bus lines and a Metro stop nearby? Is the piazza nearby welcoming and accessible? This is important in a city that has historically lived out of doors. Look also at the neighbourhood adjacent. No matter which zone you choose, it will be worthwhile to check on what's nearby: the downtown districts overlap and services not offered in yours may actually be quite close.

## KNOWING THE RIONI

Rome was divided in 10 BC by Augustus into 14 *regio*, then redivided into 22 *rioni* in medieval times, all within the Aurelian Walls. Many of the zones are still called by their ancient names, although with bisecting streets cut through over the centuries, new zones were created; now inside or outside the ancient walls, they're all called *quartieri*, and there are more than 35. To the south is EUR, and to the north are the suburbs mentioned above. Today these are all just neighbourhoods, some more convenient than others, depending on your criteria.

Officially, Rome is divided into 20 *circoscrizioni*, which are administrative and tax districts in which each resident of that area is registered; this number is due to be consolidated to 13. Unlike the Paris *arrondissement* system, however, circoscrizioni are purely administrative, and Romans identify their neighbourhood by name.

Graphic by John Zaugg

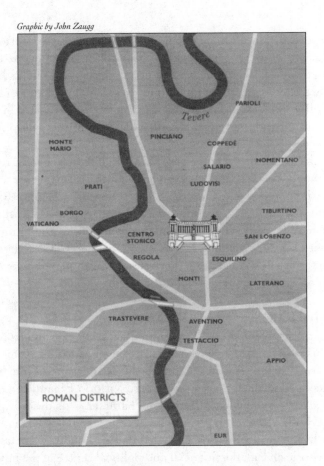

The **Centro Storico**, the *rioni* of the **Renaissance Quarter**, **Prati**, **Pinciano**, and **Parioli**, central and close to every service and convenience, are among the most expensive areas. Still toward the centre are **Ludovisi**, near Via Veneto and **Salario** just to its east; in each you can find a range of housing options, both moderate and expensive. **Trastevere**, an ancient and formerly bohemian yet still lively section, can find some moderate rents, although newcomers are turning this, too, into a trendy area.

**Monteverde Vecchio**, peaceful and green, is close to Trastevere but a world apart. The workers' districts of **San Lorenzo** and **Tiburtino** near the university, national library and medical centre, are filled with student hangouts, have a political atmosphere, and offer moderate rents. Moderate too are the areas around the **Colosseum** and the **Lateran**, with a local atmosphere despite the ever-present tourists.

L'**Aventino**, one of the original seven hills, is a coveted neighbourhood, relaxed and elegant; just south is **Testaccio**, totally opposite in character. Others such as **Fleming** or **Monte Mario** have many amenities, including their altitude — but as mentioned, they may be somewhat less convenient for those commuting to the city centre. Each one has its own advantages. Of course not all areas are described here; there should be enough, however, to form an understanding of what the city has to offer.

## Centro Storico

The area from Piazza del Popolo to Piazza Venezia and from the Spanish Steps to the Tiber is the medieval centre of Rome, the **Centro Storico**. It also comprises the **Renaissance Quarter**, a dense, wedge-shaped area past Corso Vittorio Emanuele II, but that area — somewhat different in character — is described below. Here, however, is a mixture of tourists and Romans in an area lively and exuberant, crowded day and night, yet retaining its historic charm; the financial and political centre of the modern capital; and large modernised apartments in centuries-old *palazzi* that make it a convenient and exciting area in which to live.

Centro Storico refers to an area that included the **Campus Martius** in ancient Rome. This district dominated Rome in the middle ages, and does so today. Here are **Piazza del Popolo**, the entrance to Rome for medieval pilgrims from the ancient Via Flaminia; beautiful **Piazza di Spagna**, dominated from above by the 16th century Trinità dei Monti and from below by 20th century tourists; **Piazza della**

**Rotonda**, home to the Pantheon and the ending point for a warren of narrow medieval streets; and **Piazza Navona**, begun as a stadium about AD 86 by Emperor Domitian, but from the middle ages to the last century the city's main market square — and today, some say, despite the influx of tourists each day, still the heart of Rome. Modernised throughout the millennia, but somehow escaping the periodic frenzies of destructive development, the piazzas and side streets of the Centro Storico are much as they have been for centuries, and today's modern shops and restaurants merely take the place of many that came before.

Only parts of the Centro Storico are true residential areas for Romans, although every apartment is inhabited, many by a fifth or sixth generation occupant. Some apartments — restored or remodelled — are owned as investments by foreigners who rent them out; others are lived in by politicians, writers, or film stars. Some out-of-the-way corners such as the artists' street Via Margutta hold charming residential enclaves, but rental apartments here are rare to find. So are those around the Pantheon, somehow dense with tourists and those who want to live near here as well. The area toward the south and the Corso Vittorio Emanuele II and Via del Governo Vecchio see some Renaissance palazzi with elegant apartments within, but many of these now house offices and commercial enterprises.

But the Centro Storico remains, as it has for centuries, the downtown area — the **Centro**, where much of the work of the capital is done. Here are the Rome stock market and the Senate, government and private offices, and the Romans with their businesses to serve the tourist trade. Given the number of tourists in the area, the late-night restaurants, and the tight security around the area near the Senate, this remains a good area for walking day or night, safe excepting the occasional pickpocket. Restaurants abound, as do some gentle piano bars; but the raucous nightclubs are elsewhere, meaning that this area closes down slightly earlier than some of the others.

The late Saturday afternoon *passeggiata* of Roman youth takes place along Via del Corso, the ancient road that extended from Piazza del Popolo toward the Pope's basilica in Rome. Ultimately everyone comes to the Centro, so every type of shop and convenience is within walking distance. Some narrow streets like Via Laurina near Piazza del Popolo, maintain a row of local food shops and indeed, the varied and well-stocked daily market in Piazza Monte d'Oro services all parts of the zone, and Via della Croce, near Piazza di Spagna, is convenient with its take-away food shops.

This is not one of Rome's verdant neighbourhoods: few trees, no parks. The **Pincio** can be reached by climbing up from Piazza del Popolo, and the river winds along the district's western edge. The cafes in the piazzas — famous or not — are good for relaxing along with the countless tourists, but contacts with nature in the Centro are sparse. Air pollution and noise from the heavy traffic can be unpleasant, although the new traffic control efforts are beginning to make some headway in this regard.

In fact, this is not an area in which to think about keeping a car. A permit is required to drive into the Centro Storico, and parking is difficult. Yet public transportation is available to all parts of the city. The electric minibus #119 makes a circuit around the area itself, and buses head up the Lungotevere Marzio, down Via di Ripetta and the Corso, on Corso Vittorio Emanuele II at the southern edge, and north past Piazza del Popolo at Piazzale Flaminio. The metro also stops at Piazza di Spagna and Piazzale Flaminio.

Apartments are scarce but becoming available, yet rents can be steep. But in the balancing act of Rome, this remains one of the most interesting and convenient areas of the city.

## Renaissance Rome: The Ghetto to Via Giulia
Corso Vittorio Emanuele II essentially separates Renaissance Rome (**Regola**) to its south from the medieval Centro Storico above. Winding from the river toward Piazza Venezia, this now

commercial street was from the 15th century an important papal artery. Now as Corso Vittorio, widened and redone during the rapid development of the late 19th century, it is crowded with traffic, lined with shops, and at Largo Argentina, confused with ancient ruins competing with a bus and taxi hub. On either side remain the narrow, winding streets and inhabited palazzi that were mercifully left untouched by the development. On the north are the Piazza di Spagna, Piazza Navona and Piazza del Popolo, just described. To the south — in what is a small, dense amount of space — lie the old Jewish Ghetto, Campo de' Fiori and Via Giulia, all interesting, lively and liveable, all developing during the centuries of the Renaissance, yet all distinctly different in character.

In 1555, Pope Paul IV forced some 5000 Roman Jews into a swampy, low-lying area near the Tiber, creating what is now known as the **Ghetto**, and ending what had been a long period of tolerance. Centuries of abuse followed, relaxing only after the unification of

Photo: Pomponi/Photoreporters

*Campo de' Fiori in the Renaissance Quarter, a lively and liveable area with plenty of history.*

Italy and rising again during World War II. Now the Ghetto is a thriving village, expensively shabby in its own way; the narrow dark passages opening onto the broad piazzas see remodelled modern apartments above old, cluttered shops, and modern Romans eating out or shopping in the bakeries and groceries, all with a still ancient and Jewish flavour. The Ghetto is an attraction for Romans and tourists alike. Lines form at the neighbourhood bakery late each afternoon when the *ricotta e visciole* fruitcake is ready, and the Roman-Jewish restaurants always draw crowds.

Although only a small number of Roman Jews live here, it remains the heart of the Jewish community, and the evenings see friends sitting outside and chatting, while children play nearby. Other Romans are moving in, and foreigners are buying apartments, too, raising property values considerably. This area remains as safe as any to traverse, partly owing to the 24-hour security provided by police who guard the main Rome synagogue (bombed in 1982), and partly because the neighbourhood has become so chic. From the Teatro di Marcello to Via Arenula, the Ghetto's western border, the area is one of the most sought after districts.

The streets on the other side of the wide Via Arenula — a commercial artery leading from Ponte Garibaldi to Largo Argentina — head vivaciously toward the famous Campo de' Fiori and Piazza Farnese, its neighbour. The major street in this direction is Via dei Giubbonari, typically Roman, with retail shops and trattorias thriving at the bottom of the palazzi. Campo de' Fiori itself holds the city's most famous market during the day, and in the evenings it hosts much of young Rome — eating in the pizzerias, sipping in the pubs and wine bars, going to the cinema, or just hanging out below the looming memorial to Giordano Bruno. Well lit, crowded, exuberant, this piazza is the most secular in Rome — not a church in sight.

Until the 15th century, the Campo de' Fiori was a meadow or field of flowers, as the name suggests. With the return of the Papacy from Avignon, however, the area saw new inns and commercial enterprises serving the pilgrims who returned, as well. A residential area sprang up upon its edges and still exists today. Artisans came and stayed, courtesans came and went, and the piazza was even used for public executions, including especially Bruno, the heretic who dared venture that the earth was not the centre of the universe. This remains a fascinating, hectic area day and night. Everything you need can be found within a hundred yards. There are still small hotels and artisans, shops of all kinds, delicious bakeries, interesting groceries and old trattorias — all essentially Roman despite the tourists who know this is a square not to be missed. Everything can be found around here and much of Rome comes to find it.

Just below is Piazza Farnese — strangely empty and elegant — gently reminding one that this was home to the city's aristocrats in the 16th century. In the surrounding streets — especially those like Via Pettinari — are grand Renaissance palazzi that lend testimony to the once luxurious atmosphere of the quarter. Now Piazza Farnese is primarily home to the French Embassy, housed in the gracious Palazzo Farnese. Quiet and serene, in aristocratic contrast to the constant activity of its neighbour, Piazza Farnese opens on its north to Via di Monserrato, a spare residential street with remodelled palazzi and its own rather staid demeanour.

The back of the Palazzo Farnese looks out onto Via Giulia, a 16th century fashionable street connecting St. Peter's to central Rome. Once one of Rome's most strategic streets, it begins at the ivy-covered Farnese Arch, which the Farnese family began as a bridge across the Tiber to connect two of its large land holdings. The bridge never materialised, but Via Giulia takes off from here, remaining a popular residential area of the city, inhabited by younger, professional Romans in spacious tranquil apartments. Via Giulia itself is a straight cobblestoned street. Despite the clothing and antique shops, it somehow remains peaceful, surprising in an area so dense. A bar here and there or an interesting shop front breaks up its otherwise stark demeanour.

41

Although there is every convenience and every shop in this area, there are no parks, no green spaces for kids. The area is packed with cars despite the traffic restrictions, and parking is difficult. Most streets are narrow and some are one-way. Public transportation to all parts of the city, however, can be found on the edges, on the Lungotevere and especially at Largo Argentina, on the Corso Vittorio.

And the Corso Vittorio itself, noisy and crowded, almost explodes at Largo Argentina, a chaotic, transportation hub, yet also the site of ruins so ancient that Julius Caesar was assassinated nearby. Corso Vittorio is the strategic thoroughfare between the two areas that make up the Centro Storico. It's easy to go from one to the other, to find your way in their intense sets of narrow, angular streets, and to find what you want in either of the districts that the busy street bisects. Despite seeing a deluge of tourists, these two districts that make up the Centro Storico remain the heart of Rome.

## Prati and the Borgo

An extremely pleasant and convenient quarter between the Vatican and Piazza del Popolo across the river, **Prati** is one of the most comfortable and hospitable residential districts directly in the centre of Rome. Within walking distance of the Palace of Justice and the Vatican, and on several bus lines as well as Metro A, this is a genteel, liveable neighbourhood with some tranquil tree-lined streets, and with all services and conveniences at your door.

Although close to St. Peter's and a base for pilgrims over many centuries, Prati began to flower only in the late 19th century, when after the unification it was caught up in the influx of bureaucrats coming to work in the newly created capital. In fact, the Regina Margherita bridge, connecting Prati to Piazza del Popolo was constructed only in 1891. Having been developed so recently has allowed Prati's streets to be more grid-like, more even, more navigable. Now the tree-lined broad streets boast elegant, well maintained palazzi with large apartments within — many built around World War I — offices, interesting stores, and a generally energetic atmosphere. Despite being so close to the Vatican and its constant wave of tourism, this remains a true Roman area, since it lacks ancient ruins, historic churches and other tourist attractions. It also lacks the boisterous nightlife of Trastevere, its neighbour to the south.

A solidly professional area, the residents here remain bureaucrats and officials, office workers of one sort or another who want a quiet neighbourhood and all conveniences, yet with close proximity to the centre. Thus, despite being so central, this is a family neighbourhood, although with little open space; mothers bring their children to squares such as Piazza Cavour at the beginning of Via Crescenzio, and to the small attractive park toward the south, near Castel Sant'Angelo.

The main east-west thoroughfare, Via Cola di Rienzo, stretches from Piazza della Libertà at the river to Piazza del

Risorgimento, the major bus terminus near the Vatican. This busy street is named after a flamboyant demagogue of the 14th century who led a revolt against the nobles, proclaiming Rome a republic. Calling for a united Italy, he ultimately ran politically afoul of the powerful city states and of the Pope. Excommunicated then restored, in and out of prison and power, he was eventually murdered. Now this street named for him is home to good quality shops of all sorts and an excellent covered market, the large Standa Department Store and supermarket, several cinemas, and the luxurious gourmet shops, Franchi and Castroni. A popular and crowded area, Via Cola di Rienzo and side streets are filled with double-parked cars; apartment buildings don't necessarily have garages, and public parking barely exists.

Heading north from Cola di Rienzo's end at Piazza del Risorgimento is Via Ottaviano, another major commercial street with a variety of services and shops, almost of the same quality. At its northern end is Piazza Mazzini, named after the 19th century founder of *Giovane Italia*, a group of young idealists trying to establish a unified Italy, and who was one of the early rulers of the Republic. A major commercial hub, yet with few tourists and typically Roman, the piazza also services a residential district including Piazza Bainsizza to its north.

And to the south is what was formerly known as the **Borgo**, stretching from the river and Castel Sant'Angelo to the Vatican. The name is from the Anglo-Saxon *burgh*, for town. Since the 9th century, it has been a warren of small streets and alleys in a walled area that protected the inns and hospices for pilgrims who stayed in the shadow of St. Peter's. Unfortunately, in 1936 Mussolini decided that St. Peter's needed a more prestigious, grandiose approach, and, as a gesture of reconciliation with the Papacy, began construction on the wide, straight Via della Conciliazione, dispossessing the inhabitants, destroying old piazzas and changing the atmosphere of the Borgo forever. Nonetheless, the small streets on both sides of Via della Conciliazione — those that escaped Mussolini's eye — remain interesting to explore. There are still some apartments and residential services, and there are many good moderately priced restaurants. Street names that start with *Borgo* instead of *Via* will be in this area.

The Vatican itself, on its 108 acres, provides good services to the area. Its post office is efficient, its pharmacy carries international medications, and in general the shops in its shadow are welcoming to foreigners. The thousands of Romans who come to work at the Vatican every day, the religious events, and the constant stream of tourists, keep this area busy every day of the year.

## Trastevere

When a Roman boasts *"so' trasteverino,"* more is meant than being a person who just happens to live in **Trastevere**. It means membership in a tightly-knit group of Romans who base their ancient heritage here, claiming that Trastevere is the oldest, most authentic section in Rome, the most Roman of anything and everything that is Rome. And it is true that if this isn't the exact oldest section of the city, it certainly comes close. There was already an Etruscan settlement here in 509 BC, when King Tarquinius Superbus was expelled and the Roman Republic declared. By the time of the Second Punic War in 218 BC, Rome was expanding, and

45

Trastevere was infused with dock workers, sailors and the services needed to maintain what was becoming the city's port. Jews came as merchants from the Middle East to settle here, building their first synagogue and thriving until the 16th century when they were forced into the Ghetto. Trastevere boasted the strongest gladiators in the Roman Empire, and nobles kept their gardens and orchards here, as street names such as Via degli Orti di Cesare attest. In decline after the fall of the Empire, Trastevere began again to assert itself as the workers' and artisans' quarter around the 12th century and has continued to maintain this character. Although the erstwhile poverty and violence of such a district can occasionally still be seen in some of the narrow, dark back streets, Trastevere today is one of Rome's most lively areas.

Bounded on the north by the Janiculum Hill, modern Trastevere winds itself south along with the bend in the river and ends across from the Testaccio area at Circonvallazione Gianicolense and the Ponte Testaccio. Trastevere is one district with many faces: distinctly separate neighbourhoods, for example, are created by the generally north-south Viale Trastevere, the area's most commercial street. To the east is the older neighbourhood with its small groceries, old apartments with flower-potted balconies and apartment projects, with Trasteverini working still in the warehouses and workshops and by the river front. Here too is Rome's famous flea market, Porta Portese, that is a Sunday draw. To the west is the Trastevere of restaurants and discos, of trendy shops and galleries, yet a residential and commercial district, as well.

To the north is John Cabot University, situated off Via della Lungara, another straight Papal road, on which wealthy Renaissance Romans constructed their homes. Now the university has created a different atmosphere at this end of the district, with pensioni, bars, inexpensive restaurants and services created for the student population.

After the War, many of the old Jewish families came back to Trastevere, and among the ubiquitous Catholic churches, you'll find a thriving Jewish community. There's also an Indian section, and Americans and British are finding apartments here and settling in, making Trastevere the most multi-cultural area of Rome. Still nonconformist, still independent, Trastevere has an atmosphere all its own.

The action of Trastevere centres around several piazzas, especially the lovely Piazza Santa Maria in Trastevere, home to the city's oldest official church, founded in about AD 220. By day Trasteverini pass through the traffic-free square on their way to work, stopping in one of the many bars nearby for their caffeine jolt and a chat with friends. By night, this is the recognised meeting place for locals and visitors alike to head for the nightlife — restaurants, clubs and bars — that is steadily taking over the area. And just to the south, Piazza San Cosimato hosts a varied, daily food market, crowded with the Trasteverini by day, and by night also a thoroughfare for people on their way to the restaurants and clubs. Others such as Piazza Trilussa and Piazza della Scala, with enoteche, pubs and pizzerias, also come alive in the evenings.

Trastevere is close to some of the city's major parks, lovely for strolling, relaxing, and in the case of the Janiculum to the north, for some of the best views of Rome. Villa Doria Pamphili — Rome's largest park — is to the west, and the Villa Sciarra, with its fountains and statues, is in the heart of the district. Rome's Botanical Gardens are also here.

So in its cobbled alleys and unexpected parks and piazzas, Trastevere creates a melting pot of the ancient and the modern, of tourists and locals, of tranquillity and noise. Next to a small expensive restaurant will be an old family-run trattoria, both packed with Romans from all areas of the city. Next to an artisan shop with exquisite workmanship will be one that sells electronic games, and next to one that sells expensive gifts to tourists will be a shop that caters efficiently to local needs. Junkies walk the same streets as fun-loving tourists, but the crowded, rowdy streets in the evenings turn into serious work places by day.

Apartments in the newly-trendy areas are being spruced up and rents spruced up as well, although some good prices can still be found. Buses and trams make this accessible to any other part of the city. But since everything you might want, from Porta Portese's flea market on Sunday to some of the city's most expensive restaurants, is in Trastevere, there may be no reason to leave.

For those who want to be near all this frenzy but not of it, the adjacent area of **Monteverde Vecchio** is highly popular. Almost a suburb of Trastevere, Monteverde — developed in the 19th century for the upper classes — winds peacefully down from the Janiculum and consists of gardened homes and tree-lined streets, providing a haven for those who can afford tranquillity at home and Trastevere at their doorstep — perhaps the best of all worlds.

Monteverde Vecchio should not be confused, however, with **Monteverde Nuovo**, a solidly middle class residential and commercial district to the southeast of Trastevere, bordering Villa Pamphili on its north. Comfortable postwar apartment blocks can be found here, and the area offers moderate prices on rents and all services. Circonvallazione Gianicolense to its south is a major artery connecting with Viale Trastevere, heading into central Rome.

## Parioli/Pinciano

Situated just north of the verdant Villa Borghese, **Parioli** and **Pinciano** are among the most peaceful and residential districts of Rome. Among the wealthiest too, for these are the districts where diplomats find residence, to be near their embassies. Green and hilly with tree-lined winding streets and lovely villas, bounded on the south and north by parks, Parioli and Pinciano are often considered by sojourners as excellent neighbourhoods for families with children.

Parioli itself is a large and relatively new district, built over old estates from Baroque Rome, and most current apartments and homes date no further back than the turn of the century; some, in fact, are as recent as post-World War II. In addition to the embassies that obviously impose, law firms too have discretely nestled themselves into palazzi throughout the area. The two major piazzas, Piazza delle Muse and Villa Balestra, are less congested with traffic than is usual, and some areas of Parioli even have places to park. The squares are good meeting places, with agreeable bars and cafes, in the mornings taken over by mothers and their small children. Villa Ada, a large park on the northeastern edge, too, is a meeting place for families. Adding Villa Borghese to the south and Villa Glori to the north, the green boundaries of the area create almost a sense of isolation for the area. Parioli's spirit, while certainly that of Rome, seems nonetheless removed from the cares of the city, which have yet to encroach. On weekends many people head out of the city, and the streets are a peaceful oasis, rarely found elsewhere.

Part of the feeling of remove that makes Parioli so enjoyable also makes it important to think about a car. It's easiest to get around by car, and shops and conveniences in this lofty residential district are not quite as ubiquitous as in more mixed-use zones. Some shopping takes place in Viale dei Parioli and Piazza Diogene, with their luxury shops and prices to match. But for a more complete commercial experience one heads down to Viale Regina Margherita, a large varied shopping street which serves Salario as well. Parioli's market, in Viale dei Parioli and Via Locchi, is well-stocked and high-quality.

To the south of the thoroughfare Viale Bruno Buozzi is Pinciano, a friendly, tranquil district with an atmosphere somewhat less removed than Parioli yet comfortable as well. Here a major intersection of three large thoroughfares results in Piazza Pitagora, a commercial area serving both districts. Pinciano also borders pleasantly on Villa Borghese. Large gracious apartments in this area are convenient both to Parioli and the area around Via Veneto.

## Ludovisi/Salario

Most people know **Ludovisi** as home to Via Veneto and the mystique of *la dolce vita*. But this large area stretching from the Villa Borghese down to Piazza San Silvestro and from Piazza del Quirinale to Villa Ada, contains residential pockets worth considering, and is home to Romans who go about their business, ignoring the tourists searching for something that might no longer be there. If the days of *la dolce vita* brought excitement to the area, it also made it one of the least Roman in Rome. Now, however, although the luxury hotels, shops, banks and cafes still thrive on the wealthier tourists, the celebrities themselves seem to have moved elsewhere. Tourists mingle with Romans who have come back to enjoy the conveniences of a zone with a decidedly mixed atmosphere.

A millennium ago, this area was already a wealthy suburb which eventually, along with the Roman Empire, went into decline; some ruins can still be seen peeking through, here and there. In the 17th century the area became popular with the wealthy once again, and the Boncompagni-Ludovisi had a wooded estate here, destroyed during their own development of the area into broad streets and residential palazzi in the 19th century. Palazzo Margherita, the family's second palace, was built after the unification of Italy, but lost when their fortunes declined; it now houses the United States Embassy, overseeing much of the upper section of Via Veneto. Via Veneto itself dates only from the late 19th century. Side streets house offices and apartments; lacking tourist attractions, transient visitors are few. Yet this is a well-kept, middle class area with large palazzi dating from the end of the last century and navigable streets.

Continuing down with hotels and tourist services, Via Veneto makes one wide curve, at which the stark, commercial Via Bissolati changes the area's character as it heads toward Piazza della Repubblica. Via Veneto itself ends down at the bustling Piazza Barberini, now a focus for hotels and shops, but until 1800 an open space between the villas of the Ludovisi and the Barberini. Nonetheless, from the bottom of the piazza begins Via del Tritone, the main shopping street. Good quality shops serve both tourists and Romans, from costly souvenirs to clothing and shoes. To see this area now, it is hard to remember that in 1944, in nearby Via Rasella, Italian partisans killed 32 German soldiers, resulting in the infamous reprisal at the Fosse Ardeatine where 335 Romans were slaughtered.

Actually, all streets close to the Centro are commercial: Via di Propaganda, Via Capo le Case, Via Sistina, Via Due Macelli — prowled by tourists, but frequented also by Romans — as is the more chaotic Via Nazionale to the east, where much of Rome does its shopping. Starting at the large Piazza della Repubblica, a formerly austere 19th century square, but now a bus and tourist hub, Via Nazionale is a principal artery from Stazione Termini and points east to Piazza Venezia, and it is always traffic jammed. The character of the street itself is mixed, with ratty shops and quality boutiques, cheap pensioni and good hotels. At its beginning, its eastern neighbour Esquilino holds the difficult area around the station, but as it moves down it skirts the popular subsection of Monti, with Via Panisperna and Via dei Serpenti the most prominent.

**Salario**, just above Ludovisi, runs to Villa Ada on the north. Above Piazza Fiume with its La Rinascente department store, it is a pleasant neighbourhood with an agreeable feel. Because it's considered slightly out of the centre, rents are more reasonable, as are prices in general, yet it is as convenient to the centre as any other area so close in. Here in the neighbourhood shops and

51

*Via del Tritone, a commercial street in central Rome.*

trattorias you will find fewer tradespeople speaking English, yet lacking tourists, the ambience is distinctly local. Viale Regina Margherita is the main commercial artery, just above Villa Torlonia, the district's popular park, and Mussolini's home during World War II. Yet Viale Regina Margherita's shops have apartments above, and the street cuts across a solidly middle class district of wide straight streets and reasonably priced abodes. Via Salaria is also a major shopping street.

At Piazza Buenos Aires begins the unusual sub-district of **Coppedé**, a small section so recent as to have been developed only after World War I, in a style closer to Art Deco, or what the Italians called *stile Liberty*, than any other. Designed by the Florentine architect Gino Coppedé before Fascist architecture imposed itself, this area is the least traditional in Rome, offering a rather dreamy look of somebody's most imaginative fairytale.

Charming and exciting, it clusters around Piazza Mincio, Via Brenta, and its tiny offshoot Via Dora. Piazza Mincio's central fountain decorated with toads and bees dominates the square, which is popular at lunchtime with the workers who come from Viale Regina Margherita nearby. The individualistic apartment buildings overlooking it are fantastic as well, decorated with curlicues, gargoyles, ornate scrollwork, spires and turrets. Prices here can be higher than in its surround, because the area is so special.

North from Via Salaria to Via Nomentana is the 'African Quarter,' including such streets as Viale Libia, Viale Eritrea, Viale Somalia. Not one of the city's charming districts, many of the apartment blocks were inspired by Fascist architecture. Yet, almost a city in itself, this area is more modern and efficient than its more popular neighbours, and it borders on Villa Chigi park.

## Esquilino to the Lateran

Stazione Termini dominates the atmosphere of the northern part of **Esquilino**, despite the charm of certain streets, despite the diverse services and shops on every block. It is around the Termini where the recent wave of immigrants — some legal, some not — has made its home, too many people without much income changing forever the character of a neighbourhood that still struggles to survive. Piazza Vittorio Emanuele, shabby now, was at the end of the last century the heart of a modern and choice district developed for civil servants and others coming to claim a part in the capital of a newly united Italy. No more, and the scruffy area immediately around the piazza needs to be navigated carefully at any time of day. But the neighbourhood spirit persists: the piazza in the daytime sees one of the city's most important markets; here Romans come to shop by day but leave the area to the lurking subculture by night.

Fortunately, this gloomy picture is not all Esquilino has to offer. From Piazza Santa Maria Maggiore to the Lateran, from

Piazza dei Cinquecento down to Mussolini's broad construction, Via dei Fori Imperiali, tourists and natives mix in what is basically a middle class, liveable, central district of Rome. Districts within districts are here, varying from block to block, from corner to corner. Via Merulana, a tree-lined commercial street starting at Piazza Santa Maria Maggiore and heading straight to the Lateran, sees good quality shops, casual pizzerias, and excellent bakeries and groceries, all servicing a solid residential district. And Via Cavour, making a beeline in another direction from the piazza down toward the Forum, is likewise a street of conveniences, seeing tourists only toward the end. Here in the cafes and wine bars sit people tired from walking around the Forum, and Romans heading toward the Metro on their way home.

**Monti**, historically known as Suburra, was originally one of the most ancient suburbs of Rome, lying low from the edge of the Forum to the Esquiline hill. From ancient days a seedy workers' quarter, now it is a lively neighbourhood winding around Via dei Serpenti and Via Panisperna, with little shops, artisans, restaurants and groceries. Neighbours here have known each other for decades, and the spirit is distinctly Roman. For centuries one of the shabbiest, seediest and least desirable parts of town, notorious for crime, Monti is now rather agreeable, and many newcomers are finding this area convenient. The evenings see pub-crawlers around Via San Martino ai Monti, and Romans in the restaurants and trattorias of Via del Boschetto. Although the area is crowded and dense, down and just across Via Cavour is the Colle Oppio Park and Nero's Domus Aurea, Via dei Fori Imperiali, and the Colosseum.

To the south of Via dei Fori Imperiali is the small residential and commercial district nicknamed **Celio** that seems basically to ignore its imposing neighbour, the Colosseum, constantly crowded with tour buses and souvenir stands. Yet the streets to the side — Via S. Giovanni in Laterano, Via Ostilia, Via SS. Quattro — are convenient for apartment living, and shopping is done in the narrow streets or in the broad, commercial Via Merulana above. Here is the church of San Clemente, with its layers of history reaching down to Nero's Rome. And indeed, up off Via Labicana is his Aurea palace, now situated as ruins in a park inhabited by neighbourhood families on late afternoons. Below is Villa Celimontana, another green haven close by.

## San Lorenzo to Nomentana

**San Lorenzo** is an unprepossessing area that is home to university students, medical researchers, workers, and above all, the *Sanlorenzini*, Rome's adherents of radical politics. San Lorenzo has a character uniquely its own. Just above Stazione Termini — but a world away — this small, dense and outwardly shabby area sees few tourists, although its modern history is as compelling as much in Rome's past. This is the area of Rome that battled most fiercely against the Fascists in the 1920s, again holding out against the Nazis in the Forties. Here too the radical university students in the late Sixties gathered, and even now it is common to see posters and graffiti protesting one political insult or another, or announcing an upcoming event.

The area — historically one of rebellion — was named after the 3rd century martyr San Lorenzo. When Rome demanded a tribute of all his church's treasures, Lorenzo produced a crowd of sick and destitute Christians: for this he was burned alive. In AD 330, Constantine began construction of the first of the churches to be built on San Lorenzo's burial site, culminating in the present multifaceted Basilica San Lorenzo Fuori le Mura.

Despite retaining the atmosphere of the workers' quarter it has always been, since the 1930s San Lorenzo has been the home of the University of Rome, known as **La Sapienza**, bringing thousands of students each year to the district. Also nearby is the Policlinico, an extensive training hospital. And, in Viale Castro Pretorio stands Italy's national library, **Biblioteca Nazionale**

**Centrale**, with more than three million volumes. But long before all this there was **Campo Verano**, the city's largest public cemetery, and the life of the district began with the gravediggers, marble cutters and the services needed to maintain them; although the university students steadily encroach, and gentrification is on its way, this remains a workers' district, with low houses, artisans' workshops and services for the residents.

It was this area — and the working-class **Tiburtino** that abuts to the north — that was bombed in July of 1943, the first attack on a Rome that had thought itself inviolate. Thus, much has been reconstructed, including the heavily damaged Basilica. Now post-war construction mixes with the old, and the area is crowded and dense. Yet the narrow, hastily planned streets (named after the ancient tribes of Italy), although not particularly attractive, are some of the most interesting in Rome. Piazza del Verano is one centre of the workers' district and Piazzale Aldo Moro the entrance to the university complex. To the north is Piazzale San Lorenzo, from which starts Viale Regina Margherita, connecting to Parioli, to the north. Slightly west and closer in spirit to the Termini is the modern Piazza Indipendenza. In all, this area is mixed in spirit, with both new apartments and old, shabby tenement blocks. San Lorenzo remains one of the most inexpensive districts of central Rome: small locally owned shops, trattorias and pizzerias demonstrate the existence of both workers and students mixing homogeneously in this area.

Yet just to the north in Tiburtino, the conditions improve somewhat. Although still decidedly working class, the atmosphere changes pleasantly as one moves out toward the attractive and gentle residential district of Nomentana, beginning above Viale Regina Margherita, where life centres around Piazza Bologna. Via Nomentana borders this area to the northwest: a broad, straight boulevard, tree lined and pleasant, that begins at Piazzale Porta Pia and eventually leads past Monte Sacro, a rather bland but habitable middle class neighbourhood. Popular during the Fascist era and containing Mussolini's home in Villa Torlonia, now there are few tourists, and Via Nomentana is the principal street in a solidly middle class section, with many modernised condominiums and some foreign embassies. Boutiques and good quality shops are evident throughout the area making it convenient and welcoming.

## L'Aventino

On the river just below the Palatine and past the Circo Massimo rises l'Aventino, the southernmost of the original seven hills of Rome. Actually there are two peaks to this hill, **Piccolo Aventino** being to the east of Viale Aventino, a busy thoroughfare that divides the area and its character neatly in two. Despite a feeling of peaceful remove, l'Aventino is close to all downtown areas, including Trastevere just across the river.

L'Aventino is a coveted residential area, tranquil and elegant, an oasis of charm within the centre of Rome. This is in stark contrast to the earliest history of the hill when it was inhabited by the lower classes of Romans who were separated from the more elegant Palatine by the low lying Vallis Murcia and the Circo Massimo. In fact, l'Aventino has had a mixed history: in the 6th century BC, it was a holy area with a temple to Diana at its summit. During the Republic, in proximity to the ancient commercial port on the river, the Emporium — as is Testaccio, its neighbour to the south — l'Aventino was inhabited by a class of traders and artisans. During the Empire, nobles built their villas here, and the area has since remained solidly and elegantly residential, although at certain times it was not central to Roman life. At times it became a hotbed of radical democratic ideas, and indeed even in this century it was home to rebellious anti-Fascists.

L'Aventino today is a serene haven of winding streets, walled-in gardened villas, and lovely views. At the top of the hill is a peaceful park of orange trees. And there is the famous Piazza dei Cavalieri di Malta, whose priory opens onto the charming square designed by Piranesi. There is a small market and a few shops, but generally the feeling in l'Aventino is of distance from downtown Rome, despite its easy proximity. Yet only one bus goes to the top of the hill, so it might not be as convenient as other neighbourhoods unless you decide to keep a car, and here is one of the few neighbourhoods where parking spaces can be found. Nonetheless, despite its slight inconvenience, and despite the prices for private homes here, this is one of the most desirable residential areas in Rome.

Below, Piccolo Aventino is closer to Rome in spirit and feel, although across the busy Viale Aventino, it is still an area of graceful streets and an exclusive residential area. Near to the United Nations Food and Agriculture Organization, small elegant hotels cater to visiting officials. A nice daily market in Piazza Bernini serves the entire area, and as usual, the square holds food shops to round out marketing needs.

## Testaccio

Just south of l'Aventino is **Testaccio**, a staunch, lively, workers' area by day that is also known for its trendy restaurants serving *cucina romana* to tourists by night, and for its discos and clubs that draw many in Rome until dawn. This is not one of the picturesque *quartieri*: there are no views, few sights for tourists to explore, few charming piazzas. Partly because of this, the area has retained its own traditional character, and although it is slowly becoming gentrified and may yet become an all-round trendy area, the process is slow, and the area may currently not be appropriate for a long-term stay. This may be especially true for women alone, for the winding dark street at the bottom of Monte Testaccio does not always seem hospitable. Some parts, away from the hill itself, are welcoming, and Piazzale di Porta San Paolo, alongside Piazzale

Ostiense, is a busy commercial and transportation hub. As is so common, this is an area interesting in some regards, mixed in feel, and typical of one of the many spirits of Rome. It is a part of the centre of Rome and has its history, its own character, its own point of view on just about everything. The daily market in Piazza Testaccio is one of the most popular in the city, there are some interesting shops around Piazza Santa Maria Liberatrice, and the restaurants are certainly among the best in town.

The area is built by Monte Testaccio, a hill constructed by chance in the second century AD, as workers at the Emporium — the docks for trading oil, wine and grains — threw empty amphorae onto a heap, as the contents were transferred to larger storage vats. This lasted until it was discovered that storage was better in caves, caves that paradoxically now house car mechanics' garages and some of the trendy night spots. The Emporium is now Piazza di Emporio, and Monte Testaccio (also known as **Monte dei Cocci**) is an archeologically important 34-metre hill that is closed to the public.

Other workers clustered here for trades that required the port. Streets such as Via Marmorata attest to the ancient artisans here who worked the marble that was unloaded at the port for the homes of Roman nobles, and workers of later generations re-worked the stone from ruins scattered around the city.

The low-lying malaria-prone area Testaccio declined over the centuries and only became repopulated at the end of the last century, when workers from all over the country came to help build the capital of the newly united Italy. Public housing blocks were built to house the workers, eight-storey blocks that still stand today and that are still publicly owned, inhabited by today's workers who live in the rent controlled apartments. Now even other Romans are beginning to move in, taken by the interior court-yards and apartments, somewhat lighter and more comfortable than one would from the outside suspect.

Contributing to the working class atmosphere was the construction in 1891 of the *mattatoio*, the slaughterhouse that was the meat centre of Rome, lasting until 1975, when the centre was moved outside the urban confines. The fate of the mattatoio today is uncertain; to make it into a cultural centre serving the area, some clubs have moved in, along with some services, but as yet the idea has not yet quite taken hold. Nonetheless, the presence of the businesses there contributed to the culinary reputation of the area, and it is in Testaccio that one finds much of the best Roman cuisine, both in trendy tourist-filled restaurants and trat-torias for the area's residents.

To Testaccio's south lie the large, spread-out districts of **Ostiense** and **Garbatella**. Here too is the original workers' hous-ing from the last century, but amid a middle-class district now coming up. And the areas are popular as some of Rome's exciting nightlife has been moving in. These areas, bordering on the wide Via Ostiense and the major artery Cristoforo Colombo, are convenient both to the central districts to the north and to the activities and business of EUR, their neighbour to the south.

## The Lateran and South

It is difficult to believe that the traffic-jammed Piazza San Giovanni in Laterano was a grassy field in the last century. How dramatic it must have been, with the imposing basilica at its edge. Now the piazza is traffic-fumed and noisy as traffic rushes nearby through the Porta San Giovanni, its edges lined with tourist attractions near the basilica, and with services for those coming to the ancient San Giovanni hospital in Via Amba Aradam, just off the square. But the Piazza is the end of the straight Via Merulana, laid out in 1575 and today still serving a surrounding residential and commercial area that also heads west on Via Labicana toward the Colosseum nearby.

The Lateran Palace was, until the Pope's departure for Avignon, the papal residence in Rome, and it and the Basilica gave the area a splendid lustre. Afterwards in decline, the area for centuries remained in a kind of rural hibernation, coming to life again after the unification of 1870, when it was developed to house some of the influx into the new capital. Now it is a middle-class area, somewhat bland, yet with some charming pockets of neighbourhood feel.

Just south of the Lateran is another residential and commercial district centring on Via Appia Nuova, a 'new' street only in that it was built in reaction to a toll booth on the ancient Via Appia that was installed in 1300. Thus the original road somewhat to the east — some 2000 years old — is known formally as Via Appia Antica, and informally still as the *Via Appia*, the Appian Way. Like Via Appia Nuova, it leads southeast out of the city, and is a good excursion for tourists seeking the many remnants there of ancient days. It is also an area of expensive and luxurious villas, an enclave of wealthy Romans who want to be near to the city while avoiding its congestion.

The residential area around Via Appia Nuova, comparatively recent, is popular with Romans who want the city at reasonable prices. Via Appia Nuova itself is a commercial street, broad and green, full of shops and other services. Piazzale Appio and Piazza dei Re di Roma see good shopping areas and lively Roman crowds, but few visitors passing through. Several stops on Metro A — at Ponte Colli Albani, Furio Camillo, Ponte Lungo and Re di Roma, as well as San Giovanni itself — make this district as convenient as any other to the centre of Rome, although its atmosphere seems somewhat, and agreeably, different. Here are markets, gymnasiums, department stores, small family owned shops — everything you'd want, yet with an atmosphere of a small town.

## EUR

*Esposizione Universale di Roma,* now known simply as **EUR,** is the 'new Rome,' conceived and planned by Mussolini in the 1930s: an entirely new city to glorify the achievements of Fascism, to extend Rome all the way to the sea, and to house a major world's fair in 1942, the 20th anniversary of Mussolini's march on Rome. Begun in 1937, World War II interfered, leaving Mussolini's dream unfinished and in shambles. Postwar development — first for the 1950 Holy Year and then for the 1960 Olympics — restored buildings damaged during the war, built and completed others, created new zones entirely, and finally came up with an achievement of urban planning: an interesting district of government ministries, corporation headquarters, conference and trade centres, cool parks with an artificial lake, and genteel, gardened villas and apartment complexes.

Here the Fascist architecture of square white marble monoliths mingles with high-tech buildings of aluminium and glass. Imposing edifices are gentle among shady green parks. Curving wide streets are peaceful, and often there are even places to park a car, which is important, for EUR's grandiose planning seems to have assumed that people would drive down the long boulevards, rather than walk. The broad avenues and central streets are orderly, as one would expect from Fascist planning, yet they are dramatic in their execution, and many are named after such lofty ideals as humanism, technology, industry, etc. Dramatic in itself, the enormous church of SS. Pietro e Paolo rises imposingly in its piazzale at the end of the broad Viale Europa.

The residential areas, whether of private homes or modern apartments, are truly suburban, and welcoming to the politicians, upper-middle class business owners and diplomats who call them home. Parks contribute to the feel, and the *Laghetto Artificiale*, the artificial lake, has outdoor cafes on its shores and rowboats to rent. In EUR the shops are modern and the cafes are clean, and there is no lack of restaurants, food shops, bakeries, cinemas, or any other service. The quality in the shops is at the high end, and obviously this is not one of the inexpensive sections of town. Yet close by in Laurentina is the large I Granai shopping mall, with its several floors of affordable shops and its well-stocked super-market.

Only 15 minutes from the centre of Rome to the north and the same amount from the beaches to the south, the best entry into this haven of EUR is Via Cristoforo Colombo, at war's end only a partially completed avenue surrounded by green fields. Today it is a major artery coming into EUR north from Piazza dei Navigatori, and at the south leaving it to head to Ostia and the sea. At its top are commercial establishments and the Fiera di Roma, home to trade shows of all sorts. To its south, however, are mixed in some interesting apartment complexes that are conven-ient living areas for those working in the industrial areas near Pomezia or Latina, some kilometres to the south. A straight broad artery, Cristoforo Colombo splits at the Laghetto and comes to-gether again just south of the Palazzo dello Sport, the huge sports complex completed for the 1960 Olympics, and which now hosts public sporting events.

EUR may not have the easiest access to the cultural life of Rome, nor may it be one of the most exciting parts of the city. Yet

Photo: EPT-Rome

*Art and history are a part of everyday life on the streets of the city.*

it doesn't take long to get into the Centro from the two metro stops directly in EUR or another two on its edges. And the district itself has its own attractions. There are several well known museums that draw tourists, and for all in Rome there is Luneur, the year-round amusement park. The Piscina delle Rose is Rome's most popular outdoor public swimming pool, and tennis courts are at the park at Tre Fontane. Summertime open air concerts and all year sporting events at the Palazzo dello Sport plus other special events also help to liven this essentially suburban district within Rome.

# CHAPTER TWO

# HOUSING AND SETTLING IN

Those who remember Rome as charming and inexpensive should be relieved to know that at least the charm remains today. Unfortunately, Rome is gradually catching up with the other capitals of Europe, although rents for apartments and residential hotels are still somewhat lower. Owing to recent changes in rental requirement laws, a large number of apartments have become available for rent, and landlords prefer foreigners who will not stay permanently and who will not be subject to rent control laws. In addition, landlords quote higher prices at first, for bargaining is expected. Foreigners might want to take along an Italian, whether a real estate professional or a friend, to talk with and deal with the prospective landlord. Occasionally, with persistence, or if you can find friends who know friends with a vacant apartment, even bargains can be found.

As Rome is a city of apartments, houses in the central areas are rare and these can cost around L7 million per month. In general, expect to pay an average of L1.8 million for a decent one-bedroom apartment in the city centre and about L1.2 million just outside; two-bedroom apartments can cost upwards of L2.3 million.

Residence hotel prices are state regulated as are regular hotels, and according to quality, they range between L600,000 and L1.6 million weekly. Slightly more expensive than private apartments, they are easier to find, offer more services and amenities, and are an option to consider for a short to medium length stay, or while you are looking for permanent housing.

As soon as you know your departure date, start thinking about housing. You can do a lot before you leave, and if you plan to deal with Italian agencies, you will need *pazienza*. Three months in advance is not too long to begin inquiries, to place or respond to advertisements, or to commit yourself and pay a deposit. Call weekdays, for most agencies are closed weekends. And take into account that in August neither landlords nor agents will be in town.

# SHORT TERM HOME EXCHANGE

The least expensive way to stay abroad for a few months is to exchange your home for one in Rome. International home exchange companies publish catalogues in which prospective renters from many countries list their homes, hoping to find people in the country and city of their choice who want to exchange their own for the same period of time. Generally, you pay for the listing: you describe the home, the surroundings, the amenities. You then correspond with the people who answer, send photos of the property and come to an agreement.

Make sure to start the process well in advance of your departure: catalogues are published only a few times a year, and lead time can be long. A real conversation with people at these companies can be difficult: phones are usually answered with a message asking for your name and address, so that an information packet can be sent.

- **Homelink International**: P.O. Box 650, Key West, FL 33041 (US tels: 800/638-3841; fax: 305/294-1448). Three catalogues and three supplements annually.
- **Intervac US**: Box 590504, San Francisco CA 94159 (US tels: 800/756-4663; fax: 415/435-7440). Three catalogues annually; list your home in one catalogue, but receive three. **Intervac Paris**: 230, boulevard Voltaire, 75011 Paris (France tel: 33/01.43.70.21.22).
- **Loan-a-Home**: 7 McGregor Rd., Woods Hole, MA 02543 (US tel: 508/548-4032). List your home and receive the current directory and a supplement.
- **The Invented City**: 41 Sutter Street, Suite 1090, San Francisco, CA 94104 (US tel: 415/252-1141; fax: 252-1171). Three annual listings. Listings also available in affiliated catalogues in Europe.

# SHORT/MEDIUM TERM RESIDENCE HOTELS

The **residenza** (residence hotel) has become popular for short and medium term stays. They are also convenient for lodgings while searching for permanent housing. Residences offer the same amenities as hotels, including porters, message-taking, and daily room cleaning. Suites range from studios to multi-bedroom; all have equipped kitchenettes. They offer the feeling of independence of an apartment, but with hotel type services provided. Residences are in all parts of the city. Those close to the centre, of course, are more expensive than those further out which often offer amenities such as gardens, pools, and car parks. Rates are set by the week or month, and range from L2 to 6 million monthly. Although prices may seem high, they are comparable to apartment hotels worldwide: divide the monthly cost by thirty to determine the price per day and add in 9% tax and a gratuity for the staff. See *Residenze ed Appartamenti Ammobiliati* in the Yellow Pages. Also, the tourist office should have a copy of *Accommodation Facilities in Rome and Province of Rome*.

- *Ludovisi* — **Mayfair Residence**: Via Sicilia 183, just off Via Abruzzi and between Via Veneto and Piazza Fiume (tel: 48 20 481; fax: 42 81 57 53). Small, well-maintained residence of 14 apartments.
- *Parioli* — **Residence Aldrovandi**: Via U. Aldrovandi 11, facing the Villa Borghese, near Via Veneto (tel: 32 21 430; fax: 32 22 181). Quiet, elegant residence with studios and two-room apartments. Restaurant.
- *Piazza del Popolo* — **Residenza di Ripetta**: Via di Ripetta 231, near Piazza del Popolo (tel: 32 31 144; fax: 32 03 959). Large, elegant residence with apartments of various sizes in a remodelled 17th century convent.
- *Piazza Venezia* — **Palazzo al Velabro**: Via del Velabro 16, near the river, behind the Forum (tel: 679.7879; fax: 67 93 790). Ancient palazzo restored and modernised, this is one of the more luxurious and centrally located of the residence hotels.
- *Prati* — **Residence Candia**: Via Candia 135/b, near the Vatican (tel & fax: 39 72 10 46). Moderately priced apartments of up to four rooms, free parking and a laundromat. In a courtyard off a commercial street, it is near metro/bus, markets and a supermarket.
- *Trastevere* — **Residence Ripa**: Via Luigi Gianniti 21, off Viale Trastevere (tel: 58611; fax: 58 14 550). Large, modern and well-maintained, with a restaurant and laundry within. Buses and trams nearby.
- *Vigna Clara* — **Residence V House**: Largo di Vigna Stelluti 18 (tel: 36 30 90 41; fax: 36 30 37 98). Well- situated and maintained residence in a beautiful area north in the city, near some of the international schools.

- *EUR* — **Residence Garden:** Viale dell'Arte 5 (tel: 59 21 474; fax 59 12 791). Apartments from one to four bedrooms, on one or two levels; some balconies. A large establishment with a restaurant, bank, hairdresser and laundromat within. Convenient to ministries in EUR and to the IBM headquarters.

# LONG TERM APARTMENTS

For a long stay, you should rent an apartment, but finding a good one might take some time. Ninety percent of Romans live in apartments, and although there are more apartments available, there still aren't enough apartments for a growing population. Rent control keeps turnover low, families hand down apartments for generations, and even when one becomes available, landlords hesitate to rent because Italian laws make it almost impossible to evict a permanent Italian tenant. This does not apply to transitory leases, so landlords often prefer to rent apartments at hefty prices to foreigners who are expected to leave at the end of their lease.

Apartments, of course, vary from the elegant and expensive to the shabby and only slightly less pricey. Many ancient Romans lived in apartment houses called *insulae*, and despite your feelings about some you're shown by an agent, none survive today. Some buildings, true, are hundreds of years old, but their crumbling ochre facades are deceptive; many seemingly decrepit medieval *palazzi* boast charming, well-kept courtyards and cool, modernised apartments within.

Real estate agents and relocation services are the most reliable methods to find a good apartment at a reasonable price. To search for an apartment on your own, however, look at newsstands for the biweekly English-language *Wanted in Rome* (see Chapter Nine), or *Porta Portese*, a semiweekly Roman advertising newspaper. Notice boards can be found at the **Economy Book Center** in Via Torino 136, at **The American Church of Santa Susanna** in Via XX Settembre 14, and **All Saints Anglican Church**

in Via del Babuino 153. You can also look out for signs on buildings that say *affittasi appartamento*, giving the number of rooms and whether the apartment is furnished or unfurnished. But on the whole, unless your Italian is excellent, it's best to deal with an agent or relocation service.

## Aspects to Consider

Furnished apartments *(ammobiliato)* are generally equipped with all basic needs. Unfurnished apartments *(vuoto)* often don't include kitchen appliances, light fixtures or closets, so you may have to buy them yourself and expect to sell them upon departure to someone just arriving. (The English-language magazine *Wanted in Rome* is the best source for ads for this kind of purchase or sale. See Chapter Nine.) Also, don't expect to find a cleaned unfurnished apartment or one that has been repainted and fixed up for your arrival. You'll probably have to arrange to have these things done on your own; if so, make sure you get an estimate *(preventivo)* in advance of the work, or at least a confirmation of the price and timeframe for completion of the work.

Not all buildings have elevators, and you should think twice about renting an apartment on the fourth floor of a building without one, even though the price may approach the reasonable. Although the view may be lovely, the breeze cooling, and the idea of exercise appealing, it can get tedious climbing the stairs if you're not used to it. If you wouldn't live in such a building at home, don't do it in Rome.

If you intend to keep a car, inquire specifically about parking. Some apartment buildings have garages listed, others do not. The nearest garage may not be in your building at all and may not be open 24-hours daily or weekends. This means that in an emergency or on a Sunday you may not be able to access your car. In addition, check the size of the space itself, to see if it fits your car. Many spaces are designed only for the small European car. Check to see how carefully the cars are parked.

Ask about the electrical voltage in the apartment; although most buildings have 220-volt electricity, a few have not been converted and may also have some 110/220 volt combination. Make sure you know, too, where the circuit breaker is; most apartments support up to three kilowatts, but some don't, so if you are using too many appliances at the same time, you may trip the fuse. In this regard, see if the stove is gas or electric; electricity costs are high. (See Appendix for household emergency telephone numbers.)

Find out whether utilities (including heat) are included, if there's air conditioning, who pays the garbage tax and how the garbage is picked up: often residents wrap and take their garbage down to the green containers located in nearby streets. It is important to know the telephone number and that the phone has been hooked up; otherwise it takes about a week for hookup. Ensure that there are no hidden expenses such as maintenance costs in a condominium building. Ask for an inventory from the landlord and make sure it matches what is in the apartment. Last,

71

*The residential streets of Rome can provide apartment living, access to the city, market stalls and a liberal dose of old world charm.*

find out from the landlord the requirements for leaving the apartment; some require three months written notice to return your *deposito cauzionale* (security deposit) with the accrued nterest. Some people use the deposit as the last month's rent.

Before signing a lease, hire an attorney for an hour to make sure all clauses are as they should be. A good real estate agent or relocation service should also be helpful with all of this.

# BUYING AN APARTMENT

Buying an apartment in Rome — or any property in Italy — can be extremely complicated. For example, it is important to ensure that the title is free and clear, and if anyone has the right of first refusal. When negotiating price, prospective buyers must also keep in mind the 2-5% fee of the real estate agent, the fee of the notary, the registration taxes or VAT, and the attorneys' fees. It is important to understand in advance how the carrying/service fees of the *condominio* (condominium) are assessed, how many owners are absentee landlords, when voting on condominium business takes place and how proxies are filed, and who the managing agent is. All this points to the absolute necessity of having a reliable real estate agent and a good lawyer, knowledgeable in real estate law (see Chapter Seven).

## Real Estate Agencies

Guidebooks list real estate agencies in Rome; these are primarily for vacation length rentals. Although you can eventually look for apartments on your own, at first it is helpful to have a real estate or relocation expert with you, and agents also know of apartments that have not yet been advertised. Make sure to use a licensed agent or one who has been recommended to you. Be clear in advance on how fees are charged: some agents charge a flat fee, one month's rent, or 10% of a year's rent. A few charge for showing the apartments; if this is the case with your agent, inquire in advance about a refund should you not take an apartment. The agencies listed below specialise in finding long term apartments for newcomers to the city, and all are English-speaking. (See *Agenzie Immobiliare* in the Yellow Pages, and Relocation Services below.)

- **Edwards Real Estate Agency** Via Rodolfo Lanciani 1 (tel: 86 10 871; fax: 86 11 262).
- **Genesi Realtors**: Viale Mazzini 112 (tel: 37 51 70 66; fax: 37 51 46 82)
- **Internazionale Immobiliare**: Via di Porta Pinciana 34 (tel: 48 20 441; fax: 48 71 672).
- **Nelson International Real Estate Agency**: Piazza Mazzini 27 (tel: 33 37 164; fax: 33 37 162).
- **Property International**: Viale Aventino 79 (tel: 57 43 170; fax: 57 43 182).

## Relocation Services and Help with the Bureaucracy

Relocation companies provide a variety of important services in addition to acting as real estate agents. Especially in Rome, where bureaucratic requirements are complex and changing, these agencies are extremely useful. They can deal efficiently with the current bureaucratic formalities and with providing crucial information on the intricacies of living in Rome, such as finding insurance and getting your utilities hooked up. Staff members can converse in English and are used to dealing with the concerns of new arrivals.

- **Studio Elle**: Via Bruno Bruni 98 (tel & fax: 33 25 05 21; cell tel: 0360/24 17 06). Lorena Leopizzi understands completely the bureaucracy and helps new arrivals with all aspects of coping with it. Real estate, residence and work permits, *codice fiscale*, etc.
- **Studio Papperini**: Via Ugo Ojetti 114 (tel: 86 89 58 10; fax: 86 89 65 46). Registers cars and helps with finding housing for new arrivals, documentation, hiring of household help, etc. The Italian owner, a lawyer, is expert in dealing with the bureaucracy.

Photo: Jacopo Astengo

*Distinct architectural styles characterise many Roman buildings.*

- **Welcome Home:** Via Barbarano Romano 15 (tel: 30 36 69 36; fax: 30 36 17 06). Real estate, assists with documentation and helps deal with the bureaucracy. 'Welcome Neighbour' gatherings, plus an English-language newsletter. Hosts an American Fair each September. The American owner, Yolanda Bernadini, knows Rome and its bureaucracy thoroughly.

## TOURIST OFFICES

If you arrive in Rome without accommodation, try the tourist offices below, which have lists of hotel rooms for the short term, and can sometimes help with long term lodgings.

- **Ente Provinciale per il Turismo di Roma (EPT):** Via Parigi 5, off Piazza della Repubblica, is the Rome Tourist Office (tel: 48 89 92 55; fax: 48 89 92 28). Branches at Fiumicino Airport, just past Customs (tel: 65 95 60 74) and the Stazione Termini (tel: 48 24 078). Hours: 8:15 am – 7:15 pm; closed Sunday, except at the station.
- **Enjoy Rome:** Via Varese 39, is an active, multi-service private tourist service (tel: 44 51 843; fax: 44 50 734). Commission of a week's rent is charged if an apartment is contracted for. Hours: 8:30 am – 1:00 pm and 3:30 – 6:00 pm; closed Saturday afternoon and Sunday. telephone answered until 10:00 pm M–S.

## ROOMING HOUSES

What used to be called *pensioni* are now just lower rated hotels. Rooming houses as such, those with kitchen privileges or meals served, are rare to find. The tourist offices do not keep lists of rooming houses. Enjoy Rome, the tourist service, can occasionally find rooms in private homes, screens them, and works with clients to assure a good placement. Otherwise, it's best to ask for recommendations from friends who have already found rooms.

## HOUSING FOR STUDENTS

English-language universities help their registered students find housing. In addition, during August, when Rome's universities are closed, vacated dormitory rooms *(Casa dello studente)* at several sites are turned into hostels: inquire at **Residenza Universitaria de Lollis** in Via Cesare de Lollis 20 (tel: 48 71 152). Contact **EPT** or **AIG**, listed below, for information.

A hostel can offer inexpensive short term quarters while looking for more permanent housing. The official hostel in Rome is the **Ostello de la Gioventù Foro Italico** in Viale delle Olimpiadi 61, near the Foro Italico sports complex, which is somewhat out of the centre, although near public transport (tel: 32 36 267; fax: 32 42 613). Rates for 1996 were L23,000 per night, including breakfast. **YWCA** in Via Balbo 4 near the train station offers accommodations for young women (tel: 48 80 460); basic rooms, shared bath, and a midnight curfew. Young women coming for brief stays may also inquire at the **Associazione Cattolica Internazionale al Servizio della Giovane** in Via Urbana 158 (tel: 48 80 056).

The Italian tourist offices abroad and in Rome should have copies of **Ostelli per la Gioventù**, a listing of Italian hostels, reservation requirements, plus other pertinent information. Membership in **Hostelling International** is required; membership cards can be purchased before leaving at travel agencies near universities and others that cater to budget travel as well as at hostels themselves. Reservations at hostels may be made in advance, with a credit card guarantee: the second number in each listing below is the reservations number.

- **American Youth Hostels**: 733 15th Street, NW, Suite 840, Washington, DC 20005 (tel: 202/783-6161; fax: 783-6171; reservations tel: 783-6161)
- **Australian Youth Hostels Association** 10 Mallett Street, Camperdown NSW 2050 (Tel: 02/565-1699; fax: 565-1235; reservations tel: 02/261-1111)
- **Hostelling International Canada**: 400-205 Catherine St., Ottawa, Ont K2P 1C3; (tel: 613/ 237-7884; reservations toll free: 800/663-5777)
- **Youth Hostel Association of England and Wales**: Trevelyan House, 8 St. Stephen's Hill, St. Albans, Herts. AL12DY (tel: 1727/855-215; reservations tel: 171/836-1036)

- **Youth Hostels Association of New Zealand**: Box 436, Christchurch 1 (tel: 03/379-9970; fax: 365-4476; reservations tel: 09/379-4224)
- **Hostel Association of South Africa**: P.O. Box 4402, Capetown 8000 (tel: 21/419-1853)
- **Associazione Italiana Alberghi per Gioventù (AIG):** Via Cavour 44 (tel: 487 1152; fax: 488 0492).
- **Centro Turistico Studentesco e Giovanile (CTS)** offers young visitors and students discounts on services, help with lodgings, sightseeing tours, rental cars, and more. It also sells the International Student Identity Card, the International Teacher Identity Card (see Chapter Six), and another discount card, the **Carta Verde**. The main office is in Via Genova 16 (tel: 46 79 271) Others are in San Lorenzo in Via degli Ausoni 5 (tel: 44 50 141), and in Corso Vittorio Emanuele II 297 (tel: 68 72 672).

## RELIGIOUS HOUSING

Monasteries and convents can be pleasant and inexpensive for an interim stay, if you can make do with one Spartan room. Some offer private bathrooms, others must be shared. Some require their guests to clean their own rooms, and some have curfews as early as 11:00 pm; some require guests to be Catholic. Benefits are that these institutions provide meals, they are less expensive than other lodgings, and they often have peaceful garden settings. Unfortunately, most limit stays to no more than one month, but this may be enough to allow selection of permanent housing. The Tourist Office should have a list of religious housing possibilities.

## MOVING COMPANIES

If shipping personal furniture/effects, make sure your residence certificate is in order before shipment. Without one you will have to pay customs duties and VAT tax on your own belongings. The moving companies listed below can help with all documentation and bureaucratic aspects as well as packing and shipping. Contact them well in advance to discuss procedures. In addition, if you can provide the address of your new housing, it will help them determine how best to deliver and unload furniture in what might be a narrow street or a walk-up apartment. See Chapter Three for discussion of importation. See *Traslochi* in the Yellow Pages.

- **Italian Moving Network:** Via Oreste Ranelletti 63 (tel: 66 18 18 88; fax: 66 18 21 11)
- **Bolliger:** Via dei Buonvisi 61 (tel: 65 57 121; fax: 65 57 133).
- **Gondrand:** Via Idrovore della Magliana 163 (tel: 65 74 63 40; fax: 65 74 63 55).

## THE TOBACCO SHOP

As soon as you settle in, find your neighbourhood *tabacchi* (tobacco shop). Marked by a large white T on a black rectangular sign, tabacchi, of course, carry cigarettes, candies, matches, etc. More importantly, they are the sole vendors of many of the official forms and documents necessary to cope with the bureaucracy; these also include the standard apartment lease forms (although most wind up with many handwritten additions and inserts). If there are some forms the *tabaccaio* doesn't carry, he will know where you can get them. Tabacchi also sell the *piombino* (seal) necessary for mailing certain packages, postage stamps, phone cards, and bus and metro tickets and passes.

# HOUSEHOLD HELP

If you hire a **COLF** *(collaboratrice per i lavori familiari)*, you will need to pay her social security. If you have used one of the relocation services listed above, it will help with all bureaucratic requirements. If you have, instead, inquired of friends or scanned the notice boards at churches and bookshops and hired domestic help on your own, you must go to the INPS **(Istituto Nazionale per la Previdenza Sociale)** in Via del Amba Aradam 5 to obtain the forms (tel: 77381). Bring identification and a *codice fiscale* for you and the employee (see Chapter Eight). **C/Work Agency** at Via Fienaroli 7/a (tel: 58 36 707) is one agency that provides household help, baby sitters, help for the elderly and other services.

# CHAPTER THREE

# FORMALITIES FOR STAYING

## TOURIST OR RESIDENT?

Foreigners in Italy are either 'tourists' or 'residents.' Tourists generally are in Italy for a period under three months; for stays over three months application is made in advance of departure at an Italian consulate in the home country.

To enter Italy, all foreigners need a passport; citizens of EU countries, Australia, Canada, New Zealand and the United States do not need an entry visa for visits shorter than three months. Citizens of other countries may need to obtain a visa in advance; check with the Italian embassy in your country. All non-EU nationals must register their presence in Italy within eight days of arrival; EU-nationals must register within the same time period if coming to work. Upon registration, a *permesso di soggiorno* (stay permit) is issued, which allows the person to remain in Italy. The type of *permesso* granted depends on the reason and length of the visit; the tourist stay permit is good for an initial three months.

The tourist stay permit may be renewed for additional three-month periods, but one or two renewals are generally all that are allowed.

Hotels and residence hotels will register your presence in Italy. For the *permesso di soggiorno*, if you are using the services of a relocation agency to help you get settled, it can help with all formalities, assuming all advance work has been done. (See Chapter Two.) This is the most efficient method, for dealing with the bureaucracy on your own is frustrating. Nonetheless, if you want to strike out on your own, call the **Questura-Ufficio Stranieri** in Via Genova 2 off Via Nazionale. (tel: 4686, ext/2987; info: 4686, ext/2120), and ask how to register. You will probably have to go in person. Hours are from 8:00 am-12:00 pm weekdays, and there's always a crowd. Go very early, well before opening time, even at 7:00 am. You will be given a number and told when to return for an interview; sometimes there are English-speaking personnel available. The Questura may have a computer printout of the requirements and documents needed for each *permesso*. Note also that it is at the Questura where reports of lost passports, etc. are made; in order to apply for replacement passports, tickets or traveller's cheques, a police report must have been filed.

Even those who do not need a visa for a stay of under three months may need a *permesso di soggiorno* immediately, for it is needed to work, open a bank account, rent an apartment, turn on the electricity, or buy a car. You will need to bring your passport and a photocopy, passport pictures and a completed *domanda*, an application form which is available at tobacco shops. The Questura will also have a form to fill out. Note that EU citizens generally receive their *permesso* the same day.

EU citizens are entitled to stay and work anywhere within the EU. For non-EU nationals entering Italy with a non-tourist visa, the stay permit can be anywhere from six months to two years and may be renewed upon presentation of proper documentation. If planning to work for either an Italian or foreign company with offices in Italy, non-EU citizens will need to obtain a work visa prior to departure; the *permesso* will specify exactly the type of work the person is allowed to do and the time period approved (see Chapter Four). Application for the *permesso di soggiorno* must be done in advance at an Italian consulate; the applicant may not come to stay in Italy pending the issuance of the visa. The visa will be granted only for the time indicated on the application. The Italian government objects to tourists wishing to adjust their entry status to work in Italy, and non-EU citizens may find it difficult to obtain permission to work if they have entered on a tourist basis.

The work visa is issued by the Italian consulate in your home country, and you should check well before departure to see what documents are needed and the time requirements (see Chapter Four). For example, a visa can sometimes be issued quickly if you are coming only for a fairly brief business trip. Business visitors from countries as listed above don't need a visa if the trip is projected to last fewer than three months, but if you are working at an Italian company, a visa might be recommended to avoid problems for that company with the Department of Labour. If, however, you are coming on a secondment, receipt of a visa might take up to three months.

There are specific requirements also for people coming to Italy for medical cures, for religious purposes, or for engaging in sports. Check with the nearest consulate well in advance of your planned departure.

If you have obtained a non-tourist stay permit for at least a year, you may register as a resident after just a few weeks. This is important, for a residence permit is required even to buy a car or to bring your own goods into Italy. Either use one of the relocation agencies that is expert in dealing with the bureaucracy, or go to the **Anagrafe** in Via Luigi Petroselli 50 (tel: 67101); you must bring the *permesso di soggiorno*, passport size photos, the *codice fiscale* (see Chapter Eight), and the current fee. It is open mornings only. You can also register at your *circoscrizione*, the local registry district. After registration, you will be officially listed as a resident in that *circoscrizione*. When departing for good, go back to the Anagrafe and deregister; ask for the *Abbandono di Residenza* and make sure you are no longer registered in your *circoscrizione*.

Once you have the residence permit, you must understand and abide by laws for Roman residents, such a registering at the Anagrafe every change of residence and filing appropriate tax returns. That there are many laws unknown to newcomers makes it imperative to use a knowledgeable expert such as a relocation agency, international attorney or *commercialista*. (See Chapters Two and Seven.)

## STUDENT VISAS

A tourist visa is not valid for studying in Italy. Those who speak Italian and want to enrol seriously in an Italian university must before departure obtain a student visa. A valid passport is needed, a picture, a declaration of financial responsibility, and certification from an Italian consulate in the home country that the qualifications are acceptable. Students must also have an official acceptance letter from the university or school, indicating the program to be studied, the date it commences and its duration. A notarised letter from an insurance company must attest to the student's medical insurance; British students may bring the E111 form. Note that requirements change; ask well in advance what will be needed and how long the process will take. Students from countries that do not require an entry visa may enter to study at an Italian university program of three months or less designed for foreign students.

## IMPORTATION OF PERSONAL EFFECTS

Used personal effects such as household items and furniture may be imported by foreigners with a *permesso di soggiorno* tax-free for up to six months after arrival in Italy. Work with the shippers as early as possible to discuss documentation and inventories needed. (See Chapter Two.)

One automobile may be imported, if it is more than one year old. All documentation must be brought with the car: title, registration and insurance papers. The car must have valid license plates to be driven in Italy pending transfer to Italian documentation. (See also Chapter Ten.)

## OFFICIAL TRANSLATORS

Some documents require translation by an Italian-government recognised official translator. Those below are among the English-speaking authorised translators. Also ask your relocation agency or *commercialista* for recommendations. For translators and interpreters for meetings, see Chapter Seven. See the Yellow Pages under *Traduttori e Interpreti*.

- **ABC Traduzioni**: Via R. Lanciani 74 (tel: 86 32 32 79)
- **Agenzia Barberini**: Piazza Barberini 5 (tel: 49 91 497)
- **Centro Traduttori Associati**: Via Asmara 37 (tel: 83 82 210)
- **Agenzia San Bernardo**: Piazza San Bernardo 102/c (tel: 48 85 856)
- **World Translation Center**: Via Santa Maria Maggiore 181 (tel: 48 81 039)

## ITALIAN EMBASSIES ABROAD

In most countries Italy has one embassy, located in the capital of that country. In larger countries it also has consulates, and travellers should go to the nearest consulate to determine the requirements for visas, permits, etc. Note that requirements change, that every consulate does not always have the most recent forms or information, and that the consulates may be understaffed. Applicants may have to be persistent in their requests.

- **Australia**: 12 Grey Street, Deakin, Canberra A.C.T. 2600 (tel: 6/273-3333; fax: 273-4223)
- **Canada**: Embassy at 275 Slater Street, Ottawa, Ont K1P 5H9 (tel: 613/232-2401; fax: 233-1484); Consulate at 3489 Drummond Street, Montreal, Quebec H3G 1X6 (tel: 514/849-8351)
- **England**: Embassy at 14, Three Kings Yard, London W1Y2EH (tel: 171/312-2200); Consulate at 111 Piccadilly, Manchester (tel: 161/236-9024)
- **New Zealand**: 34 Grant Road, Wellington (tel: 4/473-5339; fax: 472-7255)
- **Scotland and Northern Ireland:** Consulate at 32, Melville Street, Edinburgh EH3 7HA (tel: 131/220-3695)
- **South Africa**: 796 George Avenue, Arcadia, Pretoria (tel: 12/435-541; fax: 435-547). From January through June, 2 Grey's Pass Gardens, Capetown (21/235-157; fax: 240-146).

Italy has consulates throughout the **United States**. The Italian Embassy is at 1601 Fuller Street, NW, Washington, DC 20009 (tel: 202/328-5500; fax: 462-3605). Consulates are as follows:

- **Boston**: 100 Boylston Street (tel: 617/542-0483)
- **Chicago**: 500 North Michigan Avenue (tel: 312/467-1550)
- **Detroit**: 535 Griswold Street (tel: 313/963-8560)
- **Houston**: 1300 Post Oak Boulevard (tel: 713/850-7520)
- **Los Angeles**: 12400 Wilshire Boulevard (tel: 310/820-0622)
- **New Orleans**: 630 Camp Street (tel: 504/524-1557)
- **New York**: 690 Park Avenue (tel: 212/737-9100)
- **Philadelphia**: 100 South Sixth Street (tel: 215/592-7329)
- **San Francisco**: 2590 Webster Street (tel: 415/931-4924)

# FOREIGN EMBASSIES IN ROME

Embassies provide emergency services for their citizens in Rome and are most helpful to their country's citizens during times of crisis: they replace lost passports, and they will help in medical or

legal emergencies by referring their citizens to appropriate doctors, dentists, or lawyers; they do not, however, help people get
out of jail. They can be the liaison between the family at home in
emergency situations, as well. For non-emergencies, they also
record births, marriages and deaths of their citizens, and they can
provide advice on matters of importance, such as absentee voting
or filing taxes while abroad. Sometimes they will offer their citizens detailed information on local services that will be helpful
during their sojourn; these include lists of English-speaking doctors and attorneys, international schools, etc. (See *Ambasciate* in
the Yellow Pages.)

Some countries allow their citizens to register their presence in the country, making it easier to replace lost passports and
to be contacted in case of emergency. Information is confidential
and not released unless the person permits. Inquire of your embassy. Bring your passport and be prepared to fill out a form that
asks your address in Rome, telephone number, next of kin, etc.

Most embassies are open for consular affairs in the mornings only, or close at lunch time. Some have afternoon telephone
hours. Check to determine when your embassy is open before
going. Note also the national holidays of your own country, for on
those days the embassy will no doubt be closed.

- **Australia**: Via Alessandria 215 (tel: 85 27 21; fax: 85 27 23 00)
- **Canada:** Via Zara 30 (tel: 44 59 81; emergency tel: 033/37 72
  71 95)
- **Great Britain** Via XX Settembre 80/a (tel: 48 25 441; fax: 48
  53 324)
- **Ireland**: Piazza Campitelli 3 (tel: 69 79 121)
- **New Zealand**: Via Zara 28 (tel: 44 02 928; fax: 44 02 984)
- **South Africa**: Via Tanaro 14/16 (tel: 85 25 41)
- **United States:** Via Veneto 119/a-121 (tel: 46741; fax 46 74 22
  17). Emergencies also handled at Department of State (US
  tel: 202/647-5226). Ask for the duty officer.

Always carry a copy of the first pages of your passport with you. Write the emergency number of your embassy on the back, along with other pertinent information that would help you in case of emergency. If you lose your passport, report it at the Questura and take the report and two passport photos to the Consulate. If you have the *permesso di soggiorno*, you must carry it with you at all times.

# Chapter Four

# WORK AND STUDY

## WORK PERMITS

Foreigners who intend to work in Italy must have the *permesso di soggiorno per lavoro* (work permit). EU nationals may work in Italy upon receipt of the work permit, and they may use the state employment services freely. After receiving the stay and work permits, register at the **Ufficio di Collocamento** in Via R. Vignale 14 (tels: 72 13 779; 72 99 11). Like an employment agency, this is also a place to look for a job. Questions may also be answered at the **Ispettorato del Lavoro** in Via Cesare de Lollis 6 (tel: 44 49 32 97).

Non-EU citizens may obtain the work permit under specific conditions. Employees of a home-based company coming to work at a branch in Rome may obtain a work permit. So may prospective employees of an Italian company who have a written, formal job offer: the employer will apply for the work permit and send it to the person in advance of departure for Italy, so the entry visa can be obtained from an Italian consulate. The employer will have had to prove that the position could not have been filled from the local market, as only jobs that no Italian can fill may be offered to foreigners. These jobs are rare. For people who do not have pre-arranged jobs, however, finding a salaried position will be difficult, if not impossible. Unemployment in Italy has been hovering around 12%, and employment practices favour Italian citizens first, EU citizens next.

There are two other categories in which a non-EU citizen may apply for a work visa.

- An **'independent worker'** is someone working for a non-Italian company and coming to Italy on a particular company related project; a work contract and request letter detailing the type of work to be done are required in addition to other standard documentation.
- **'Self-employed'** people are qualified professionals hoping to offer their services on a freelance basis. Professional credentials, a detailed resume, and documentation demonstrating the capacity and need to work in the field will be required. Applications are filed directly with the nearest Italian consulate. After the appropriate ministries have approved the application, the consulate will be notified, and the applicant then continues the process for the stay permit. This all takes time, and six months in advance is not too soon to start.

All workers, no matter how categorised, must obtain a *codice fiscale* (tax identification number) described in Chapter Eight.

## WORK OPTIONS

Thinking about working in Rome requires some ingenuity, and there are some options to explore, as long in advance as possible. It will probably be impossible to arrive in Rome and find a job; in addition, changing the visa status once a tourist visa has been issued is also difficult.

Teaching in an international school is a possibility, but you need to start the search very early — no later than January for the following September. You will need to provide excellent qualifications: college degree, teaching certificate, proof of experience, etc. Several organisations such as **International Schools Services (ISS)** hold recruiting fairs (US tel: 609/452-0990). Addresses of international schools in Rome can be found in Chapter Five; substitute teaching in these schools is also a possibility. Universities are listed at the end of this chapter.

Teaching English privately is a possibility, but as an occupation in an Italian school or a language school, don't count on it. This is an increasingly popular occupation for young expatriates, and EU citizens are arriving in droves each year with official credentials for teaching ESL. People who want to teach English privately should be well prepared, making sure to bring good grammar books and ESL workbooks (some are available at English-language bookshops; see Chapter Fourteen). People with RSA/ TEFL certificates should look under *Scuole di Lingua* in the Yellow Pages. *Wanted in Rome* (see Chapter Nine) carries ads, and the **International House** (tel: 446 2602) in Via Marghera 22 offers courses and has a notice board. You can also post your own notices at the English-language bookshops, or at the University of Rome. The best time to look is in early Fall, just before the semester and courses begin.

Some people with writing experience provide their local newspaper with freelance articles or a 'Letter from Rome' on a regular basis, arranging in advance the type of material to be covered, the length of the articles, method of payment, etc. Query letters to magazines and newspapers concerning specific articles also sometimes bring results. Otherwise, finding writing or editing jobs once you're in Rome — despite terrible English translations of most Italian materials — will be impossible. To pursue writing opportunities, you will need a computer, probably with a modem: see Chapters Nine and Fourteen.

To begin inquiries, make sure you have an Italian translation of your resume. It is also helpful to have business cards should you be asked to an interview, as they are exchanged automatically upon first meeting. When responding to an advertisement, make sure to send a neat, informative and detailed cover letter with your resume. Although resumes are important, personal contacts are even more so.

Being an *alla pari* (au pair), a live-in nanny in a family home, is a possibility, receiving room and board and some spending money in return for taking care of children and sometimes doing the housework. *Alla pari* do not need a work permit, but working full-time in someone's home may not provide the Italian experience one has come for; these are, nonetheless, official positions and the head of the family must register the person with the *Questura* and assume responsibility for the person during the time of the contract. Make sure you understand the requirements of the family before accepting a position.

Occasionally the **UN Food and Agricultural Organization (FAO)** in Via delle Terme di Caracalla hires English speakers for administrative positions, for whom special visas are then given. Application forms are at the gate. The tourist industry also occasionally hires foreigners for short term work, as English speakers are always needed; see the newspapers for listings.

## STUDYING ITALIAN

It's important to make an effort to speak Italian as soon as possible, especially if you are looking for a job. Although shopkeepers in the city centre will speak English to tourists, and although many younger Italians have studied English in school, outside the city centre it is rare to find English speakers. If you want to communicate with government offices, schools, or businesses, don't assume that people speak English. Upper level managers in international businesses often speak several languages. Nonetheless, it is not only polite to make every effort to speak the language of their country, it will help you understand more quickly the Roman culture and how it works. Romans are encouraging of those who try to speak their language, no matter how badly at first. Italian language schools offer both intensive and casual courses. Look in the Yellow Pages under *Scuole Varie — Scuole di Lingue* and in the English-language publications described in Chapter Nine.

- **Dante Alighieri**: Piazza Firenze 27 in the Centro Storico (tel: 68 73 722). Traditionally taught lessons for all levels. Business Italian and cultural classes as well.
- **DILIT**: Via Marghera 22, just above Stazione Termini (tel: 44 62 602; fax: 44 40 888). A well established school with a variety of courses and cultural activities.
- **Italia Idea**: Piazza della Cancelleria 85, just off Corso Vittorio Emanuele II (tel: 68 30 76 20; fax: 68 92 997). Both intensive and extensive group courses, individual programs, and evening programs.
- **Leonardo da Vinci**: Corso Vittorio Emanuele 39, at Largo Argentina (tel: 67 98 896; fax: 67 95 185). Morning or afternoon classes for individuals or groups of all levels. Cultural courses as well.
- **Torre di Babele**: Via Bixio 74, near Stazione Termini and just off Via Principe Eugenio (tel: 70 08 434; fax: 70 49 71 50). Intensive and non-intensive Italian language courses for groups and individuals. Student outings around Rome help with conversational experience.

## UNIVERSITY STUDY

Those who speak Italian fluently and want to enrol in an Italian university must before departure obtain the student visa, as described in Chapter Three. Write the university directly, or the Italian consulate near you; the Italian embassy should have application forms. Otherwise, when applying in Rome, see below.

The **Università di Roma (La Sapienza)** in Piazzale Aldo Moro is near San Lorenzo. The largest university in Italy, more than 100,000 students filter through; about 5% are foreign students. Founded in the 14th century, La Sapienza has been in this location only since Mussolini moved it here in the 1930s, hence the fascist architecture of enormous, austere, square buildings. The main building of the Administration (**Economato**) is in Piazzale Aldo Moro 5 (tel: 49911). The **Segreteria Stranieri**, which advises foreign students, is in this building (C-2); hours: 8:30 am-noon, Monday, Wednesday and Friday. For a small fee, **Nuovo Centro Servizi Universitari**, a private service at Viale Ippocrate 160, helps with enrolment, registering for courses and other bureaucratic matters; with the fee come discounts to a variety of services throughout Rome (tel: 44 55 741; fax: 44 55 743). The **Ufficio Centrale Studenti Esteri in Italia (UCSEI)** in Lungotevere dei Vallati 14 (tel: 68 80 40 62) works with students who are already enrolled. Other important Italian educational institutions are:

- **L.U.I.S.S.**: Viale Pola 12 (tel: 67 48 67 20; fax: 84 12 956). Well respected private university founded in the early seventies. Programs in political science, business and law. There is also a School of Journalism.
- **Università Gregoriana**: Piazza della Pilotta 4 (tel: 67011). A Church-run school, it offers courses in religion, philosophy and political science. Excellent library.

Other options for university study include taking courses or degrees given in English from a variety of higher institutions with degree-granting programs in Rome. (There are many more than those listed below.) **The Association of American College and University Programs in Italy (AACUPI)** in Corso Vittorio

Emanuele II 110 has information, and can offer various types of advice on dealing with the bureaucracy (tel: 68 80 47 52). And sometimes information can be had from the Ministry for Universities and Scientific Research (toll free tel: 167/01 96 36).

- **The American University of Rome**: Via Pietro Rosselli 4 in Monteverde Vecchio (tel: 58 33 09 19; fax: 58 33 09 92). An accredited independent college offering bachelor degrees in various disciplines. Also a two-year A.A. degree program and continuing education programs. Summer sessions. For information, write Director of Admissions at address above.
- **John Cabot University**: Via della Lungara 233, in Trastevere (tel: 68 78 881; fax: 68 32 088). A full English-language university, offering degree and auditing courses in business administration, international affairs, English literature and art history. Run on the quarter system, the sessions begin in September, January, April and June. It is affiliated with Hiram College in Ohio, USA.
- **European School of Economics**: Largo del Nazareno 25 (tel: 67 80 503; fax: 67 80 293). Undergraduate degrees in international business, and a one-year graduate course.
- **Loyola University of Chicago**: Via Massimi 114/a, north at Monte Mario (tel: 35 58 81). Founded in 1962, an accredited undergraduate college offering courses in a variety of subjects, primarily in the Classical World, the Renaissance and contemporary Europe. A number of other Catholic colleges are affiliated. No summer sessions. For information, write Loyola University of Chicago, Rome Center of Liberal Arts, 6525 N. Sheridan Road, Chicago, Ill 60626 USA (US tels: 800/344-ROMA; 312/508-2760).
- **St. John's University Graduate Center Rome**: Pontificio Oratoria San Pietro, Via Santa Maria Mediatrice 24 (tel: 63 69 37; fax: 63 69 01). Accredited university offering MBA in international finance and executive management.

95

- **Tech Rome**: P.O. Box 3172 Ruston, LA 71272 (US tel: 800/ 346-8324). Louisiana Tech's Europe campus, offers six-week Summer programs in Rome and up to 13 hours semester credit, with more than 40 courses to choose from. Open to non-degree students as well.
- **Temple University Rome**: Lungotevere Arnaldo da Brescia 15 (tel: 32 02 808; fax: 32 02 583). Programs for a semester or year for undergraduate students in architecture, liberal arts, Italian studies, visual arts and international business. Tyler School of Art graduate program offers courses in painting/ drawing, sculpture, photography, print making, photography, and more. Write International Programs, Office of Vice Provost, Conwell Hall, 5th Floor, Temple University, Philadelphia, PA 19122 (US tel: 215/204-4684).

In addition, check with the **Council on International Education Exchange** office in your country. The CIEE administers study abroad programs, university enrolment service, internships. The Rome office is in Via della Lungara 233, in Trastevere (tel: 68 32 109; fax: 68 93 701).

## Non-credit Courses and Seminars

Look in the media, both Italian and English, for other courses, one-time seminars or lessons in a variety of fields; as in any large city, there are many to choose from. The weekly events guides *Trovaroma* and *Roma C'è* list current opportunities. The English language **Economy Book & Video Center** in Via Torino 36 offers an extensive series of interesting seminars and workshops each year, from wine tasting to writing, from watercolours to Dante's *Divine Comedy* (tel: 47 46 877); Economy publishes its own calendar of events and courses.

For more specialised study, there are options in all fields: look in the English-language publications, the events guides and in the Yellow Pages. The **Centro Sperimentale di Cinematografia** in Via Tuscolana 1524, for example, offers a wide variety of courses pertaining to film, and foreign students are welcome (tel: 72 29 41). Adjacent to the famous **Cinecittà**, this is Italy's largest film school. The **Gruppo Archeologico Romano** in Via degli Scipioni 30/a has an English-language program in art history and gives archeological lectures, tours and trips (tel & fax: 39 73 40 87).

It's also rewarding to take **cooking classes** in a country that has such a distinctive cuisine. Some of the language schools offer their own classes, and there are cooking schools such as **A Tavola con lo Chef** (At the Table with the Chef) in Via dei Gracchi 60 (tel & fax: 32 03 402); English interpretation is available. For courses in Italian, try **Pepe Verde** in Via S. Caterina da Siena 46, near the Pantheon (tel & fax: 67 90 528). It offers cooking courses of all sorts, including classes for 'men in the kitchen.'

# LIBRARIES

When first visiting the English-language libraries, bring identification with you. Some also require proof that you are a resident, albeit temporary. Some charge for use. The last two listed below are Italian libraries of importance; each *circoscrizione* also has its own public library. And the English-language universities listed above have libraries that are available for use. Note that in Italian, library is *biblioteca* and a book shop is a *libreria*. (For book shops, see Chapter Fourteen.)

- **USIS (American Embassy Library)**: Via Veneto 119/a, at the United States Embassy (tel: 46 74 24 81). Current periodicals and reference materials on American political and social affairs. Some recently published nonfiction and fiction works. Hours: weekday afternoons.
- **American Academy in Rome**: Via Angelo Masina 5 (tel: 58461). Library use with a recommendation from a professor at home, documenting need. Researchers must bring evidence of their project.

- **British Council Library**: Via delle Quattro Fontane 20, off Piazza Barberini (tel: 48 81 979). A cultural centre, with much research online, and a film and lecture program. Members may borrow books. Closed the end of July and August.
- **The British School of Rome**: Piazzale Winston Churchill 5, off Viale Bruno Buozzi (tel: 32 22 155). Open to visiting British scholars and students; photo and documentation of research need required. Hours: 9:30 am-1:00 pm and 2:00 pm-7:30 pm weekdays.
- **Centro di Studi Americani**: Via Caetani 32, near the Ghetto has a library open to students of Anglo-American subjects (tel: 68 80 16 13). Check for opening hours.
- **Santa Susanna Church**: Via XX Settembre 15 (tel: 48 27 510). Large lending library, open to all. Open Sunday, Tuesday, and Thursday mornings; Wednesday and Friday afternoons; closed Monday and Saturday.
- **Biblioteca Nazionale Centrale**: Viale Castro Pretorio 105 (tel: 4989). The Italian national library, it holds all Italian books published. Open 8:30 am-7:00 pm weekdays. Open Saturday morning; closed August.
- **Biblioteca Universitaria Alessandrina**: Piazzale Aldo Moro 5 (tel: 44 41 565). La Sapienza's main library, specialising in philosophy, history, literature, social sciences and economics. Hours: 8:30 am-1:30 pm and 2:00 pm-6:00 pm; open Saturday morning. Open to the public.

# CHILDREN

As you might suspect, Romans love children. Children travel free on public transit (under four years old and under three-feet-three-inches tall), they pay no admittance at museums and galleries, and they are welcome in restaurants. Most restaurants have high chairs *(seggioloni)* and will try to place a family with a young child at a comfortable table. Italians tend to make a fuss over children, tweaking and patting, and this may take some getting used to, although it has only the most friendly and respectful intent.

Getting your children set for a long stay in Rome is not difficult. For babies, disposable diapers and pureed foods are readily available at pharmacies and supermarkets. Inoculations required are basically the same as those worldwide (DPT, Polio, Hepatitis B) and English-speaking pharmacists and doctors are available. Childhood diseases in Rome are no different than anywhere else, but be prepared for the usual colds and sore throats, especially if your children go to school. See Chapter Six for health related issues.

# SCHOOLS

Selecting a child's school, of course, will be based on considerations other than just the location or reputation of a school: the age, character and language ability of the child should be considered, as well as the expected length of stay in Rome and planned return into home country schooling. Some long-term foreign based parents prefer private international English-speaking schools throughout the child's educational career; others start their children out in the international schools and after a period of adjustment and language learning slowly move their children into the local school system. The curriculum in the Italian school system is demanding, and no special attention is given to students without fluent Italian.

In Rome there is a good selection of international English-language schools and most provide the high scholastic education required by European schools. The international curriculum is stringent and of high academic quality, for entrance into European universities is at a premium. These are all private schools, and may seem expensive, but they are generally in line with international private academic schools; in addition to tuition, a registration fee is usually charged. Sometimes, especially with entry of more than one child, reduced tuition is available, as are scholarships. As most of the schools are out of the city centre, transportation is usually available at extra cost. Many of the schools have sports and after school programs. Consider purchasing the *ISS Directory of Overseas Schools*, distributed by Peterson's Guides (US tel: 800/338-3282). The English-language magazine *Wanted in Rome* publishes an annual directory of Rome's international schools. The embassies should have complete lists as well

For pre-schoolers of ages 3-6 there are private *scuole materne*, which often have daycare opportunities for toddlers as well. (Also see *Nidi d'infanzia* in the Yellow Pages). English-speaking teachers can help your child get acclimatised to the new environment. These schools accept children for morning hours only, for afternoons or all day. Transportation is usually available at extra cost. Lunch is often included in the costs.

- **Greenwood Garden School**: Via Vito Sinisi 5, north off the Cassia (tel & fax: 33 26 67 03). Children from ages 2-6 are taught on the American/British system.
- **Kendale Primary International School**: Via Gradoli 86, to the northwest at Tomba di Nerone (tel & fax: 33 26 76 08). Both the US and UK curriculum from 3-10 years of age. Discounts for more than one child.
- **Socrate Bilingual School**: Via Casale San Nicola 150, in the Cassia zone (tel: 30 89 09 08; fax: 30 89 55 02). An Italian/English curriculum from nursery school to high school.
- **Casa dei Bambini**: Viale di Vigna Pia 2, to the south of Trastevere (tel & fax: 55 87 851). An authorised Montessori School, with English spoken. Hours are flexible, according to needs of parents. Closed August.
- **Ambrit International School**: Via Filippo Tajani 50 (tel: 55 95 305 fax: 55 95 309). Kindergarten, primary and middle school students through 9th grade. Students must have fluent English and an above average student record. Pre-acceptance interview.
- **American Overseas School of Rome**: Via Cassia 811 (tel: 33 26 48 41; fax: 33 26 26 08). American curriculum in classes from pre-kindergarten through high school. Computer lab and instruction. An international mix of students. Boarding is an option for grades 8-13.
- **Marymount International School**: Via di Villa Lauchili 180 north, off the Cassia (tel: 36 30 17 42; fax: 36 30 17 38). US and international curriculum from ages 3-18.
- **The New School**: Via della Camilluccia 669 north, near Monte Mario (tel: 32 94 269; fax: 32 97 546). Coeducational and established in 1972, it takes children from 3-18 years. English

101

curriculum, plus preparation for SAT, British university qualifiers. Transport available.

- **Rome International School**: Via Morgagni 25, off Viale Regina Margherita (tel: 44 24 33 28; fax: 44 24 30 90). British curriculum for students from 2-13 years, including a mother/toddler play group. Fees do not include bus, lunches, swimming, tennis or field trips.
- **St. George's English School**: Via Cassia, La Storta (tel: 30 89 01 41; fax: 30 89 24 90). British curriculum, for children 3-18 years of age, kindergarten-high school. Half-day kindergarten available. Hot lunch, sports, books and field trips included.
- **St. Stephen's School**: Via Aventina 3, in l'Aventino (tel: 57 50 605; fax: 57 41 941). Coed high school founded in 1964, offering American and international baccalaureate. Day and boarding programs for ages 13-19. Full sports program.

## SCOUTING

There are active scouting troops for all boys and girls from six to seventeen years old, from Cub and Boy Scouts to Girl Scouts. Because troop leaders and meeting locales change, call the Community Liaison Office of the American Embassy for current information (tel: 46 74 23 34).

## PLAYGROUNDS AND CHILDREN'S ATTRACTIONS

Some of Rome's larger parks have playgrounds *(parco giochi)*, and most have some kind of children's attractions; parks are generally open from early morning to dusk. Smaller neighbourhood parks are generally filled with parents and children during the morning and after the afternoon nap. For sporting opportunities such as bowling alleys and swimming pools, see Chapter Thirteen.

- **Villa Borghese** is accessible to any central area. Rental rowboats on **Giardino del Lago** (9:30 am-1:00 pm and 2:00 pm-7:00 pm) and bicycles are nearby. Pony rides, an amusement park, ducks, mini-trains and the **Cinema dei Piccoli** in Viale della Pineta 15 shows cartoons (tel: 85 53 485). Paved paths for roller skating and biking. The **zoo** is in Viale del Giardino Zoologico 20 (tel: 32 16 564).

- **Villa Ada**, convenient to Parioli and Salario, has two playgrounds, plus a roller skating rink, carousel, rowboats, and pony rentals. Generally full of young children and their nannies — and older skateboarders.
- **Villa Balestra**, just north of Viale Bruno Buozzi, offers a playground and rides in pony carts.
- **Villa Glori**, in the same area, just above Via Maresciallo Pilsudski, has a playground and pony rides.
- **Villaggio Olimpico**, off Corso di Francia, has a good playground and a roller skating facility.
- **Villa Celimontana**, near the Colosseo/Lateran districts, has a large playground and a bicycle track, as well as outdoor theatre performances in clement weather.
- **Villa Sciarra**, off Via Calandrelli, is a popular park in Monteverde Vecchio. It has a playground with swings, a sandpile, a workout course for older children, a carousel, a roller coaster and an aviary.
- **Gianicolo**, on the hill behind Trastevere, has a splendid view of Rome. Donkey rides in summer and puppet shows on Piazza Garibaldi afternoons (except Wednesday). A cannon is shot daily at noon. Rome's botanical gardens are here: entrance on Via Corsini. Open daily, but hours vary seasonally.
- **Villa Doria Pamphili**, Rome's largest park, to the west of the Gianicolo, has a large playground, running tracks, pony rides, an aviary, and paths and gardens of interest.
- **Parco Schuster**, near Piazzale S. Paolo, is a small park with merry-go-rounds and bocce courts.
- **Baby Park**, in Via Tiburtina in San Lorenzo, has a playground, merry-go-round and jungle gym.

# STRUCTURED ENTERTAINMENT

Few museums are designed especially for children, although many will be of interest. There are, however, some puppet theatres and special events: to find out what's going on each week, look in *Trovaroma*, which is the Thursday supplement to *La Repubblica*, or in *Metro* or *Roma C'è*. Many of the famous attractions will be of interest to children: throwing a coin into the Trevi Fountain, climbing to the dome of St. Peter's, watching the changing of the guard at the Quirinale Palace, and at Christmas there is **Befana**, the children's fair in Piazza Navona (see Chapter Fifteen). Note that the **Biblioteca Centrale per i Ragazzi**, the children's library, is in Via San Paolo alla Regola 16 (tel: 68 65 116). There is a small selection of books in foreign languages. Opening hours vary, and the library is closed for two weeks in August. Residents may borrow books.

- **Puppet Theatre**: Via di Grotta Pinta 2 (tel: 58 96 201). Puppet shows in English. Sundays at 5:00 pm.
- **Teatro dei Satiri**: Via di Grotta Pinta 19 (tel: 68 71 639). Puppet shows, often in English. Closed summers.
- **Teatro delle Marionette degli Accettella**: Via Giovanni Genocchi 15, in EUR (tel: 51 39 405). Sort of a children's cabaret theatre, it has performances on Saturday and Sunday at 4:30 pm. Closed August.
- **Teatro Mongiovino** in Via. G. Genocchi 15 (tels: 86 01 733). Traditional puppet shows in Italian. Tuesday-Friday at 10:00 am, Saturday and Sunday at 4:30 pm.
- **Grauco** in Via Perugia 34 shows children's cartoons at 4:30 pm on Saturday and Sunday (tel: 78 24 167).
- **Hydromania**: Vicolo Casal Lumbroso, at Exit 33 of the Grande Raccordo Anulare (tel: 66 92 844). Large water park with an Olympic-sized pool, slides, water massage, 'kamikaze,' tennis courts and *calcetto*.
- **Acqua Piper**: An aquatic park in Via Maremmana Inferiore, about 15 miles from the city centre at Guidonia (0774/3 26 538).

Shuttle bus from the city centre. Pools with waves, water slides, pools for toddlers, pony rides, electronic games, restaurant and picnic area.

- **Luneur**: Via delle Tre Fontane (tel: 59 25 933). The city's year-round amusement park in EUR. Ferris wheel, merry-go-rounds, a roller coaster, haunted house, other carnival attractions, and a miniature golf course. Hours vary according to the season.
- **Oasi Park**, year-round amusement park in Via Tarquinio Collatino 56-58, near Cinecittà (tel: 76 96 21 12).
- **Bomarzo Monster Park** is 60 miles north of Rome near Viterbo, off Highway A1, or by train to Attigliano and then a local bus (tel: 0761/92 40 29). Built in the 16th century by an eccentric nobleman, there are giant stone monsters scattered throughout a pleasant wooded park, and kids can climb all over them and explore a rather strange house.

## EATING OUT WITH CHILDREN

Children are welcome in most Italian restaurants, especially in local neighbourhoods and in areas such as the Cassia, near the international schools. There are times, however, when a burger is just what is called for, and Rome obliges with many fast food emporia. Afterwards, you can find ice cream in *gelaterie* in any neighbourhood. In addition, if there are particular cereals or peanut butters or other favourite foods that are missed at home, you might look for them at **Castroni** or **Ruggeri**, or in the other international groceries described in Chapter Twelve.

- **Big Burg**, fast-food chain. One is in Via del Tritone 212 (tel: 67 94 129), convenient to the Centro Storico.
- **McDonald's**: Piazza di Spagna (tel: 69 92 24 00); Piazza della Repubblica 40 (tel: 48 15 510); Piazza Sonnino 39 (tel: 58 97 127); Corso Vittorio Emanuele II 137 (tel: 68 92 04 12); in EUR at Piazzale Don Luigi Sturzo 21 (tel: 59 11 683).

105

- **Burghy**, fast food chain. Piazza della Rotonda 14 (tel: 68 75 643); Via Cola di Rienzo 157 (tel: 68 74 225); Via Barberini 2 (tel: 48 71 257); Stazione Termini (tel: 48 28 935); and at Cinecittà Due (tel: 72 21 172).

## A NIGHT OUT

For nights out, arrange for a baby sitter as long in advance as possible; don't call on weekends and expect to find a sitter available. Rates vary according to time of day. Ask your friends or at the international schools for recommendations. English-speaking baby sitters often advertise in *Wanted in Rome* and *Metropolitan*, English-language publications described in Chapter Nine, and they put up notices on the bulletin boards of such churches as All Saints and Santa Susanna (see Chapter Sixteen). You can try calling the English-language universities, which post baby sitting opportunities on notice boards (see Chapter Four). Also see the weekly events magazine *Roma C'è*.

- **La Luna Nel Pozzo**: (tel: 30 16 541; fax: 30 16 552). Babysitting, cooking, help for the aged, parties, dog watching, plant watering, etc. English spoken.
- **Crescere Insieme**: (tel: 55 65 133). Baby sitters, parties, help for expectant and new mothers.
- **Hallo Baby**: (tel: 33 80 703). English-speaking baby sitters available.

# CHAPTER SIX

# STAYING HEALTHY

## BEFORE YOU LEAVE HOME

Ensuring good health while abroad should begin before you leave home. Arriving in Rome requires no particular medical precautions or vaccinations. If you haven't had a tetanus shot within the last ten years, however, you should consider updating your inoculations whether you are travelling or not. And, if you are bringing children, make sure to bring a copy of their inoculation records; DPT, polio, and Hepatitis B vaccinations are required of all children.

Daily living in Rome should pose no problems. The water is safe, milk is pasteurised, and raw vegetables can generally be eaten with no qualms. Even the water bubbling from spigots in the street is drinkable (unless there is an *acqua non potabile* sign). It's all sanitary and travellers needn't hold back in fear of becoming ill.

Any concerned person may call the **United States Center for Disease Control's** hotline to hear recorded, current international health information, including how to avoid and treat

107

travellers' diarrhoea (US tel: 404/332-4559; fax: 332-4565). There is also a booklet, *Health Information for International Travelers*, which may be purchased for US$6.50 from any US Government Printing Office shop or ordered from The Superintendent of Documents, US Government Printing Office, Washington, D.C. 20402 (tel: 202/512-1800).

American travellers should call US State Department's **Overseas Citizens Services Center** for automated, current Consular Information Reports for all major countries, which are updated as the situation of a given country warrants (tel: 202/647-5225; fax: 647-3000). British travellers should call the **British Foreign and Commonwealth Office** (tel: 171/ 270-4129). Canadians should call the **Ministry of Foreign Affairs** (tel: 800/267-6788).

Although Rome itself offers no particular health risks to the traveller, your own existing health conditions will, of course, accompany you wherever you go. When travelling abroad, instant identification of a long standing condition may be life saving. If you have a chronic illness such as diabetes or a heart condition, think about wearing an identification bracelet that details the condition and gives a 24-hour medical reference to call. Keep a list of your allergies and other emergency information with your passport.

- United States — **Medic Alert** records health information and sells identification bracelets (tel: 800/432- 5378). Medic Alert has a 24-hour service, so any doctor worldwide can obtain current information on a member. The person's name and condition are engraved on the bracelet, as is the hotline number to be called collect. It takes about six weeks to receive the bracelet and to have health information recorded.
- United Kingdom — **Medicalert Foundation**: 21 Bridge Wharf, 156 Caledonian Road, London N19UU (tel: 171/833-3034). Records medical information for members and issues a metal emblem with the person's name and condition engraved, and the 24-hour Medicalert worldwide telephone number.

- Worldwide — **International SOS Assistance**: (U.S. tel: 215/244-1500; England tel: 181/744-0066; Switzerland tel: 22/347-6161). Subscription service offering referrals for medical and personal emergencies, evacuation, etc. SOS centres are worldwide.
- Worldwide — **Europe Assistance Worldwide/Worldwide Assistance Incorporated**: (British tel: 181/680-1234; US tel: 800/821-2828)

In addition, consider how to treat your existing conditions should it become necessary. Make sure to consult your physician before departure to discuss medication alterations at the beginning of time changes.

- **American Diabetes Association**, 1660 Duke Street, Alexandria Va 22314, issues *Travel and Diabetics* (tel: 800/232-3472). You can also get a list of diabetic organisations abroad from The Diabetic Traveler (tel: 203/327-5832).
- **British Diabetic Association**: 10 Queen Anne Street, London W1M 0BD (tel: 171/32301531).
- **Canadian Diabetes Association**: 15 Toronto Street, Suite 1001, Toronto, Ont M5C2E3 (tel: 416/-363- 3373).
- **International Diabetes Federation**: International Association Center, Rue Washington 40, B1050 Brussels, Belgium (tel: 2/647-4414).

Be sure to carry your important medications on board with you when you fly, for checked luggage can go astray. If your medication includes syringes or other items that might be questioned, carry with you some proof of their medical need. To avoid needless questions, make sure that your prescriptions are in their original, labelled containers. Make sure you have with you a copy of your eyeglass prescription and an extra pair of glasses.

# ENGLISH-SPEAKING DOCTORS

Finding English-speaking doctors in Rome can be done before departure. The **International Association for Medical Assistance**

**to Travelers**, a worldwide non-profit association, provides its members with a list of screened and approved English-speaking doctors abroad; the physicians agree to a preset fee schedule. Membership in IAMAT is free, but donations are encouraged. To receive a list of doctors and IAMAT centres in Rome: in the United States write IAMAT at 417 Center St., Lewiston NY 14092 (tel: 716/754-4883); in Canada, write 40 Regal Road, Guelph, Ontario N1K1B5 (tel: 519/836-0102); in New Zealand, write P.O. Box 5049, 438 Pananui Road, Christchurch 5 (tel: 03/352-9053; fax: 352-4630).

Most credit card companies will help Gold Card holders find a doctor (or a lawyer) abroad. They assist in making arrangements for emergency evacuation, for transporting others as needed, or in relaying messages to those concerned. Call your credit card company to find out about its health related services and to obtain its 24-hour telephone number. Generally, toll-free numbers are not dialled from abroad, but there are area code numbers at which the credit card company will accept collect calls. VISA participates in this referral program, and it also provides an emergency Italian number for those eligible to participate (toll free tel: 167/819 014). In addition, you should call your own credit card company at home and request an informational brochure.

Once in Rome, of course, you should be able to find other doctors or specialists through your friends and colleagues or the concierge at your lodgings. The embassies also have current lists of English-speaking general practitioners, specialists, and dentists.

# HEALTH INSURANCE

If your current company is sending you to Rome, the personnel department should be knowledgeable about health insurance coverage for employees abroad; check to see how you will be covered and the extent of the coverage. If you will be working for an Italian company, you will have the residence permit and other documents that allow you to enter the Italian system, wherein all people, even foreigners, are covered. All foreigners in Rome may receive treatment for health emergencies.

Otherwise, if you have health insurance, contact your carrier to find out whether you are covered for both emergency and routine claims when out of the country and how to file a claim. Some carriers provide full coverage and require only the same physician-completed documentation as at home: name of doctor, diagnosis, date and description of treatment, and fees paid. Some companies offer travel insurance riders to be added to the main plan for the length of the stay.

For short stays, Americans might try **Access America** at 600 West Broad Street, Richmond VA 23230 (tel: 800/424-3391); that has varied coverage. And **Travel Assistance International** at 1133 15th Street NW, Washington D.C. 20005 (tel: 800/821-2828), offers emergency assistance coverage for up to a year. For long term insurance, you might start your inquiries with **Wallach and Company** at 107 West Federal Street, PO Box 480, Middleburg VA 22117 (tel: 800/237- 6615), which offers several long-term plans, including Health Care Global and MedHelp.

Coverage, costs, deductibles and exclusions vary. Since Italy has good medical and emergency facilities, you should determine what additional coverage you need and what you are willing to pay for. Some policies include coverage for trip cancellation and lost luggage; this may duplicate other insurance that you hold, so you may not want it. In addition to determining policies concerning exclusions and preexisting conditions, questions to ask would include what kind of forms and receipts are necessary, what the deductible is, whether prescriptions are covered, whether payment up front is necessary and what the time line is for reimbursement.

Registered students should consider buying an **International Student Identification Card (ISIC)** before departure, and faculty should consider the **International Teacher Identification Card (ITIC)**. They both provide some accident, illness and hospital insurance in addition to other services. The card is valid for 16 months, beginning in September. Cards are available at many travel agencies that cater to students, or in Rome at the **Centro Turistico Studentesco Giovanile**, in Via Genova 16 (tel: 46791; fax: 46 79 205). Card holders may call collect to London for help (24-hour tel: 44181/666-9205).

Students up to 23 years can obtain insurance for up to ten months from **International Travelers Assistance Association** at PO Box 5375, Timonium MD 21094 (tel: 800/732-5309). Its **TravMed** program includes $50,000 of medical benefits and $200 of dental emergencies at $2 per day.

Older Americans should be aware that Medicare does not cover travel abroad (except for Mexico and Canada) and should investigate Medigap policies that supplement Medicare, offering coverage against catastrophes abroad. The **American Association of Retired Persons** (US tel: 800/ 523-5800) and the **National Council of Senior Citizens** (US tel: 800/ 596-6272) offer Medigap coverage and some emergency coverage abroad.

Canadians are covered by the national health plan only to the amount that similar services would be covered at home, so most travellers buy additional insurance. Provincial Ministry of Health Offices should have information on how to cover health services abroad. And travel agents can inform you about additional insurance.

British travellers should obtain an E111 form before departure. All EU citizens are entitled to receive health services throughout the EU. The E111 is available from post offices and the Department of Health and Social Security, which offers a booklet, *Health Advice to Travellers*. In Rome the E111 should be exchanged for a Temporary Resident's Form 503E at a **Unità Sanitaria Locale (USL)** office. USL offices are listed in the phone book and are open weekdays. Or, apply at the main USL in Via Ariosto 3, near the Lateran (tel: 77301); bring the *permesso di soggiorno* and *codice fiscale* (see Chapter Eight). Enrolling for a year costs L750,000, but this may cost less than private insurance. Note that medical visits and medications are not free. Be prepared to pay for tests, x-rays and other laboratory costs and to pay small fees for clinic visits. The British Embassy in Via XX Settembre 80 will provide a list of English-speaking doctors; (tel: 48 25 441). And check on supplemental insurance with your travel agent, for brief stays may not be worth the effort of dealing with the Italian bureaucracy.

Non-EU citizens who wish to enrol in the health system must bring an identity card, a residence, work or study permit, and the USL form indicating their doctor. The national insurance department, **INPS**, handles non-EU requests (tels: 59051; 77381). Decentralised, INPS is in each *circoscrizione*.

## HEALTH PROBLEMS AND PHARMACIES

Any sudden changes in diet or climate can cause brief discomfort. This may very well be true in Rome if you suddenly start overdoing it on the potent Italian coffee, or drastically increasing your intake of olive oil which, like any other oil, is a laxative. In addition, Rome in the summer can be extremely hot, and the heat combined with air pollution from the street clogging traffic can bring on allergies or aggravate asthmatic conditions.

The chlorinated water, safe to drink, is extremely rich in minerals — especially calcium. To cope with the calcium, Romans themselves often drink bottled water. In addition to the more famous **San Pellegrino** brand, inexpensive bottled water is readily available — both naturally carbonated and still — and such slightly fizzy brands as **Uliveto, Ferrarelle**, and **Acqua di Nepi** are available in any food shop. **Acqua Panna** and **Acqua Vera** are good still waters. There are many others.

*Farmacie* (pharmacies) generally are just for health and baby related products, although some — especially the *erboristerie* (herb and natural pharmacy shops) — carry items of a broader range. If you need cosmetics, try a *profumeria*, which specialises in name-brand beauty products; pharmacies generally carry only those that are hypo-allergenic. Although pharmacies used to dispense many common medicines freely, the situation is changing, rules are tightening, and some common remedies can no longer be had without a prescription. Thus, it might be wise to bring small supplies of anti-diarrhoea medications and antihistamines if you are prone to digestive or respiratory problems. Women who tend toward yeast infections might take along one of the over-the-counter clotrimazole kits with cream and suppositories. Think of the particular brands of pharmaceuticals you regularly use and take some along for use until you get settled.

This is especially true for those who are bringing children. Check with your paediatrician to determine which medicines and other items you should have with you until you can set yourself up with a paediatrician in Rome. Make sure to bring a copy of your child's health records, especially inoculation records, as mentioned above. Make sure all inoculations are up to date.

Pharmacies carry such standard items as toothpaste, aspirin, ibuprofen, cough syrup and throat lozenges, sunscreen, mosquito repellent, mild sleep aids, tampons and contraceptives, and more. Be aware of the dosages on pain relievers and other such products. Ibuprofen, for example, often comes in dosages of 400mg, double that sold in some other countries.

If you have prescriptions that need regular refilling, make sure you arrange this before you leave home. Take as much with you as is practical and ask your physician to write a prescription using the generic (often Latin) name of the drug. When speaking to a Roman pharmacist about prescriptions, it will be helpful if you can be specific about the name of the condition, as many names are based on the Latin and are recognisable even to those who don't speak English. Check with your medical insurance company: if it covers medications, it will usually cover a vacation length amount bought in advance; with a letter indicating a longer term abroad, larger amounts may also be covered.

Pharmacies are recognisable by their external signage, an illuminated cross. Most pharmacies close at lunchtime; in general, hours are 8:30 am-1:00 pm and 4:00 pm-8:00 pm. One pharmacy in each district stays open 24 hours on a rotating basis. Each pharmacy should have a sign posted in its window indicating which pharmacy in the district is open on which night, and there should be a list in the daily newspapers. For a complete list of permanent 24-hour pharmacies, consult *In caso di emergenza* in the *TuttoCittà* supplement to the telephone book. For information, call 110. Home delivery of prescriptions is available to those over 65 or disabled (tel: 28 89 41).

Until you find a 24-hour pharmacy in your neighbourhood, try one of these.

- *Corso Francia* — **Giudice:** Corso Francia 174/176 (tel: 32 91 650).
- *Ghetto/Campo de' Fiori* — **Arenula:** Via Arenula 73 (tel: 68 80 32 78).
- *Laterano* — **Primavera:** Via Appia Nuova 213 (tel: 70 16 971).
- *Ludovisi* — **Gellini:** Corso d'Italia 100 (tel: 44 24 97 50).
- *Trevi* — **Internazionale Barberini:** Piazza Barberini 49 (tel: 48 25 456).

- *Parioli* — **Tre Madonne**: Via Bertoloni 5 (tel: 80 73 423).
- *Prati* — **Farmacia Cola di Rienzo**: Via Cola di Rienzo 213 (tel: 32 43 130).
- *Quirinale* — **Piram**: Via Nazionale 228 (tel: 48 80 754).
- *Termini* — **Farmacia Grieco**: Piazza della Repubblica 67 (tel: 48 80 410).
- *Termini* — **Della Stazione**: Piazza dei Cinquecento 49 (tel: 48 80 019)
- *Trastevere* — **Portuense**: Via Portuense 425 (tel: 55 62 653).
- *Via del Corso* — **Del Corso**: Via del Corso 242 (tel: 67 92 983).

Most have some international brands of medicines. **Farmacia Cristo Re dei Ferrovieri** in Stazione Termini is open daily from 7:00 am-11:30 pm (tel: 48 80 776). **Farmacia Trinità de'Monti** in Piazza di Spagna 30 (tel: 67 90 626) carries some international products as does **Farmacia del Vaticano**, by the Porta Sant'Anna (tel: 69 88 34 22); bring your passport and prescription.

## Erboristerie
*Erboristerie* are pharmacies that also dispense herbal medications not requiring prescriptions. *Valeriana*, made from the herb valerian, for example, is a popular sleeping aid, available without a prescription. Pharmacists are knowledgeable, and shops usually carry a wide variety of dietetic and natural products, as well.

- *Centro* — **Euronatural**: Via delle Colonnelle 1 (tel: 67 87 408).
- *San Silvestro* — **Erboristeria di M. Messegue**: Piazza San Silvestro 8, in the Galleria (tel: 67 97 294).
- *Piazza di Spagna* — **Antica Drogheria Condotti**: Via Mario de' Fiori 24 (tel: 67 89 896).
- *Piazza del Popolo* — **Farmacia di Ripetta**: Via di Ripetta 23 (tel: 32 10 257).
- *Trastevere* — **Antica Farmacia S. Maria in Trastevere**: Piazza S.Maria in Trastevere (tel: 58 03 776).

116

- *Trastevere* — **Antica Farmacia S. Agata**: Piazza Sonnino 47 (tel: 58 03 715).
- *Trionfale* — **Erboristeria La Strega II**: Largo Trionfale 10 (tel: 37 51 73 56)

# EMERGENCY AID/HOSPITALS

A **Pronto Soccorso** sign at a hospital means emergency medical aid is available. Public hospitals have *pronto soccorso*; private clinics do not. The list below shows the emergency rooms by district. (See Appendix for emergency telephone numbers.)

- *Cassia* — **San Pietro Fatebenefratelli:** Via Cassia 600 (tel: 33581).
- *Lateran/Esquilino* — **San Giovanni**: Via dell' Amba Aradam 9 (tels: 77051; 77191).
- *Monteverde Nuovo* — **San Camillo**: Circonvallazione Gianicolense 87 (tel: 58 70 46 66).
- *Parioli/Salario/Tiburtino/Esquilino* — **Policlinico Umberto I**: Viale del Policlinico 255 (tel: 44 62 341; anti-poison tel: 49 06 63).
- *Piazza del Popolo/ Centro* — **San Giacomo in Augusta**: Via A. Canova 29 (tel: 36261).
- *Prati/Trastevere* — **Santo Spirito**: Lungotevere in Sassia 3 (tel: 65 09 01).
- *Trastevere/Ghetto* — **Fatebenefratelli**: On the Tiber Island: Piazza Fatebenefratelli 2 (tel: 68 37 299).
- *Trastevere/Aventino* — **Nuovo Regina Margherita**: Via Emilio Morosini 29 (tel: 58441).

There are several specialised hospitals as well, each with *pronto soccorso* facilities.

- **Bambin Gesù**: Piazza San Onofrio 4 (tel: 68591). The leading children's hospital.
- **Centro Traumatologico Ortopedico (CTO)**: Via San Nemesio 28 (tel: 51 49 11). Broken bones.

- **European Hospital**: Via Portuense 700 in Trastevere (tel: 65 97 59). Rome University's school of cardiac surgery; all branches of medicine are practised. Translators and some English-speaking doctors available.
- **Istituto Dermopatico dell'Immacolata** dei Monti di Creta 106 (tel: 66461). Skin care. Surgery, plastic surgery, tumours, etc.
- **Ospedale Israelitico**: Via Fulda 14, specialises in geriatric problems (tel: 65 58 91; appointments toll free: 167/01 00 48)
- **Ospedale Oftalmico**, in Piazzale degli Eroi 11 (tel: 39 73 62 03). Specialises in eye problems.
- **Policlinico Gemelli** in Largo Gemelli 8 (tel: 30 15 40 36). Anti-poison centre (tel: 30 54 343).
- **San Eugenio**: Piazzale Umanesimo 10, in EUR (tel: 5904). Burn centre.

There are several private, English-speaking hospitals and facilities without emergency wards. Patients may be transferred to these hospitals after having received emergency treatment elsewhere. English-speaking outpatient care and referrals are also available.

- **Salvator Mundi International Hospital** in Viale delle Mura Gianicolensi 67 is a popular private hospital accessible to Trastevere and Prati (tel: 58 89 61). No emergency facilities. English spoken; help with reimbursement of health insurance.
- **Rome American Hospital**, in Via Emilio Longoni 69 (24-hour tel: 22551; physician's weekday tel: 22 55 290). Full-service private hospital. Coronary care centre and ambulance service with intensive care mobile unit. English-speaking doctor on call. Help with reimbursement for insurance.
- **International Medical Center** in Via Amendola 7 has English-speaking doctors on call, a mobile first-aid center and a coronary unit, aids in admission to hospitals and clinics, and has a 24-hour referral service; it will also set up appointments and offers other services (tels: 48 82 371).

• **Ambulatorio Samo** in Piazza Navona 49 (tel: 68 80 61 45). Homeopathic health centre. General medicine, paediatrics, gynaecology, psychological consulting, acupuncture, and otolaryngology. Laboratory tests are available, as well as general surgery. English-speaking doctors available. Open weekdays.

## Getting to the Hospital
If you are driving to a hospital in a medical emergency, wave a white handkerchief or tissue, or tie one to the radio aerial, and honk your horn; traffic will let you by. The **Croce Rossa** is a public ambulance service (tel: 5510), but it may not have enough medical equipment or trained personnel on board; request that a doctor be on board. **Medital** has well equipped ambulances (tel: 167/49 14 91), as does the **Croce Bianca** (tel: 81 81 011). In all cases be explicit about needing a doctor and equipment on board.

## Dental Needs
Dentists in Rome are well trained, and all needed services are readily available. Yet, it is always best to have all needed dental work completed before leaving home. If you are concerned that a tooth might soon have problems, bring dated x-rays with you, to avoid excess x-rays. For private English-speaking dentists, get a list from the American or British embassy, or see the *English Yellow Pages*.

For dental emergencies, call or go to **Ospedale G. Eastman** in Viale Regina Elena 287/b, near San Lorenzo and Tiburtino (tel: 84 48 31). It can handle dental emergencies on a 24-hour basis.

## HIV/AIDS Information
The Ministry of Health has a toll-free number for information and referrals concerning **AIDS**: call 167/86 10 61. For information on **AIDS** treatment, call 58 75 212. In addition, try **POSITIFS** *(Associazione persone sieropositive e con AIDS)* in Via di Valle Aurelia 111 (tel: 63 80 365). **OSA** offers medical advice and care for AIDS

119

patients (tel: 167/86 90 27). The **Associazione Nazionale Lotta all'AIDS** is in Via Barberini 3 (tel: 48 20 999). The **Centro Mario Mieli** in Via Corinto 5 has a gay health service, including HIV testing (tel: 54 13 985; fax: 54 13 971). AIDS testing is generally available at all major hospitals.

## Problems with Coping

The Community for Healthy Living, established by the American Embassy, provides preventive mental health programs for Americans in Rome (tel: 46 74 21 90). **The Samaritans** in Via Giovanni in Laterano 250 will listen — in confidence — to people who are lonely or otherwise troubled (tel: 70 45 44 44). Hours: 1:00 pm-10:00 pm.

There are several facilities for help with alcohol and substance abuse. **Alcoholics Anonymous** meets at St. Paul's in Via Napoli 58 (tel: 48 83 339), and at St. Andrew's in Via XX Settembre 7 (tel: 48 27 627). There are also meetings of **Narcotics Anonymous** and **Al-Anon**. Call the churches for schedules.

## Births and Deaths

All births while out of your home country should be registered immediately at your embassy or consulate. Inquire as to procedures for ensuring citizenship at home for new births. British citizens who were not born in Britain, or whose parents were not, should obtain a leaflet and information from the embassy, as passing on citizenship is not automatic. The birth will be recorded also with the city; obstetricians or the local hospitals will follow the appropriate procedures.

Notify your embassy if there is a death in your family. All deaths must also be officially recorded with the city of Rome. The attending doctor or hospital will know the current procedure for official recording of a death. The city's *obitorio* (morgue) is at Piazzale del Verano 8 (tel: 44 56 220).

120

# Chapter Seven

# BUSINESS MATTERS

Italy is rated as the fifth industrialised nation in the world. Although none of its industries dominate, it is competitive worldwide in automobiles, machinery, chemicals and pharmaceuticals, textiles and shoes; iron, steel and cement, and robotics also feature heavily in the economy. Italy's was an agricultural economy until World War II, yet the country is a net food importer: much of its land is not suitable for farming and its few natural resources are primarily in natural gas, fish, and marble. A large part of its economy has been based on the transformation of raw materials, mostly imported, into a finished product. There is a considerable difference in the geographical make-up of Italy: the North is primarily industrialised, with double the *per capita* income of the agricultural South.

Over the years Italy's economic performance, despite continuing political uncertainty, has been steadily improving, and international trade — especially growth in exports — continues as an important priority. Some 55% of its exports are to EU countries, and about 10% to the United States; its imports follow much the same ratio. In broad terms, Italy is a net importer of energy, chemicals and metals, and a net exporter of manufactured goods and textiles. Its agricultural output focuses on cereals, wine, and olive oil.

The business atmosphere in Italy is in the process of major change. The Italian government, until recently having controlled some 20% of the country's economy, is seeking to align its policies with other EU countries, and some of the largest government holdings are being privatised. This includes the government's heretofore tightly-controlled telecommunications, energy and electricity monopolies. In addition, many of the large traditionally family run industries such as Fininvest, Fiat, Pirelli and Olivetti, long dominant in the Italian economy, are turning over the reins to a younger generation that has trained management expertise, international ambitions, and multinational connections. This is all making an increasingly welcome atmosphere for foreign investment: branches of multinational corporations and international commercial chains are opening in major Italian cities, and new opportunities are also taking hold for businesses on a smaller scale and for joint Italian-foreign enterprises.

Italy is open to foreign investment, and 100% foreign ownership of a corporation is allowed. No screening procedures are directed solely at foreign investment, although the government reserves for itself the right to review mergers and acquisitions over a certain financial level, and it may block mergers for 'reasons essential to the national economy.' Only a few industries, such as domestic air transport, aircraft manufacturing, railways, and tobacco manufacturing are closely regulated or prohibited to foreign investment.

One of the new opportunities taking hold is franchising, with approximately 15% of the retail trade controlled by franchises: fast food, sports clothing and shoes, beauty products, and houseware are strong in this area, and couriers, computer software and hardware, and management consulting are growing. Italians are beginning to consume frozen foods, bottled speciality drinks, imported beers, and non-traditional ethnic foods. And the need of the Italian export market for raw materials is constant: forest products, skins and hides, soybeans and grains.

# BUSINESS CONSIDERATIONS

While first considering a business enterprise in Italy, make sure to avail yourself of all information from government trade agencies — both Italian and foreign (see below). Economic information is most concisely available from foreign sources. In initial planning, note that in August nothing will get done and there is nobody around to do it. This also means that if you are opening a shop or other business that depends on the year-round participation of the public, you should feature in your planning the disappearance of Romans from the city in August. This also holds true around Christmas and the New Year.

It is especially important to take into account the labour pool you will need for labour laws are strictly regulated. Foreigners may be offered only jobs that no Italian can fill; EU nationals seconded to Italy, however, do not require work permits. In addition, benefits costs such as Social Security contributions are high, and can account for up to 45% of the total labour cost. There are eleven national holidays; employees generally get three to four weeks of vacation annually, plus five personal days off. Strikes are less frequent than in the past, but labour and union rights are importantly upheld since the Workers' Statute of 1970.

Most important is that meeting the requirements of the bureaucracy in Italy, always difficult, is getting no easier. If there was previously a seemingly impossible tangle of arcane requirements and regulations to wade through, it is now compounded by new programs to eradicate the corruption heretofore so widely rampant throughout the system. *Mani pulite* is the 'clean hands' effort to create a more honest government and corporate structure, while figuring out who in the past was guilty of what. Progress is being made on some fronts, yet dealing with the bureaucracy in Italy is still a matter of overcoming its ever-present red tape.

## Permits, Approvals and Taxation

The legal and tax structure for private industry is also complicated, and it is said that Italy is a country with 250,000 laws. Many of these laws seem to the cynical only to be called upon in reference to a permit or form someone currently needs. Industrial projects require a multitude of approvals and permits, long to accomplish, and in general, foreign investments often receive close bureaucratic scrutiny. Nonetheless, the overhaul of the government is proceeding apace, with some new laws added, some antiquated ones repealed, with the result that currently, although the system is actually becoming more manageable, it may seem less understandable. It is thus crucial when starting a business or doing business in Italy to have the best advice and representation possible: a good attorney specialising in your field, international accountant, and *commercialista*. In the end, there are profitable opportunities for business on all levels.

## Business Climate in Rome

Rome, of course, is the site of thousands of years of history and culture that draw millions of tourists each year, and it is the political and bureaucratic centre of the country. Yet it is only the country's third-ranked industrial city. The main financial centre, including the main stock exchange, is in Milan; although there is a Roma Borsa, it is less important, and Roman stockbrokers increasingly access the Milan exchange electronically. The heaviest manufacturing industries such as steel and automotive are headquartered in the northern cities including Milan, Turin and

Genoa. Nonetheless, Rome claims to lead the Italian field in computer enterprises, engineering companies, research, and public communications. In fact, with 2000 small businesses, 40,000 stores, and five multi-service commercial centres, Rome — with its resident population now heading towards four million — is a viable commercial centre, servicing also the more than ten million visitors filtering through each year.

# SETTING UP A BUSINESS
People ready to start a business in Rome must first ensure their own ability — or that of their agents — to remain and do business in Italy, by obtaining the *permesso di soggiorno* and *codice fiscale* (see Chapters Two and Eight). The next step is to consult an attorney and *commercialista*, the people most qualified to offer expert advice on the appropriate legal form for business enterprises, the taxes and liabilities associated with each, as well as recommending other needed technical help; they can also help with the permits mentioned above. A good attorney should help you choose the simplest business structure possible and will help take care of all bureaucratic requirements. Each type of business requires different forms and applications; some require a business license. All individuals and firms doing business in Italy must be registered with the local **Chamber of Commerce, Industry and Agriculture**, a quasi-government office. To register, an agent of the company must produce a power of attorney notarised at an Italian consulate in the home country. In Rome, work with your attorney, and for information contact the **Unione Italiana delle Camere di Commercio, Industria, Artigianato ed Agricoltura** in Piazza Sallustio 21 (tel: 47041).

## Legal Forms of Business Enterprise
• **Ditta Individuale** (sole proprietorship). Some may require a permit; trade names must be registered.

- **Società in nome colletivo-snc** (general partnership). Partners have unlimited liability for obligations.
- **Sede Secondaria** (branch of a foreign corporation). Filing with Italian courts and Register of Enterprises required.
- **Società in accomandita semplice-sas** (limited partnership). Minimum of one partner with unlimited liability and one with limited liability.
- **Società a responsibilità limitata-SrL** (corporation). For small and medium-sized businesses.
- **Società per Azioni-SpA** (joint stock corporation). Minimum capital requirements; governed by shareholders.

## Legal and Management Assistance

There are quite a few English-speaking attorneys practising in Rome, and your embassy should have a list or suggestions, including some Italian, English-speaking firms. Relocation agencies can also be helpful in finding the appropriate specialist. Look also in the *English Yellow Pages* (see Chapter Nine). Although foreign lawyers may not appear in Italian courts, most foreign lawyers are allied with Italian attorneys and work closely with them. It is considered unethical for Italian lawyers to advertise, and Italian law does not permit lawyers to accept cases on contingency or percentage basis; be sure to discuss fees in advance. Some of the firms have offices in other countries as well, making international dealings convenient.

- **Tonon e Associati**: Via Toscana 30 (tel: 42 87 10 33; fax: 42 74 47 08). Italian international firm with offices also in Milan, New York, Los Angeles and La Paz. **Danilo Tonon**, partner.
- **Alegi & Associates** in Via XX Settembre 1 (tel: 48 20 147; fax: 48 71 149). **Peter Alegi**, an American lawyer long established in Rome.
- **Studio Legale Associato Frères Cholmeley Bischoff**: Viale Bruno Buozzi 47 (tel: 80 80 133; fax: 80 80 134). **Donald Carroll**, American partner in an international firm.

- **Sinisi, Ceschini, Mancini & Partners** in Via Carrara 24 (tel: 32 21 485; fax: 36 13 266). Offices in Milan, Atlanta, San Diego and Athens. **Roberta Ceschini** and **Vittorio Sinisi**, partners.
- **Grippo, Associati e Simmons & Simmons**: Piazza Sallustio 9 (tel: 48 70 920; fax: 48 28 562). British-Italian firm with offices in London, Paris, Brussels, Lisbon, Hong Kong, Shanghai, Abu Dhabi and New York.

There are also several internationally known management consulting firms that can offer advice on management, taxes, and accounting procedures.

- **Arthur Andersen**: Via Campania 47 (tel: 47 80 51; fax: 48 23 684)
- **Coopers and Lybrand**: Via Quattro Fontane 15 (tel: 48 18 565; fax: 48 14 636)
- **Ernst & Young**: Via Romagnosi 18/a (tel: 32 47 51; fax: 32 47 55 04)
- **Peat Marwick Fides**: Via Sardegna 40 (tel: 48 26 251; fax: 48 71 280)
- **Price Waterhouse**: Via Bosio 22 (tel: 44 24 20 98)

Note the subtle differences between the various types of Italian accounting experts, although in some instances they overlap: a *commercialista* is a certified accountant with a degree in economics and commerce who, having passed the qualifying exam, may prepare taxes and review contracts to ensure accuracy, that all the legalities are being met, and that the contracts are beneficial to their clients, as much as possible; a *ragioniere* is also an accountant, often without a degree but who is knowledgeable in all facets of financial bureaucracy, an administrator who keeps a firm's books and who can assure a business that all government requirements are being met. Last, a person used in all negotiations is a *notaio*, a notary public, a public official who guarantees signatures and documents.

## Business Guides

A helpful guide is *Business Guide to Italy*, published by **Connect** at Via Lorenzo Valla 40, 00152 Rome (tel: 58 09 690; fax: 58 80 851). Articles with hands-on information are written by international lawyers and accountants doing business in Rome, and in the back there is a directory of services and products. Connect also arranges meetings and luncheons for business networking.

The **British Chamber of Commerce** in Via Camperio 9, Milan, issues a helpful publication called *Britaly*, an informative guide to doing business in Italy (tel: 02/87 77 98; fax: 86 46 18 85).

Americans should ask the IRS Forms Distribution Center, P.O. Box 25866, Richmond, VA 23289 for Publication 953, *International Tax Information for Business*; also request other publications that help Americans in international business. In Rome, inquire at the IRS office at the Consulate.

## United States Trade Promotion

The United States and Foreign Commercial Service at the United States Embassy in Via Vittorio Veneto 119/a, is the agency for trade promotion and assistance for United States exporters (tel: 46 74 22 02; fax: 46 74 21 13). It sponsors programs to help American exporters find buyers, locate agents and distributors, and find optimum trade opportunities. It organises trade missions and appears at trade fairs. It produces Industry Sector Analyses, country specific market information for a variety of industries. There are also publications on taxation issues, and on United States/Italian legal and accounting practices. In Washington, it is part of the International Trade Administration, Department of Commerce.

Anyone can receive information from The National Trade Data Bank at the U.S. Commerce Department. It is a comprehensive source of world trade data and an excellent source of global market research for prospective foreign business ventures. Through its Stat-USA section, automated information on the availability of its products is available to anyone by fax. A CD-ROM on the U.S. Global Trade Outlook and 119 Industry Trends Tables is available for US$24.95. Call or write STAT-USA, U.S. Department of Commerce, Room H-4885, Washington DC 20230 (US tel: 202/482-1986).

## British Trade Promotion

Great Britain has several government sponsored programs to help British commercial interests in Italy. The Director of Trade Promotion is headquartered at the Consulate in Milan in Via San Paolo 7, and it is this office that coordinates Britain's commercial efforts throughout Italy (tel: 02/72 30 01). In Rome, there is an active Commercial and Economic Section at the British Embassy in Via XX Settembre (tel: 48 25 441). The offices offer marketing information services, export representative services, assessments of overseas companies, representation at major trade fairs, seminar arrangements, and more.

In Great Britain, The Overseas Trade Services (OTS) sets policy and oversees activities of the diplomatic posts abroad. Its personnel comes from the Foreign & Commonwealth Office and the Department of Trade and Industry. Contact Business in Europe, Department of Trade and Industry, Kingsgate House, 66-74 Victoria Street, London, SE1E 6SW. The DTI sells Export publications, including country profiles to help investors build a picture of the market (tel: 0171/510-0171; fax: 510-0197).

## Chambers of Commerce

Chambers of Commerce, generally corporate membership organisations, provide information and networking possibilities. The headquarters for the Chambers of Commerce of Great Britain and the United States are both in Milan.

- **British Chamber of Commerce**: Via Camperio 9, Milan (tel: 02/87 77 98; fax: 86 46 18 85)

129

- **American Chamber of Commerce in Italy**: Via Cantu 1, Milan (tel: 02/86 90 661; fax: 80 57 737) For information in Rome, call John Fanti, the honorary representative (tel: 51 86 11).
- The **Italian-Canadian Chamber of Commerce** is in Via delle Quattro Fontane 15 (tel: 48 83 979).
- The **Australian Chamber of Commerce** is in Via Barberini 86 (tel: 47 43 565).
- **Camere di Commercio Internazionali**: Via XX Settembre 5 (tel: 48 82 575).
- **Unione Italiana delle Camere di Commercio, Industria, Artigianato ed Agricoltura**: Piazza Sallustio 21 (tel: 47041)
- **Camera di Commercio di Roma**: Via de' Burró 147 (tel: 67 91 309)

For contacts outside Italy the **Assocamerestero**, the association of Italian Chambers of Commerce Abroad, has offices in 17 countries including the United States and England. It connects business people to Italy, facilitating international trade. It issues an annual *Business Atlas* listing the Italian Chambers worldwide and gives financial statistics about all countries. In Rome, Assocamerestero is in Via Flaminia 21 (tel: 32 15 660).

The main office of the **Italy America Chamber of Commerce** is at 730 Fifth Avenue, Suite 600, New York, NY 10019 (tel: 212/459-0044). In England, contact the **Camera Commercio per la Gran Bretagna** in 296 Regent Street, London WIR6AE (tel: 0171/637-3153).

## Trade Fairs

Trade fairs are a good way of test marketing a product and determining public interest in it. Attendance at the trade show can also expand your professional contacts and customer base, and of course, scout the competition. Some government agencies take part in trade fairs throughout Italy (and the rest of the world) and help their citizens determine the most effective manner to publicise their products. Milan has the largest fairgrounds in Italy, and it hosts some 75 trade shows each year; there are others throughout the country, including Rome. The largest trade fairs in Italy are BIT (tourism), MIPAN (machinery), SMAU (information technology), SIM (furniture), LEVANTE (industrial and consumer goods), MAC (chemicals), AUTO (automobiles), and SAMOTER (building machinery). Others of importance concern pharmaceuticals, natural stone, wine, and footwear.

- **Fiera Milano:** Largo Domodossola 1, 20145 Milano (tel: 02/49971; fax: 49 97 71 74)
- **Fiera di Roma:** Via dei Georgofili 7, 00147 Roma (tel: 51781; fax: 51 78 205)

# GOVERNMENT OFFICES

The government of Italy is divided into three spheres: the Parliament, the Government (the executive branch), and the Judiciary. The President of the Republic, with some responsibilities in all three spheres, and the constitutional court work to maintain an equilibrium among the branches. Government ministries and offices are in the capital. The Presidential offices, Senate and Parliament are in the city centre, while many of the other ministries are situated further out, some in EUR.

- **Ministry of Foreign Affairs:** Piazzale della Farnesina 1 (tel: 36911)
- **Ministry of Foreign Trade** Viale America 341 (tel: 59931)
- **Ministry of Finance**: Viale Boston 20 (tel: 59971)
- **Ministry of Industry**: Via Molise 2 (tel: 47051)
- **Ministry of Interior**: Palazzo del Viminale 7 (tel: 4651)
- **Ministry of Justice**: Via Arenula 70 (tel: 68851)
- **Ministry of Labor**: Via Flavia 6 (tel: 46831)
- **Ministry of Post and Telecommunications**: Viale America 201 (tel: 59581)

- **Ministry of Transport and Navigation**: Piazza della Croce Rossa 1 (tel: 84941)
- **Ministry of Universities and Research**: Piazzale Kennedy 20 (tel: 59911)

**United Nations**

The headquarters of the **United Nations Food and Agriculture Organization** (FAO) are in Viale delle Terme di Caracalla (tel: 52251). There is a general **U.N. Information Center** in Piazza San Marco 50 (tel: 67 89 907).

# BUSINESS CUSTOMS

Despite functioning in a high-tech modern industrial society, Rome and its business customs persistently remain Mediterranean at their core. Don't expect government offices or your business colleagues to operate on a nine-to-five schedule. Although *orario non-stop* (open all day) is catching on, businesses and offices outside the direct centre generally experience some extended closure at midday. Some traditional business lunches take place, yet many busier people, especially those with international dealings, routinely take sandwiches at their desks. Government offices may not be open in the late afternoon, although some may be open one or two afternoons a week. In general, morning office hours can be from 8:30/9:00 am to 1:00/1:30 pm. They start again between 3:00 and 5:00 pm and stay open until 7:00–8:00 pm. Make appointments well in advance, and try to avoid setting meetings for early morning or just after lunch; mid-morning, late afternoon, or early evening can be most effective. Despite the Roman tendency to take time casually, you should always be on time for a meeting and apologise if you are not.

Italian business works best using the personal approach. Be professional, yet personable and friendly. Make sure to follow up all meetings, and schedule follow-up visits. Acknowledge all correspondence and provide information requested in a timely fashion to your Italian contact or counterpart.

Make every effort to speak Italian, at whatever level you can, both to be polite in business situations and for protection of your interests, although even fluency in the language will not be enough to guide you through the arcane bureaucracy for which Italy is famous. Do not assume that Italian government officials on any level speak English or will do so in their business dealings even if they can. High level people in international business often have several languages, but it is courteous to begin by speaking their language. Write introductory business letters in Italian; if you can't do it, get someone to translate your correspondence for you. If the reply is written in English, future letters may be written in English. Trade literature, catalogues and instructional brochures should be in Italian, and complex oral presentations, no matter in which language presented, should be accompanied by written documentation in Italian.

The business lunch or dinner is an important event. Take every opportunity to meet new people and to further your contacts. Expect to spend several hours over a multi-course business meal, especially in initial negotiating stages. Despite the myth of heavy drinking Italians, alcohol is usually enjoyed only at meals, generally a bottle of good wine, with an occasional *aperitivo* of vermouth before. If it is your treat at the restaurant, sometimes it is best to arrange with the restaurant proprietor beforehand that you get the bill. Romans will generally *fare la scena* (make the gesture to pay), no matter whose invitation it was orginally.

## Interpersonal Customs
Italians are courteous and friendly in business situations, and will exchange flowery pleasantries for a while at the beginning of business encounters. Nonetheless, if you are speaking Italian, always use the formal third-person singular, and begin by using the

133

person's honorific and last name. This is true in all situations, whether professional, personal or commercial. Do not assume that just by meeting you are automatically on a first name basis. Address a woman as *signora*, and men either as *signore*, or *dottore*, since everyone with a college degree is a dottore. Medical doctors are also *dottore*, unless they are affiliated with a university, in which case say *professore*. A woman in this situation, of course, would be a *dottoressa* or a *professoressa*. Attorneys are addressed as *avvocato* and engineers as *ingegnere*.

## Business Cards

The exchanging of a *biglietto da visita* (business/visiting card) is an important opening in any professional situation, although not at social occasions. Thus, many Italians have two such cards. One is seen as a private card, with just the person's name, address and telephone number, this one to use in personal situations, to enclose with gifts, and to give to those you would want to have your home address. The actual business card will display the person's name and honorific, position title, company name, address, telephone and telefax numbers.

Despite someone's job title, it can sometimes be difficult to tell from a business card who actually has the power in a corporation. Family-run industries formed after World War II are now seeing the younger generations making their way to the top. The previously corrupt corporate structure, riddled with patronage positions and held together by an increasingly evident system of bribes and payoffs, is in the process of being examined. An Italian saying is that the less information on a business card, the more important the person.

Italian business cards are often slightly larger than those used in the United States or Britain, are generally printed (or engraved) black on white. You can order them from any **tipograpfia** or **centro per fotocopie**. For basic business cards, use one of the machines that for approximately L10,000 will print cards instantly in a variety of print styles and sizes. Machines can be found throughout the city, in supermarkets such as Standa and UPIM, and near Largo Argentina in Via Arenula 85.

## Networking

No matter where you do business, personal contacts are one key to success. There is an active expatriate community in Rome for both professional and social contacts; people tend to be welcoming to newcomers in both areas, and sometimes the two categories will overlap. Welcome Home, described in Chapter Two, hosts neighbourhood coffee meetings and publishes a newsletter targeted to the new arrival in Rome. In addition, the organisations listed below are valuable for making both professional and personal contacts. Note also that the Rome group of **Rotary Club** is at Lungotevere Flaminio 22 (tel: 32 26 434), and **Lion's Club International** is at Via Piave 49 (tel: 42 87 07 78).

- **American Club of Rome**: c/o Marymount School, Via di Villa Lauchili 180 (tel: 32 95 843). Helps Americans in Rome to meet each other, with monthly luncheons, guest speakers, dinners and an annual tennis tournament.
- **American Women's Association of Rome**, Hotel Savoy, Via Ludovisi 15 (tel: 48 25 268). Monthly meetings, tours, trips, seminars and an annual member directory.
- **Canadian Women's Association of Rome**, hosts coffee meetings, luncheons and a variety of cultural activities for Canadian women (tel: 36 30 08 43).
- **Commonwealth Club**: contact Mary Handley at American University of Rome, Via Pietro Rosselli 4, hosts monthly lunches with guest speakers from embassies. A good place to meet diplomats and people in international enterprises (tel: 58 33 09 19).
- **Flagg**: Federated League of Americans Around the Globe (tel: 48 20 147). Concerns itself with interests of Americans worldwide.
- **Professional Women's Association**, Hotel Savoy, Via Ludovisi 15 (tel: 63 90 244; 58 31 03 32). Monthly meetings, guest speakers, workshops, newsletter.
- **Republicans Abroad-Italy**, Via Archimede 164 (tel: 68 53 16). Raises money during election years, helps with voter registration, has occasional meetings and represents the Republican Party in Italy. **Democrats Abroad** is headquartered in Milan.
- **Rome Labour Party** is an active group of those involved in British politics (tel: 63 84 227).
- **Santa Susanna Guild**, at the American Church of Santa Susanna is a women's group open to English-speakers. Hosts social and charitable activities. Administers the church library, organises 'coffee Sundays' and hosts a Fall Festival (tel: 48 27 510).

## Office Space and Conference Facilities

Rome does not have one business district as such. The Centro Storico contains many of the offices and seats of government, as well as of private firms, but it is also the area most populated by tourists. A wider commercial and office district stretches to the Stazione Termini on the east, west to the Tiber, and to Parioli on the north. Many law firms have their offices in Parioli, and it is also popular with embassies. The Vatican, with its separate government and services, is west of the river, bordered by Prati, a more modern section of apartments, shops, and offices. Many government and private offices and international headquarters are centred in EUR and heavy industries and their headquarters are south of the city.

As in any expanding city, offices are in every building in which the rent is affordable. In central Rome they have taken over many of the ancient formerly grand palazzi, and in EUR they are in more modern buildings specially built. Convenience for one's particular needs is the key. Narrow streets in the centre are difficult to traverse, and in the Centro Storico itself cars may enter and park only with a permit. Yet it is, of course, the centre of the city. Parioli is accessible by car, as is EUR, and parking is easier in both districts. EUR is accessible by metro, but it is somewhat out of the centre, which may or may not be important, depending on the type of business activity.

If planning to rent offices, take into account the length of time you will be staying. Commercial leases generally run a minimum of six years, and the leases may be terminated by either landlord or tenant with six months notice, with certain exceptions. Complexities in rental laws and contracts make it imperative that an attorney be consulted before any lease is signed. Make sure to use a reputable, highly recommended and licensed real estate agent.

If, however, you are staying for a shorter period, consider renting a temporary office; many offer furnished space, telephone and fax facilities, secretarial help, and other services. Prices are competitive and terms are flexible: offices can be rented by the hour, day or month in many convenient areas of the city. Some have conference facilities as well.

- *Parioli* — **Centro Uffici Parioli**: Via Lima 41 (tel: 85 30 13 50; fax: 85 30 13 29). Furnished offices and conference facilities. Multilingual secretaries and translators, a mail, fax and telex address.
- *Centro* — **Day Office**: Via Sistina 123, near the Spanish Steps (tel: 47 40 400; fax: 47 81 84 44). Offices by the day, week or month. Conference facilities available.
- *Piazza della Repubblica* — **Rome at Your Service**: Via Vittorio Emanuele Orlando 75 (tel: 48 25 589; fax: 48 44 29). Office Centre. Computers, fax, secretaries, etc. Translators and interpreters.
- *Piazza del Popolo* — **Executive Service**: Via Savoia 78, just off Piazzale Flaminio (tel: 85 43 241; fax: 85 35 01 87). Short term office space, receptionist and secretarial services.
- *Lateran* — **Your Office**: Via Appia Nuova 59, near the Lateran (tel: 70 47 55 15; fax: 70 05 408) Office rental, secretarial service, mail and fax addresses, conference room.

As noted, some of the office rental companies have facilities for conferences, and as in any city, the major centrally located hotels are set up for conferences as well. Note that a large meeting is a *congresso*. A lecture is a *conferenza*.

- **Cavalieri Hilton Hotel**: Via Cadlolo 101 (tel: 35091). A splendid view of the city and garden like setting, with extensive conference capabilities; not as conveniently located as those toward the city centre. Shuttle bus service is available.
- **Sheraton Hotel**: Viale del Pattinaggio (tel: 5453). Convenient for meetings in EUR.
- **Hotel Atlante Star**: Via Vitelleschi 34 (tel: 68 73 233; toll-free: 167/86 20 38). Near the Vatican, meeting rooms, phone and fax capabilities.

138

- **Residenza di Ripetta**: Via di Ripetta 231, just off Piazza del Popolo (tel: 32 31 144; fax: 32 03 959). A centrally located hotel offering a variety of conference services.
- **Executive Business Centre**, in the Domestic Departures Wing of Fiumicino Airport (tel: 65 95 26 07; fax: 65 95 26 30). Hosts meetings in its conference rooms, provides offices. Multilingual staff.

## Interpreters and Translators

Interpreters and organisers are available for meetings of all sizes. For interpreters at large meetings, try **CRIC Consorzio Romano Interpreti di Conferenza** in Via dei Fienili 65 (tel: 67 87 950; fax: 67 91 208). **Euronet** in Piazza Mazzini 27 arranges all facets of large meetings and provides interpreters and translators (tel: 37 51 46 54; fax: 37 51 80 67). Interpreters and translators of written materials can be also retained at those listed below. In addition, see *Traduttori ed Interpreti* in the Yellow Pages.

- *Parioli* — **Melograno Congressi**: Via Chelini 9 (tel: 80 80 892; fax: 80 80 999)
- *Parioli* — **VIP Services**: Via dei Monti Parioli 25 (tel: 32 00 283)
- *Trastevere* — **A7 Congress and Translation Center**: Via dei Colli Portuensi 589 (tel & fax: 65 32 740)
- *EUR* — **Lead On**: Via delle Montagne Rocciose 62 (tel: 59 15 521; fax: 59 15 981)

## Editorial Services

**Alphabyte** in Via SS. Quattro 42, near the Colosseum, provides complete publishing services, from original concept to printed product (tel & fax: 77 20 41 43). Editing, layout, translation and proofreading of catalogues, newsletters, articles, books, etc.

# CHAPTER EIGHT

# MANAGING YOUR MONEY

Even if you never use a *carta di credito* at home, you should consider the regular use of one in Rome, especially during a short to medium term visit and in the absence of a local bank account. First, it reduces the amount of cash you need to carry. Second, you can pay your bill each month from your own cheque account. Third, card companies generally get the most favourable rates of exchange — just 1% over the interbank rate. Although rates fluctuate, postings will likely be at a better rate than had you exchanged money to pay cash in a shop or restaurant. Gold Card holders are entitled to special services, including emergency referrals to doctors and lawyers.

In addition to charging many purchases, you can get periodic cash advances at competitive rates from banks and *bancomats* (automatic teller machines) with a Visa or MasterCard, although you will likely have to pay an interest rate that historically has been a little higher than the usual rates. They may, however, be no higher than the fee charged for exchange at Roman banks. And these cards seem to be accepted in more places than the **American Express** card. Yet during a short to medium term stay in Rome, having an American Express card can be very helpful.

American Express card holders who have enrolled in the Cash Express Service can, with a PIN (personal identification number), get lire any time from the cash machine outside the American Express office; as arranged in advance, this is debited to the person's bank account. Personal cheques may be cashed as well. The limit for cash transactions is US$1000 in lire every three weeks. (Gold Card holders may cash up to US$5000.) People who have used their charge cards can find out each month at the office the amount of the bill and pay it there with a cheque. Anyone can receive funds wired from any American Express office in the world. Other Amex services are useful as well: there is a *poste restante* and helpful travel agency (tel: 67641). American Express traveller's cheques are cashed free of charge. Refunds and lost traveller's cheques can be handled efficiently, as well as replacing lost credit cards (tel: 167/87 20 00).

The **American Express** office is in Piazza di Spagna 38 (tel: 67641; Gold Card holders and foreign residents: 72 28 02 23; lost cards, toll free: 167/86 40 46). Hours: 9:00 am-5:30 pm weekdays, until 12:30 pm Saturdays; hours change according to the season.

**Diner's Club**'s office is in Piazza Cavour 25 (tel: 32 13 841; lost cards, toll free: 167/86 40 64).

**Servizi Interbancari** in Via Quattro Fontane 22 (tel: 47 49 21) is a banking group that services **MasterCard** (lost cards, toll free: 167/01 85 48) and **Visa** (lost cards, toll free: 167/87 72 32; Gold Card: 167/81 91 04). Sevizi Interbancari will issue stop orders and notify banks of a lost card, but it does not replace cards.

Before departure, call your credit card company to find out the 'closing date' for your account, the date the monthly bill is set; also ask for a customer service number which you can call either toll-free in Italy or collect from Rome. Then, at the closing date each month, call to find out the bill and send a cheque from your home account. The same telephone number can be called for questions about your account.

## THE NEED FOR CASH

Despite the convenience of credit cards, don't be surprised that some restaurants and shops don't accept them. Much of Rome remains a cash society, and small shops, *trattorie* and *pizzerie* generally prefer *contante*. If you are planning to make a large purchase outside the city centre, check in advance to make sure credit cards are accepted.

You will, of course, need some lire immediately, at least enough to get into the city from the airport. If you can't bring lire with you, exchange only what you'll need for a day or so; the rates at airport currency exchanges *(cambio; bureau de change)* and hotels aren't as favourable as at major banks or centrally located currency exchanges, and commissions can be high. Beware, however, of currency exchanges that advertise 'no commission,' for they generally have disadvantageous rates of exchange. The *cambio* however, tends to be open longer hours than banks, and it is worth checking several; even on the same block the rates can differ. The main post office at Piazza San Silvestro has a currency exchange, as does the post office in Via Terme Diocleziano 30. See also **Thomas Cook** below, and *Cambia Valute* in the Yellow Pages.

As mentioned, banks offer competitive exchange rates, but they often charge a commission, usually a percentage (1-2%) of the monies changed. If, however, you can find a bank that charges a commission on the transaction itself, rather than the amount transacted, exchange enough each time to limit the number of times you must do so. Cash may be obtained inside the bank on major credit cards such as Visa or MasterCard; bring your passport.

Visitors may bring in and take out of Italy up to 20-million lire in cash; amounts higher must be declared to border guards. Before departure, keep track of exchange rates by checking your daily newspaper. Try to buy when your currency is high, even if it is well in advance of departure. In Rome, the *International Herald Tribune* also lists current rates, and they are posted at the *cambio* and other points of exchange.

Although not entirely reliable, *bancomats* may accept Visa and MasterCard credit cards; some will also accept Eurocheque cards. All must have a PIN. All have limits as to how much cash may be withdrawn per day. The **Plus** bank-card system operates through the Banca di Roma and Banca Nazionale del Lavoro; with a PIN, their *bancomats* should dispense lire, the equivalent in your home currency being debited from your account or charged to your credit card. **CIRRUS** bank debit cards are also accepted at some Banca Nazionale del Lavoro *bancomats*. Note that not all *bancomats* of a bank accept the same cards; check the pictures by the machine itself to see if the symbols for Plus or CIRRUS are displayed. There are also automatic exchange machines in which you insert your own currency and you receive lire at current rates; rates are usually disadvantageous.

Remember that a PIN is necessary to access the cash machines, along with the card. Generally in Europe the PIN is four numbers only, not letters; before departure, make sure at your bank that your PIN conforms to European standards. Note that in any case using the *bancomat* with a foreign card can occasionally be risky; if the machine doesn't recognise the card, it could demagnetise it or not release it, making financial transactions difficult until the card is retrieved or replaced. Often a telephone number is displayed to call in case of lost cards. Also, the *bancomats* don't work all the time, so it's always good to keep some cash in reserve. CIRRUS and Plus depend on the link between the Italian banks and computerised phone lines; sometimes cash is denied if

143

the link is not established. All this being said, however, with persistence this is generally a convenient way to keep supplied with cash from a home bank account.

Never exchange currency with people outside official exchanges or banks, or on the street. Counterfeit currency floats around, and this is how to get it.

# TRAVELLER'S CHEQUES

Bringing traveller's cheques is a good idea for early expenses, until you set up a permanent financial system. Traveller's cheques are replaceable if lost, and if you buy those whose companies have offices in Rome, the process can be fairly speedy. When cashing traveller's cheques, bring your passport.

American Express cheques can be cashed at Piazza di Spagna (lost cheques tel: 167/87 20 00). The international currency exchange, **Thomas Cook**, has several offices and also charges no fee for cashing its own cheques, but charges 2.5% for all other transactions (lost cheques tel: 167/87 20 50). MasterCard is also accepted for cash. Again, since there is a flat fee per transaction, exchange enough so that you don't have to do it very often.

Other issuers are widely known as well and have a collect number to call should your cheques become lost. **Barclays** (toll-free tel: 167/87 41 55), **Citicorp** (tel: London tel: 44171/982-4040), **Visa** (toll-free tel: 1678/74155) and **MasterCard** (U.S. tel: 212/974-5695) issue their own traveller's cheques; upon purchase ask for the procedure to report lost cheques.

# MONEY FROM HOME

If you are in need of emergency funds while in Rome, you can receive a wire transfer from home within hours of it having been made. The sender pays the fees based on the amount sent; these are fairly expensive, so this should be seen only as an emergency measure. Nonetheless, as mentioned, the service is available at

American Express (U.S. 800/866-8800), and it is also available from **Western Union** (toll-free tels: 176/01 38 39; 167/01 68 40; US 800/325-4176). There are several Western Union agencies in Rome:

- *Piazza di Spagna* — **Agenzia Tartaglia**: Piazza di Spagna 12 (tel: 67 86 079; fax: 68 41 560). Open weekdays and Saturday morning.
- *Prati* — **Mail Boxes, Etc.**: Via Ennio Q. Visconti 12 (tel: 36 12 849; fax: 32 26 712). Open weekdays and Saturday morning.

## ROMAN BANKS

For an extended or permanent stay in Rome, a local bank account is crucial, but it may not be worthwhile for stays of just a few months, or even a year. You must apply for a *codice fiscale*, which is a tax number, universally used for identification (see below). These, plus a passport, a *permesso di soggiorno*, a sizeable deposit and sometimes a letter of reference from your own bank should get you an account, although a few banks will also ask for proof of employment. Roman banking can be inefficient, so if you will need to pay your bills at home in your own currency, it is better to keep your home bank account current, to use one of the international banking services below, or to rely on a combination of methods.

One advantage of dealing with a Roman bank is that you can arrange to have some of your local bills — electricity and telephone, for example — paid directly from your account. The concept of writing a cheque and mailing it to pay your everyday bills doesn't exist in Italy. Most people go to the post office to pay their bills in cash. Banks may — or may not — charge a small fee for automatic bill paying, but in any case you avoid the lines at the post office, and you can avoid the steep penalties incurred by paying bills late.

Some of the largest banks with many city branches are listed below. These are convenient to work with, yet sometimes the smaller banks will offer special incentives and more personalised

145

services. Compare the banks, their services and fees charged. This is not as easy as it sounds. Although banks are required by law to post prominently their economic terms and conditions, they generally refer only to the maximum charges or minimum levels of interest paid. Banks are also allowed to change interest rates and charges at will, if upon opening an account the customer has signed the routine contract. But since the changes must appear on the bank statement, it is important that the customer read each statement upon receipt; if the changes are disadvantageous, change banks. The customer has 15 days from receipt of notification of the change to withdraw without penalty from any bank contract. The statements sometimes also reflect mistakes, so ask for a monthly statement and read it carefully.

Ask your friends where they bank. Find out everything you can in advance about how your own specific banking needs would be handled. Some accounts charge for services, but there are non-paying accounts as well. Note that for tax purposes, banks automatically withhold 30% of all interest earned, and this will figure in your taxes. Interest is paid once annually, and a statement explains accruals and amounts withheld.

Most banks issue cards to their account holders to use at the *bancomats*. Occasionally they run out of cash and sometimes the computers break down, but they generally function well and are handy. But as all *bancomats* are linked, when cash is available it is available everywhere, and when one machine is down, they all are. Some banks charge their customers for using the *bancomats* of other banks; inquire when you open an account.

Note that your account may not be credited the same day as you make a deposit, and in fact, banks 'play the float' for a few days before crediting the customer's account. Make sure you have enough in your account at all times to cover your cheques, as a cheque returned for insufficient funds can result in you being blacklisted at banks for up to several years.

As with any business transaction in Rome, the personal approach will make your bank business more efficient. Once you have decided on a bank, introduce yourself by name to the branch manager and establish a personal relationship. Explain what your banking needs will be.

Banking hours are usually 8:30 am-1:30 pm and 2:30 pm-4:30 pm. A few banks are beginning to stay open nonstop. Note that the day before a holiday banks often take a *semi-festivo* and close at 11:00 am; when a holiday falls on a Tuesday or Thursday, banks may even make a *ponte*, a bridge to the weekend. And, on December 24 and 31, and on August 14th, banks close at 11:30 am. Look in the Yellow Pages under *Banche ed Istituti di Credito*.

- **Banca Nazionale del Lavoro**: Via Vittorio Veneto 119 (tel: 47021)
- **Banca Nazionale dell'Agricoltura** Via Salaria 231 (tel: 85881)
- **Banca Commerciale Italiana**: Via del Corso 226 (tel: 67 12 45 43)
- **Banca di Roma**: Via del Corso 307 (tel: 67001; fax: 67 00 54 35)
- **Credito Romagnolo**: Via Vittorio Veneto 74 (tel: 48 99 31)
- **Banca Nazionale delle Comunicazioni** in Stazione Termini (tel: 48 26 838). Open nonstop weekdays; Saturday mornings.
- **Istituto Bancario S. Paolo di Torino**: Via della Stamperia 64 (tel: 85751)
- **Deutsche Bank**: Largo del Tritone 161 (tel: 67181)

## International Bank Accounts for Citizens Abroad

Another way to manage finances is to use the overseas programs of **Citibank** or **Chemical Bank**, New York banks that provide international financial services, the costs depending on the transactions required. Chemical Bank's program is called **International Employee Banking** (US tel: 212/638-0300). Citibank's is **Personal Banking for Overseas Employees (PBOE)** (US tel: 212/307-8511). Used by many international corporations for their employees based overseas, both programs also work with individuals. You open a Citibank cheque account, for example, arrange for your salary — or other funds — to be deposited directly, instruct Citibank which bills (such as mortgage or insurance) to pay each month and change the address on those bills to PBOE. For cash in Rome, Citibank helps arrange an account at a Roman bank and transfers funds upon request. A statement is sent each month detailing all activity, including the transaction charges. Charges are per transaction, plus a monthly fee. Chemical Bank's services are much the same; its transaction costs are slightly higher, but there is only one annual fee.

There are a few American and British bank offices in Rome, such as Chase Manhattan, Barclays, and Republic National Bank; although some have functioning bank branches in Milan, in Rome they are offices for commercial and business purposes only and don't offer personal customer services or cashing facilities. No teller windows or cash services are provided.

### Tracking Your Investments

A few international investment firms and stockbrokers have offices in Italy, or a toll-free number to call, either to invest or for customer service. **Merrill Lynch** is in Largo della Fontanella di Borghese 19, just off Via di Ripetta (tel: 68 39 31; fax: 68 39 32 31). **Fidelity Investment's** toll-free number in Italy is 167/87 40 93. And **Dreyfus** provides a number to call collect, 24-hours a day (US tel: 516/794-5452). Ask your stockbroker how best to track your investments.

# HOW MUCH WILL IT COST?

Forget the old stories about how cheap Italy is. Assume that costs are much the same as at home: local goods will be cheaper, imported more expensive. Fresh fruits, vegetables and cheeses are inexpensive, as are local wines. Yet some items such as meats, gasoline, cigarettes and canned goods may be more expensive than you're used to. Goods in tourist areas will cost more than in outlying neighbourhoods, but note that the tax is included in the price quoted. A nice dinner out will be comparable to fine restaurants in any cosmopolitan capital; a meal in a local establishment may be cheaper. The cinema costs approximately the same, as do theatre and sporting events. Appliances cost more, owing to high duties, but the prices of computers are slowly becoming more competitive with other countries. Utilities tend to be expensive. Think about carrying a small calculator with you at first to compare the prices in Rome with those at home, especially on large purchases.

## CODICE FISCALE

If you open a bank account or do any kind of paid work, even as an independent contractor, you must obtain a *codice fiscale*, which is a universal identification number. It is required for all official documents, and for any transaction that has financial implications, even for hooking up gas and electricity in an apartment or for buying a car. Relocation services are of the greatest help with the bureaucratic requirements; if your Italian-language ability is sufficient you can go to the **Ufficio Distrettuale delle Imposte Dirette** in Via della Conciliazione 5, near the Vatican (tel: 68 80 38 95). Hours: 8:30 am-noon, weekdays. Bring your valid *permesso* and passport.

## SOCIAL SECURITY

Some countries have bilateral agreements with Italy concerning social security to avoid double taxation of employees. This applies to both the United States and Great Britain which issue booklets that detail the arrangements and the rights of their citizens working abroad; these should be available at the Departments of Social Security in both countries, or at the appropriate embassy in Rome.

149

# ITALIAN TAXES

If you earn income for services performed in Italy, whether you are paid in Italy or abroad, you may be subject to Italian tax. This also applies to interest earned on local bank accounts. Depending on bilateral agreements between countries, you will probably not be double taxed at home. Consult with your employer, a *commercialista* or other tax advisor to determine your tax status. The Italian tax department is the **Ufficio Distrettuale delle Imposte**.

Italian taxes must be paid by May 31. There are no extensions allowed, and penalties for late payment or filing are extremely high. Taxes are complicated; again, make sure to consult a commercialista or tax specialist before taking financial actions with tax ramifications.

## Tax Filing in Rome

All people must determine their tax status at home and in Italy while living abroad. Some countries have bilateral agreements with Italy to avoid double taxation on earnings, but this does not mean that no tax forms in the home country are to be filed. British citizens should contact Inland Revenue, EC Unit Room S20, West Wing, Somerset House, London WC2R 1LB (0171/438-6254).

Americans can get *A Tax Guide for U.S. Citizens and Residents Abroad* or the *Overseas Tax Package* from the Internal Revenue Service Forms Distribution Center, PO Box 25866, Richmond, Virginia 23289 (tel: 202/874-1460). The IRS office in Rome, on the second floor at the American Consulate, offers tax help and advice (tel: 46 74 25 60). Everyone should also check with their own home state's tax department before departure, for requirements vary widely.

## Help with Taxes

English-speaking tax consultants in Rome are available: ask for recommendations among your friends or at your consulate.

Consultants all offer tax advice, help prepare returns, handle audits, and offer business related services; they will also suggest referrals to other experts, as needed. Note that your consulate may also be able to answer questions concerning filing of taxes in your home country.

- **Sally M. Silvers**: Piazza Sallustio 3 (tel: 47 45 416; fax: 33 01 291; cell: 47 47 069). An experienced attorney specialising in tax, corporate, and other bureaucratic matters for English-speaking expatriates.
- **Vincent P. Gambino**: Via Sistina 48 (tel: 67 81 398). Specialist in American taxes. Worked previously at the United States IRS office in Rome.
- **Donald Carroll**: Viale Bruno Buozzi 47 (tel: 80 80 133; fax: 80 80 134). Specialist in American taxes, wills and estates. Partner in bilingual firm that can also handle Italian tax questions.
- **Danilo Tonon**: Tonon & Associati, Via Toscana 30 (tel: 42 87 10 33; fax: 42 74 708). Italian firm with specialists in taxes and finance; international offices in Milan, New York, La Paz, and Los Angeles.

## Purchases and Italian Sales Tax

The value added/sales tax in Italy is known as **IVA** *(imposta sul valore aggiunto)* and with some qualifications is refundable to non-EU nationals. IVA is generally included in the price quoted or marked on the label. If you spend more than L300,000 in one shop, ask for a certificate for the IVA along with the itemised receipt; a passport is generally required. (Obtaining the forms can be difficult outside the tourist area, as shops sometimes claim not to have the forms or to participate in the refund plan.) Upon leaving the European Union present the receipt and the unused goods at the Customs desk at the airport. The invoice will be stamped, and then it must be sent back to the shop within 90 days from the date of its issue. The shop will then reimburse for the IVA. Note that if you visit other countries within the EU after you leave Italy, the paperwork and refund procedures are made at the airport of the final EU country visited.

Shops indicating **Tax Free for Tourists** will record information from your passport and give you a voucher if you have spent the minimum amount (info tel: 59 21 537). After having brought the goods to Customs for the validation stamp, bring the voucher to the Tax-free Refund Counter for an immediate refund in cash. In some airports the counter is within the duty-free shop.

IVA is about 19%, so although it varies with the item purchased it's worth going through the bureaucracy to get your refund. It's also worth the slight bit more you might pay by going to a well known store.

## Customs and Sales Tax Refunds

Returning British travellers should read *A Guide for Travellers*, available from HM Customs and Excise, Dorset House, Stamford Street, London SE19PY (tel: 171/202-4227). Although many British travellers believe there are no limits on tax-free goods purchased within the EU, this is not true. There are limits for bringing back tobacco, alcoholic goods, perfume and some other goods. There are no limits on goods bought for personal use on which taxes have been paid. In addition, EU nationals should note that all duty-free shopping exemptions for travel within the EU are due to be abolished in 1999.

- **Australian** citizens may bring back goods up to AUS$400. *Customs Information for Travellers* is available from the Collector of Customs, GPO Box 8, Sydney NSW 2001 (tel: 2/226 5997).
- **Canadian** citizens may bring back CDN$500; above that, the duty is 15%. Canadians should request a copy of *I Declare/Je Declare* from Revenue Canada at 2265 St. Laurent Boulevard south, Ottawa K1G4K3 (info. tel: 613/993-0534).

- **Irish** citizens should determine the limits on tobacco and alcoholic goods allowed in duty-free. Other goods up to IR£460 may be brought in tax-free. Contact Revenue Commissioners, Dublin Castle (tel: 1/679-2777).

- **New Zealand** citizens may bring back goods up to NZ$700; *Customs Guide for Travellers* should be available from New Zealand Customs, 50 Anzac Avenue, Auckland (tel: 9/337-3520).

- **South African** citizens may bring back goods tax-free up to R500. Over this limit, goods are taxed at 20%. *South African Customs Information* is a booklet to be requested from the Commissioner for Customs and Excise, Private Bag X47, Pretoria 0001, or at the embassy in Rome.

- **United States** citizens may bring in duty-free US$400 worth of goods. *Know Before You Go* details general information including duty free items, how to mail gifts, what items are restricted or prohibited to import, etc. *International Mail Imports* describes how to mail packages home from abroad. Write U.S. Customs Service, P.O. Box 7404, Washington D.C. 20044 (tel: 202/ 566-8195). Foreign-bought automobiles must conform to EPA emission standards; for information, order *Buying a Car Overseas? Beware!* from the EPA Public Information Center, PM-211B, 401 M. Street, S.W., Washington, D.C.

# Chapter Nine

# COMMUNICATIONS

## GLOBAL ROME

In its own idiosyncratic way, Italy has entered the global village. You should have no doubt about this on your first foray to downtown Rome, where on every street, in every car, and at every restaurant table, you'll see people talking and gesticulating into their cellular phones.

Actually, the Rome telephone system remains problematical. The service can be unreliable and, in addition, telephone numbers are being standardised at eight digits. Hospitals, ministries and other important public institutions often have only four or five digit telephone numbers; the more important the function, the fewer the numbers. Standardisation is a long process, and not only will you find numbers ranging from six digits to eight, you may also find that the next time you try to call, a number might well have changed. Sometimes the telephone book will specify the prospective number as well as the current one; the second entry will say *prenderà* and will give the number to come. On the other hand, if you have a phone number but don't remember to whom it belongs, call 1412 for the right name and address; dial the area code and the number. (For operator assistance telephone numbers, see Appendix.)

## THE YELLOW PAGES

The *Pagine Gialle* (Yellow Pages) are divided into two sets of books: *Lavoro* and *Casa (Work* and *Home)*. There is an alphabetical index in the first volume which indicates the page that category will be found on and in which set of books it appears. There is also a listing for all Italian *numero verde* toll-free numbers (prefix: 167). Do not assume that every business or person is listed, either in the Yellow Pages or in the *Elenco Telefonico* (white, alphabetical listing). In addition, some businesses are listed under the proprietor's name rather than the name of the business. Thus, if you have found a business, restaurant or service that you will want to visit again, be sure to ask for a *bigliettino* (business card) and keep it for future reference.

To find services designed for the English-speaking community, get *The English Yellow Pages*, published in Via XX Settembre 5 (tel: 474.0861, fax: 474.4509). This helpful L10,000 guide for English-speakers contains addresses and telephone numbers for many services in four major Italian cities. It is sold in English-language book shops and in others, including Feltrinelli.

## PUBLIC TELEPHONES

Using public telephones requires fortitude. Trying to hear yourself — or anyone else — while talking on a street-corner phone, can be a disaster. Instead, go to an office of **Telecom Italia** (formerly **SIP**) and use the metered telephones in *cabine* (booths). No premium is charged over the cost of the call; one pays after the call. The cheapest time to make long distance calls is Monday-

Saturday 10:00 pm-8:00 am and all day Sunday; there is another slightly reduced tariff after 1:00 pm on Saturdays. Of course the telephone offices aren't open at the cheapest times, except for that by the main Post Office in San Silvestro, which is open until about 11:00 pm daily.

Most public phones accept **schede telefoniche** or **carte telefoniche** (telephone cards). You can buy phone cards for either L5000, L10,000 or L15,000 from any telephone company office, such as in San Silvestro, at Stazione Termini or in just about any tabacchi. The cost of the call is deducted while you speak, and there is a display that tells how much time is left on the card. Local calls begin at L200 and are timed. Break off the perforated corner of the card and insert it into the telephone according to the diagram on the phone.

**Telefoni a scatti** are metered phones with operators. These, as mentioned above, can be found at telephone company offices, and also in some bars. There are booths in the Stazione Termini (hours: 8:00 am-11:00 pm; 9:00 am-noon and 5:00 pm-10:00 pm Sundays). In Villa Borghese parking lot, the hours are 8:00 am-9:30 pm.

Many phones take L100, 200 or 500 coins or **gettoni** (tokens) available from machines in train and bus stations. They are worth L200 and are sometimes given as change for purchases. One gettone covers about a five-minute call; make sure to have enough, or you could be cut off in mid-sentence. You can deposit more than you think you'll need; at the end, pushing the button should bring you unused tokens.

### International Calls
For making international calls while travelling or until you have a permanent telephone number, the most convenient method is to use a *calling card* from your home long distance carrier. This is especially true if you are staying in a hotel or someone else's apartment. If you

don't already have a calling card, arrange to get one before your departure; some cards also require a PIN. To use a calling card, you dial a toll-free number and are immediately connected with an operator from the home-based company who then places the call; some companies allow dial-in access. The cost shows up on your next month's telephone bill. Calls cost more than at home, but less than if you went through a hotel operator. Usually the companies charge a flat fee plus a per-call surcharge; there is no difference in rates between any particular time of day. At the end of each month, you call your telephone carrier collect (collect numbers are provided) ask how much you owe, and send a cheque. The numbers can also be used to call collect, which is, of course, more expensive.

- **AT&T**: 17 21 011 (US info tel: 800/874-4000). Universal card holders may use the card with a pin number; the cost will be posted on the next month's charges (collect tel: 904/448-8661; Rome tel: 167/877.472).
- **MCI Direct**: 17 21 022 (Customer service toll-free 167/879.073; US info tel: 800/444-2222).
- **Sprint**: 17 21 877 (US info tel: 800/877-4646)
- **Canada Direct**: 17 21 001 (Canada info tel: 800/561-8868)
- **British Telecom**: 17 20 044. (UK info tel: 0171/728-8660)
- **Australia Direct**: 17 21 061
- **Telecom New Zealand**: 17 21 001
- **Telekom South Africa**: 17 21 027

People with accounts with Telecom Italia will find rates cheaper than the calling card option above. There is also an *Italia in Diretta* calling card for use when travelling. However, compare international rates with those of the callback systems described below.

New discount international callback systems are increasingly popular. There are several different procedures for use. Check them out and see which suits: some allow calls from pre-selected numbers, while others allow calls from anywhere. Often a central number is called and the caller hangs up, only to be called back within seconds. Then the call is placed directly. Faxing from the registered number is possible at the same low rates. Rates among these carriers vary as well, yet major savings can be had from any of them. The *International Herald Tribune* often carries ads for these callback systems. Although many are based outside Italy, they are available to anyone.

- **DirectLine International:** Via Savoia 78, Rome. (tel: 85 43 241; fax: 85 35 01 87).
- **Telegroup:** 505 N. Third Street, Fairfield, Iowa 52556. (US tel: 515/472-5000; fax: 472-4747 )
- **Telegroup France**: 8, rue Témara BP 234, 78104 Saint Germain-en-Laye, France (tel: 331/01.30.87.99.00; fax: 39.21.15.66)
- **Telegroup Italy:** Via Lazzaretto 19, 20124 Milan. (tel: 02/67 07 18 00)
- **Kallback**: 417 Second Avenue W., Seattle WA 98119 (US tel: 206/ 284-8600; fax: 270-0009)
- **New World Telecommunications**: 1402 Teaneck Road, Teaneck NJ 07666 (US tel: 201/996-1670; fax 996-1870)
- **Phone Depot**: 141-14 Jewel Avenue, Flushing New York 11367 (US tel: 201/907-5315; fax: 907-5111)

### Pulse/Tone Dialling

Roman phones operate on pulse dialling, not tone. If you will be checking your voice mail or using other computer-operated phone systems, you can buy at suppliers such as Radio Shack a **tone dialler**, which changes the frequency to one that can access tone-sensitive telephone computers. There are two models: one with memory, one without.

## ONLINE SERVICES

Using a computer for electronic mail (E-mail) is easy and cheap, and it can keep you in constant touch with your business or family in a manner in which lengthy, expensive, and occasional telephone calls cannot. A compatible modem, the right software, an Italian telephone plug, a call to a local number and a message sent are all it requires. Messages can be sent any time to be picked up at the convenience of the recipient, so time differences are not problematic. Messages can be written off line and uploaded, and messages received can be downloaded to read off line, making the process even more economical and efficient.

The Italian telephone plug is large, with a triangle of three prongs. Plugs into which the more universal RJ11 can be inserted can be obtained at electronic gadgetry stores. If you can't find one, try the section on Appliances in Chapter Fourteen. Otherwise, in Rome look for a plug or a *cavo* (cord) with a *spina telefonica* (telephone plug) and a modular plug for the computer end. In addition, think about getting a multiple telephone plug in Rome; using one will help you avoid having to take out the telephone plug to insert the modem plug each time.

It's a good idea to bring an extra copy of your communications software along with backups of system, document and diagnostic disks. Power surges are frequent; be sure to buy a **para fulmine** (surge protector). For computer repair and technical support, see Chapter Fourteen.

### Adjusting to the Italian Dial Tone

Not all modems can automatically read all telephone systems. If you get a message that says 'no dial tone,' it is likely that the modem is searching for a different, steady dial tone, not the intermittent Italian signal. In this case you will have to change the commands in your software. Because the Italian telephone works on the pulse system, not touch tone, codes that say *DT* will probably have to be changed to *DP*. In addition, the dial prefix will probably need to be changed to *X3*, which allows the modem to bypass the signal. For instance, if your dial prefix at home is *ATX2DT*,

159

you may have to change it to *ATX3DP*. If you are using software that dials automatically, you may have to change the modem initialisation or dial prefix, according to the software instructions. If dialling manually, you may have to type the following prefix before the access number: *AT [OK] ATX3 [OK] ATDP*. In a residence hotel, you may also have to dial a zero to get the outside line. Thus, if your software dials automatically you will have to put a zero in front of the access number, usually followed by a comma, since the Italian telephone system is slow: a comma indicates a two-second pause, allowing slower telephone systems to dial at their own speed. If composing the number manually, your screen might look like this: *AT [OK] ATX3 [OK] ATDP,0, [access number]*.

## The Roman Internet

To access E-mail and the World Wide Web, Roman Internet networks provide local access telephone numbers in Rome and toll-free numbers throughout Italy. Italian Internet providers offer much the same services as in any other country: software is provided for access to E-mail *(posta electronica)* bulletin boards, chat lines, and the Web. They also provide technical support. Internet use is increasing rapidly in Italy, up to a half-million users in 1996. Thus, new providers including Telecom Italia will be coming along swiftly. Currently, try:

- **Technimedia/MC-link**: Via Carlo Perrier 9, east of the city centre (tel: 41 89 21, fax: 41 73 21 69; E-mail: mc001@mclink.it)
- **Agorà Telematica**: Corso Vittorio Emanuele II 39 (tel: 69 91 742; fax: 69 92 01 23; E-mail: agora@agora.stm.it)
- **Unidata SRL**: Via San Damaso 20 (tel: 39 38 73 18; fax: 39 36 69 49; E-mail: info@uni.net)
- **Italia On Line**: Salita del Poggio Laurentino 18 (tel: 59 29 90 91; toll-free 167/26 61 98; fax 59 16 541; E-mail: info@iol.it.)

### International Providers

Some international Internet providers allow access to their sub-
scribers from abroad, but they are sometimes hard to find or arrange. Most Internet handbooks list commercial Internet providers, and they often list the points of access. After joining an Internet
provider, you must sometimes — not always — ask to be included
on their foreign accounts or set up your own account with the
foreign communications system. Another option is to have your
home Internet messages forwarded to your mailbox on another
network to which you subscribe, such as MCIMail or
CompuServe. Inquire also at the Internet providers above.

Until recently, the international Internet and most other
online networks such as **MCIMail** and **CompuServe** accessed
through one central **Infonet** number in Milan, but MCIMail now
has a local number, and CompuServe has its own node in Rome,
as does **America Online** (see below). They all have online help
that gives clear information and instructions about how to access
their global services, including the Internet.

CompuServe's direct line in Rome supports up to 9600 baud,
which is slow, but fast enough to access the World Wide Web
(access tel: 51 95 73 47). With dial tone problems, those using any
of the Information Manager software should go into 'Special, Ses-
sion Settings, Modem,' and change the initialise string to include

161

the *X3* and the *DP* as appropriate. There is no surcharge for using basic services. Outside Rome, you will be charged the regular toll; dial the Rome prefix 06. For information on how to access CompuServe worldwide, when online type GO PHONES. For customer support, use online help if you can; you can also call CompuServe (US tel: 614/457-8600). Compuserve's online **Italian Forum** can answer questions about Italy.

To use AOL's services in Rome, you will need to download the AOLGLOBALnet software file and make changes to your setup; instructions online are clear (Rome access tel: 85 30 16 21). With dial tone problems, go into 'Setup, Commands Edit, Modem, Dial Prefix' and add the *X3* and *DP* as appropriate. There is an hourly surcharge. If you are able to access and have problems, write online help; if not, call AOL Customer Support (US tel: 703/264-1184).

## Infonet

MCIMail uses **Infonet**, a central access provider used by several networks including some international Internet networks; different log on codes ensure connection to the right network. (Rome access, tel: 23 15 728; Milan, tels: 02/21 57 814, 21 55 072.) For MCIMail, set your communication parameters to *7 data bits, even parity* and *1 stop bit,* unless you are uploading or downloading binary files, in which case they will stay at 8 data bits, none parity and 1 stop bits. Make sure the dial prefix in your communications software is correct.

Until recently, the Milan access numbers were clearer than the Rome number, and when accessing late at night, early morning or on weekends, rates were low. Static no longer seems to be a problem on the Rome line, but if you use the Milan numbers, remember to insert the 02 city code before the access number. Connection can be slow, so put a comma between the city code and the number. For Rome, dial without the area code. (If these numbers don't work, they might have been changed; online instructions should have current numbers.)

After you see that you are connected, log on by pressing <enter> several times, to establish the modem speed. You should see #. Type *C* and press <enter> again. When you see *Center>*, type your network's instructions for log on: for MCIMail type *MCI,MAIL*; for Internet, enter the identification code given by your provider. At this point, you should see 'Communication Established;' proceed with your usual log on and password, disconnecting as usual.

Don't be surprised if you don't see on the screen some of the responses you type while logging on, such as the *C* after the # prompt. Just keep going. And, if you see strings of gibberish letters at the beginning of the log on, it's usually just static; keep going.

For technical support the MCI office in Via Po 2 will offer limited help by referring you to a technician (tel: 85 53 368; fax: 85 58 964); in-depth help can also be had (toll free tel: 167/87 04 09). For Italian speakers, an MCI technical assistance number is (0523) 76 88 43.

## Occasional Internet Access

Bookshops, cybercafes and tourist offices are beginning to offer access to the Internet. Currently, try one of these:

- **Libreria Bibli:** Via dei Fienaroli 28 (tel: 58 84 097) Bookshop that stays open late.
- **Drome Cybercafe:** Via dei Latini 49 (tel: 44 61 492). Cafe in San Lorenzo.
- **Internet Point:** Via Genova 16 (tel:48 25 124). In the basement at CTS tourist centre.
- **Pizzeria Forum:** Via San Giovanni in Laterano 38 (tel: 78 87 531). Pizzeria near the Lateran.
- **Xplore:** Via dei Gracchi 83 (tel: 32 41 757). Twenty computers for access in Prati.

## Videotel

If you have a modem, you may also access **Videotel**, a service of Telecom Italia, which offers automated information on a great number of subjects, from finances and economics to up-to-date telephone numbers and addresses, from information about public transit to options for entertainment. Costs are reasonable, both for access via modem which is charged by the minutes on line, or for monthly rental of Videotel equipment.

# THE POST OFFICE

Unfortunately, the stories about the inefficiencies of the Italian postal system tend to be true, but don't get discouraged. Knowing how to use the state system, plus knowing the alternatives, means that your letters, documents, and larger shipments can generally arrive safely. The main post offices are open all day. There are also small substations in most neighbourhoods. The substations are open from 8:30 am-2:00 pm weekdays and 8:30 am-noon on Saturdays. Look for a yellow sign with a large PT. For general postal information in Italian, dial 160.

It is important to know the location of your nearest **ufficio postale** (post office); unless you are having bills deducted automatically at your bank, it is the place where you pay your telephone, gas, electricity and other bills, as well as buying stamps and mailing letters.

**Posta Centrale** in Piazza San Silvestro 18/20 is Rome's main facility (tels: 6771; 67 84 736). There is a currency exchange and a **fermo posta** where you can receive mail for a small fee. Mail should be addressed to you at the address above, plus *Ferma Posta,* 00186, Roma Italy. Bring your passport for identification. **Postacelere** delivers within 48 hours in Italy and internationally. There is a fax service, but at this writing, it did not include America or England. Another main facility is in Via Terme di Diocleziano

30, near Piazza della Repubblica. Both are open Saturday mornings. Other main post offices are as follows:

- **Fiumicino Airport** (tel: 65 01 06 51)
- **Aurelio**: Via Federico Galeotti 49 (tel: 66 23 006); also Via Accursio
- **Belsito**: Piazzale delle Medaglie d'Oro 46 (tel: 35 49 71 04)
- **Cassia:** Via Grottarossa 56 (tel: 33 10 88)
- **EUR**: Viale Beethoven 36 (tel: 59 26 856)
- **Monte Sacro**: Viale Adriatico 136 (tel: 81 83 390)
- **Nomentano**: Piazza Bologna 39 (tel: 44 24 44 06)
- **Ostiense**: Via Marmorata (tel: 57 43 809)
- **Prati**: Viale Mazzini 101 (tel: 37 51 65 61)
- **Appio-San Giovanni**: Via Taranto (tel: 70 04 350)
- **Stazione Termini** (tel: 47 45 640)
- **Centro Pacchi** in Piazza dei Caprettari, near Sant'Eustachio (tel: 68 80 59 01). This office insures packages; others send, but don't insure. Packages may be fastened with tape, but must also be secured with string. For book rate, secure with string only. Hours: 8:25 am-3:15 pm; open Saturday morning. Another Centro Pacchi is in Via Viminale off Via Terme di Diocleziano. Nonstop: 8:30 am-7:30 pm; Saturday, open at 11:30 am.

A postcard with more writing on it costs more to mail than a postcard with 'wish you were here!' A lengthy message is considered a letter, so the card gets charged at the letter rate. All cards, letters and packages should be sent *via aerea* (air mail) or *espresso* (express), but still expect lengthy delays. You can also register *(raccomandata)* letters and packets, ask for an *avviso di ritorno*, a return receipt. Most tobacco shops carry *francobolli* (stamps) — at least theoretically: they often seem to be out of just the denominations you want, and they also don't always know exactly the right amount for the letter you want to send. It's better to brave the lines at the post office, especially if you are not sure of the weight of the item to be mailed.

165

Post your letters in the red mailboxes on walls outside each post office, near tobacco shops and in other places around the city. Most mailboxes have two slots: the one on the left is for Rome only and the other is for all other destinations.

More reliable is the efficient **Vatican Post Office**; the clerks speak some English (tel: 6982). The Vatican, of course, is an independent state, so you must use Vatican stamps, which are the same price as Italian stamps, and you must mail your letters in blue Vatican mail boxes. There are two post offices in Piazza San Pietro and one inside the Vatican Museum. Hours: 8:30 am-7:00 pm; weekdays; 8:30 am-6:00 pm Saturday. The Museum's post office is closed Saturday and all are closed on Sundays and church holidays. During the summer, one of the offices moves to a trailer closer into Piazza St. Pietro.

## Rush Mail

For rush/priority mail service, you can use international couriers. Most have pickup and delivery. These may be worth the extra cost, to assure safe and timely delivery of your documents.
- **DHL:** Via Carlo Botta 41 (toll-free tel: 167/34 53 45)
- **Federal Express:** Pickup and delivery only (toll free tel: 167/ 83 30 40)
- **UPS:** Via della Magliana 329 (tel: 55 26 03 73; toll free 167/82 20 55)
- **Mailboxes, Etc.:** Via Ennio Q. Visconti 12 (tel: 36 12 849; fax: 32 26 712). and Via Anastasio II 321 (tel: 63 36 09). Packs and mails, uses UPS, Federal Express.

## Courier Services

There are several courier services using moto delivery within Rome. One of the largest is **Speedy Boys** (tel: 37 25 656). Try also **Presto** (tel: 39890), **Pony Express** (tels: 3977; 39 72 24 04), or **Boy Express** (tel: 70 24 802). See *Corrieri* in the Yellow Pages.

## Faxes and Photocopying

Faxing, of course, is the fastest and most reliable way to send a letter; sometimes it's easier to make a business appointment by fax than by phone. Faxes are popular in Rome and many people have them in their homes as well as at work. Most hotels have a fax for guest use. If, however, you are staying in an apartment, you will probably have to find a public fax; one shouldn't be difficult to find at a nearby tobacco shop. Use also the fax in the atrium of **Stazione Termini** or in the American Express office, where both sending and receipt of faxes is available using any major credit card. There are photocopy shops in every neighbourhood.

- *Piazza Barberini* — **Sandy**: Via San Basilio 58 (tel: 48 18 533)
- *Via del Corso* — **Centro Copia Palombi**: 54 Piazza dei Santi Apostoli (tel: 67 81 125)
- *Corso Vittorio* — **Edi Pro**: Via di San Pantaleo 63/65 (tel: 68 80 16 34)
- *Corso Vittorio* — **Tecnorama**: Corso Vittorio Emanuele 337/a: (tel & fax: 68 64 354)
- *Monteverde* — **Monteverde**: Viale di Villa Pamphili 55/b (tel: 58 33 10 45)
- *Pantheon* — **Eurocopie di Pienicci Valler**: 79 Via Monte Brianzo (tel: 68 74 387)
- *Prati* — **Berus**: Via Cicerone 72 (tel: 32 35 504)
- *Prati* — **Mailboxes, Etc.** Via Ennio Q. Visconti 12 (tel: 36 12 849)
- *Trastevere* — **Xeromania**: Via San Francesco a Ripa 109 (tel: 58 14 433; fax: 58 17 505)
- *Via Veneto* — **FAT**: Via Boncompagni 53 (tel: 48 20 405; fax: 48 15 886)

# ENGLISH-LANGUAGE PUBLICATIONS

Most of the large centrally located *edicole* (newsstands) and the train stations regularly stock foreign publications. The major international magazines such as *Time*, *Newsweek*, and *The Economist* are available, albeit sometimes in scaled down editions, and other magazines can be found in the English-language book shops (see Chapter Fourteen.) The *International Herald Tribune* is issued every day but Sunday (and carries the *New York Times* crossword puzzle). *USA Today* is published weekdays. The *Wall Street Journal Europe*, the *Nikkei Weekly* and the *Financial Times* are all current. The *European*, an English-language general newspaper published in Europe, is available, as are such British newspapers at *The Times* or *The Guardian*.

*Roma C'è*, the weekly events listing, has an English-language section. Look at newsstands also for *This Week in Rome*, a tourist-oriented events listing; at hotels, look for the monthly *Where*, a more extensive English-language magazine that also lists useful addresses.

*The Informer* is an English-language monthly publication available for L60,000 by subscription and for L6,000 at international bookstores (tel: 02/93 58 14 77; fax: 93 58 02 80). It offers 'hard information' and 'friendly advice' on laws, taxes, the bureaucracy, etc., for foreigners living in Italy. Write: Via dei Tigli 2, 20020 Arese (Mi).

In addition, there are several local English-language semi-monthly publications. *Metropolitan* covers news of interest and some Rome-specific items. *Wanted in Rome* carries news of interest to English-speakers in Rome, classified ads, notices of upcoming events. They are both sold at major newsstands. *Nerone* is an occasional tabloid available at the English-language bookshops. The **Economy Book and Video Center** in Via Torino 136 publishes *Happenings*, a listing of cultural events and happenings for English-speaking residents of Rome.

# RADIO AND TELEVISION

It's hard to find scheduled English-language news on commercial television or radio; only on satellite channels are international channels regularly scheduled, including the American CNN and the British BBC. Some hotels have satellite hookups; for shops that sell parabolas and install hookups, see Chapter Fourteen.

The three **RAI** television channels are state-owned. Historically, they were aligned with the various political parties which broadcast news programming with a particular slant; this, however, has recently changed. Most now have a more homogeneous mix of programming, including news, sports, talk shows, documentaries, soap operas, movies and miniseries. **Canale 5, Italia 1,** and **Rete 4** are part of the Mediaset network owned by former Prime Minister Silvio Berlusconi's Fininvest Group, and they tend toward lighter programming. **TeleMonteCarlo,** owned by film producer Vittorio Cecchi Gori, has a varied mix, including good films and some late night English-language news when at about 2:00 am it often hooks up with CNN; his group also includes **TeleMonteCarlo2/Videomusic. Tele+1** broadcasts films, **Tele+2** broadcasts sports, and **Tele+3** is a varied mix of cultural offerings; all are pay channels. There are many smaller, regional channels as well.

Also previously aligned with political parties were the public radio stations, but now they are basically similar. **Radio 1** (89.7FM and 1332AM) has more news and social issues programs; **Radio 2** (91.7FM and 846 AM) adds music to its mix of programming; and **Radio 3** (93.7FM), has more classical music than the others. There are quite a few private FM frequencies that broadcast modern music: **Radio Mambo** (106.85Mhz) airs lively Latin American music. And **Radio Kiss Kiss** (97.25FM), from Naples, is entertainingly unpredictable in its mix. **BBC World Service** broadcasts at short wave (15.070MHz) in the mornings and on medium wave (648KHz) at night. **Vatican Radio** (93.3FM and 1530AM) broadcasts news in English at 8:00 am and noon, Monday-Saturday.

# Chapter Ten

# TRANSPORTATION

## MAPS AND GUIDES

In this city that has been evolving for two thousand years, the streets are not laid out in any particular grid, and there is no order to their names. The first thing you'll need is a map. Maps are sold at newsstands and bookstores, and are given away at the tourist offices, in various shops and currency exchanges. For a more detailed *stradario* (street atlas), the telephone company issues a supplement to the phone book called *TuttoCittà*, a large paperback detailing clearly defined neighbourhoods. It also lists postal codes, bus routes and information for emergencies. *TuttoCittà* should be in your apartment along with the phone books or in your residence hotel. If not, call the telephone company (tel: 187). A smaller street atlas — to be carried in a briefcase or pack — is *Strada Roma*, published by Lozzi, with colourful pages and a spiral binding. To carry in a pocket, look at newsstands for *Roma Facile (Easy Rome)*.

# WALKING

Walking is the most efficient way of getting around in the city centre. But it can be challenging. Traffic is constant and there are so many 'rush hours' that they seem to merge into one long day of congestion. The four busiest times are 7:00-9:00 am and 1:00-2:00 pm daily, when people go home for lunch and schools let out. Traffic is heavy again between 4:00 pm and 5:00 pm and then after the shops close, between 8:00 pm and 9:00 pm.

While walking, be sure to cross at the *strisce* (zebra crossings), at which all vehicles must stop for pedestrians. Sometimes it seems like a dangerous game, with drivers trying to 'psych out' pedestrians, trying to keep them from entering the zebras, but eventually the cars do stop. Actually the Romans are adept at driving in crowded conditions, manoeuvring in tight situations, and going around pedestrians while hardly slowing their speed. But jaywalking is definitely discouraged: walk when the signs say *avanti* and stop when they read *alt*.

# BUSES

**ATAC** is the extensive bus and tram system. There should be a listing of bus routes in any street atlas; if not, buy one at newsstands or get one at Stazione Termini. An information booth is outside in Piazza dei Cinquecento, a major bus hub *(capolinea)*, and there are sometimes people at others such as Largo Argentina or Piazza San Silvestro (info tels: 46 95 44 44; in English: 46 95 22 52). The transport system works pretty well, given the traffic and street repairs all vehicles must contend with, meaning that sometimes waits for the bus may be long. Plans for improving the system come and go, depending on funding, yet improvements should be made in time for the jubilee year 2000, when millions of pilgrims are expected. Make sure to verify that bus routes listed in your guides still exist and are current. Also note that some buses do not return by the same route, so check on the return route before boarding.

171

Each *fermata* (bus/tram stop) is marked with a yellow or green sign that indicates which buses stop there and the routes they take. Buses and trams are conspicuously orange and they generally run from 5:30 am until midnight; there are some 28 late night buses, and the bus sign lists those that offer *servizio notturno*. You must stand under the sign and flag down the bus in order for it to stop, but if the sign says *pass*, the bus will not stop there.

Several buses in particular should be noted: Bus **No. 110** is a four-hour city tour; guideless but with an English-language brochure available, the bus leaves Piazza dei Cinquecento at 3:00 pm in summer and 2:30 pm on winter weekends. **No. 116** is a blue shuttle bus in the Via Veneto–Via nazionale areas. **No. 119** is an electric minibus that makes a circuit of the city centre, including Piazza del Popolo, Piazza Navona, the Pantheon, Piazza Colonna and Piazza di Spagna. But **No. 64**, the most convenient route from Stazione Termini to the Vatican, is known to be heavily frequented by tourists, and thus, unfortunately, by pickpockets. Watch out for your belongings on this — and on all other buses.

**COTRAL** in Via Volturno 65 operates the bus lines to the environs (tel: 59 15 551). Although there are few English speakers, you can call for airport bus information (tel: 65 95 45 52). Hours: 8:00 am-6:00 pm weekdays; closed Saturday afternoon and Sunday.

## THE SUBWAY

The **Metropolitana** is the subway; entrances are marked by a red sign with a white M. The metro is a quick and easy means of transport to many parts of the city; unfortunately at present it is not extensive enough to cover the entire city. New lines are now under construction. The fact that there is a metro at all, however, is somewhat a triumph: every time construction workers started to dig, more layers of archeological history were uncovered. Ancient relics became fodder for lengthy scholarly studies, slowing the progress of mass transit. By now, however, although the metro may not go exactly where or when you want, it is efficient and should soon have a broader city coverage. As in any other crowded public vehicle, people should be careful of their belongings and should be alert late in the evening in empty stations.

At present there are two metro lines: *Linea A* (orange) and *Linea B* (blue). The lines run, more or less, in the shape of an X, with their junction under Stazione Termini. Line A starts in the northwest at the Vatican (Ottaviano) and runs to the southeast to Via Tuscolana (Anagnina). Line B runs from the northeast (Via Rebibbia) to EUR in the southwest (Laurentina). Hours: daily from 5:30 am-11:30 pm.

## The Fares

Tickets must be used on all public transport; cash is not accepted. *Biglietti integrati* are single tickets valid for 75 minutes on any number of buses or trams, or for one ride on the Metropolitana. The current fare is L1500. The *Biglietto Integrato Giornaliero* is a one-day ticket; currently it costs L6000. Most economical, however, are the weekly and monthly passes. The *Carta Integrata Settimanale* is the weekly pass at L24,000, and the *Abbonomento mensile* costs L50,000 and is valid for the calendar month, no matter when purchased. Information on passes and fares is available at the tourist offices as well as at ATAC stands.

People with single tickets enter the bus at the back and time-stamp the ticket in the machine. Inspectors ride the buses looking for scofflaws; fines are steep, L50,000 for each offence. The weekly and monthly *tessere* (passes) are not stamped, but must be shown to the inspector if asked. Those with *tessere* may also enter from the front of the bus. All exit from the centre doors. Tickets and passes can be bought at ATAC stands (such as in Largo Argentina or Piazza dei Cinquecento) and at *tabacchi*. Make sure not to run out of tickets, especially if you use the bus at night: it's hard to

173

find them once the shops close. After midnight, tickets can be bought on the night buses.

Tickets may also be bought at the vending machines at some bus hubs and in metro stations; these take coins, and some will change L1000 notes. Don't expect metro station attendants to make change, and there are times when tickets at stations are unavailable. Keep an extra ticket with you, and for regular use, get the monthly pass.

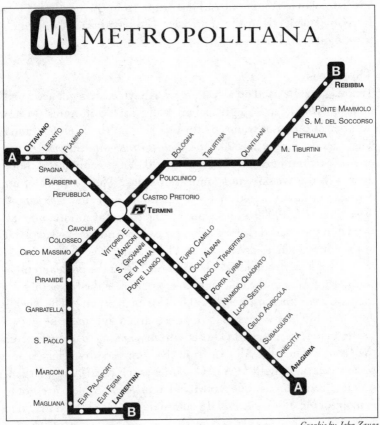

*Graphic by John Zaugg*

# TAXIS

Given the heavy traffic, sometimes it seems it would be faster to walk rather than be stuck in traffic and watch the meter of a cab. Nonetheless, taxis are useful and generally available (except at rush hours or when it's raining). Licensed taxis must be yellow or white, bear a *taxi* shield on top, and have a meter. Don't take unlicensed cabs, not at Stazione Termini or anywhere else. Make sure the meter is set at zero before your ride begins. There is a night-time surcharge, one for Sundays and holidays and for carrying baggage.

Taxis sometimes can be hailed from the street, but more easily called by phone or found at *capo stazioni* (stands) in each neighbourhood. Taxi stands are marked by a blue sign with white letters saying *Taxi*. If you call a cab, expect to be charged from when the taxi leaves the stand. There are stands at Stazione Termini and at Piazza del Risorgimento, in Piazza Sonnino, at Largo Argentina and in all the tourist areas.

Taxis may also be booked in advance, although there is generally a surcharge for booking. Call: **Cosmos Radio Taxi** (tel: 88177), **La Capitale** (tel: 4994), **Radio Taxi Roma** (tels: 3570 or 63898), **Roma Sud** (tel: 6645) or see *Taxi* in the Yellow Pages. The telephone numbers of taxi stands in the various neighbourhoods are listed by zone in the white alphabetical listing. Callers will be told how long it will take for the cab to arrive and which cab to expect, using the name of a city and a number, such as *Siena 41*.

# DRIVING IN ROME

Driving in Rome is a challenge. Traffic is unceasing, drivers are hurried, and they try to gain advantage and infiltrate into any small opening in a lane. Many streets are narrow, and some two-lane roads often see cars four abreast. Yet the traffic situation is improving. In an effort to reduce traffic and pollution, a *fascia blu*

175

zone has been created to allow only limited vehicular traffic into the city centre; a permit is required. Some 100 outlying garages have entered into an agreement with the city in which the parking fee is nominal for those who leave their car and take public transport into the city centre.

Parking in Rome has been as bad as in any other capital city, but this too is improving. *Parcometri* (parking meters) costing L2000 per hour are being introduced; residents of the neighbourhoods have special parking privileges. Look for blue lines painted on the street, and for the machine with a blue background and large white P. Meters take exact change or prepaid tickets bought at *tabacchi*. After paying, take the receipt and place it prominently on the dashboard so that it can be read by the traffic police.

There is still some free street parking, but be aware of street signs that limit hours and days. *Sosta Vietata* means 'No Parking,' and *Zona Rimozione* means that cars will be removed/towed. Parking is permitted where the curb is painted white. Yellow markings indicate handicapped parking. If you park illegally your car may be towed to one of the municipal lots; you'll have to pay a fine of at least L150,000 to retrieve it. It's best to use the underground car parks, which are also marked with a large P. There are small car parks around the city; larger ones are at Villa Borghese, in Via Ludovisi, and in Via Marescotti in Trastevere.

If your car gets towed, call the **Vigili Urbani** (tel: 67691; 67 69 838); given the car's make, registration number and license plate and where it had been parked, they will tell you to which *deposito* (pound) it has been taken, and give you the telephone number of the pound. You will need to take with you your driver's license, proof of authorisation to use the car, and enough cash to pay for the car's retrieval.

Obey all laws. Wear your seat belt at all times. The city speed limit is increasingly being enforced (50 kph in urban areas). And don't talk on your mobile phone while driving – even though the Romans do, it's against the law.

*Photo: Pomponi/Photoreporters*

*Street corner markets are an added hazard when negotiating Rome's thoroughfares.*

Driving is expensive. *Benzina* (gasoline) is sold by litres, not gallons. As of October 1996, a litre of gas cost between L1800 and 1850, and the price was due to rise. Both leaded and unleaded *(senza piombo)* are available. Regular gas is called *super*. Street pumps and garages throughout the city sell gas. Many of the larger stations take credit cards, and some have pumps that take banknotes. The smaller stations may take only cash. The most important gasoline providers are ESSO, Shell, Mobil, AGIP, IP, ERG, Tamoil, and Q8. Stations close at lunch time and in the evening around 7:00 pm. After hours, some have self-service pumps that require L10.000 bills. The stations on the **Grande Raccordo Anulare** (the ring road – see diagram on the next page) are open 24-hours, as are the more convenient AGIP stations in Lungotevere Ripa and Piazzale della Radio, and the IP station in Via Salaria at Viale Somalia; also just past the GRA on The Cassia.

177

Note also that speedometers register kilometres, although miles are often shown in smaller figures on the speedometer. To convert from one to the other, multiply the kilometres by .62 to get miles, or multiply miles by 1.6 to get kilometres. Thus, one kilometre is .62 miles, and five kilometres are 3.1 miles. One mile is 1.6 kilometres, and five miles are 8 kilometres.

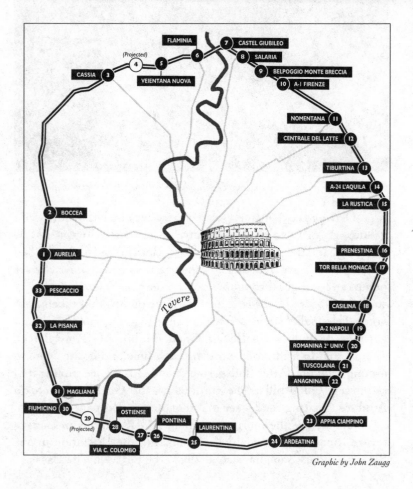

*Graphic by John Zaugg*

## Driver's Licenses

The **International Driving Permit** is essential. Although it is not said to be required, not all police will accept foreign drivers' licenses, so it's advisable to have one, or to have your own license translated into Italian. For the international permit, inquire of your home automobile club: Americans at the AAA, Canadians at the CAA. British drivers can get a translation of their driver's license from the AA or RAC. The **Italian Automobile Club (ACI)** in Via Marsala 8 can provide a document certifying that a driver's license is valid (tel: 49981, information tel: 4477); another head-quarters is in EUR, in Via Cristoforo Colombo 261 (tel: 51 49 71). Smaller offices are in every *circoscrizione*.

EU nationals may convert their licenses to Italian licenses easily, and some American states have reciprocal agreements with Italy; people from those states whose licenses were valid before the residency permit is given may automatically convert their licenses; inquire at the consulate. In general, non-EU citizens must have a residence permit and then take out a learner's permit *(foglio rosa)*. Both the written and driving examinations must be taken, as well as the passing of an eye examination. The ACI can provide information in English as to how to proceed (tel: 49981); in Italian, call the **Motorizzazione Civile** (tels: north 88 02 011; south 50 03 201). Driving schools can help with the paperwork, and some give the eye exam themselves. One recommended driving school is **Motorclub**, in Via Anastasio II 49 (tel: 60 37 74).

The ACI can be helpful in many ways. ACI is comparable to other automobile associations: it provides 24-hour emergency services (hotline tel: 116), and although membership is not required, those who are members of related organisations elsewhere receive some free services and preferential rates. Non-automobile services include tourist assistance, weather reports, information on cultural events, and more. If the warning triangle required to be carried in each car is missing in yours, the ACI can provide one;

179

the triangle must be used in case of emergency breakdown. (For emergency numbers, see Appendix.)

## Car Rental

One of the Romans' greatest weekend pleasures is to take a drive out of town. There are automobile rental agencies such as AVIS, Hertz and Europcar at the airports, at Stazione Termini and in several other convenient locations in town. There is usually English-speaking personnel. See *Autonoleggio e Motonoleggio* in the Yellow Pages.

If your plans are already set for a car trip on a particular date, reserve the car in advance before departure from home, locking in rates that are considerably lower than those at the same Italian agency. Most agencies such as AVIS, Hertz, Budget, and National have special all-inclusive rates if you reserve and pay for the car in advance. Note that most rentals are stick shift; automatic transmission is rare and costs more. Of course there are Italian rental agencies, but renting from an international company is generally better in the long run: fewer billing errors, easier checking procedures, etc. If you rent in Italy, you must figure in the tax of 19%. Renters must be at least 21 years old.

Check with your credit card company and automobile insurance carrier to determine what kind of supplemental insurance you should take when renting a car; some is provided automatically if you use a credit card, and some car insurance may not be valid abroad. You should also inquire about an **International Insurance Certificate**, certifying that you have liability insurance. In Italy, generally it is the car that is insured, not the driver.

## Importing your Own Car

If you have owned your car for twelve months, you may import it tax-free into Italy. Once in Italy you should arrange for Italian registration and Italian license plates, and you must have third-party liability automobile insurance. Collision, fire and theft coverage are optional, but highly recommended.

Your car must also adhere to Italian specifications, and must pass an inspection. Converting the car in Italy to meet specifications may be difficult, as models and parts are not the same.

**Cars must have:**
- White front parking lights, separated from turn signals.
- Turn signals in front, side and rear.
- Approved catalytic converter.
- No retractable headlights; no sealed beam headlights.

If your car tends to break down, ship some spare parts with the car; it's not always easy to get identical parts abroad, especially for older cars, or even for Japanese cars of new make. You may also want to ship oil, air filters, fan belts and automatic transmission fluid with your car. If your car model is one that is sold in Italy, you may want to contact a dealer to determine what adjustments will be needed and which parts are available. Discuss also with the shipping company the paperwork needed for the importation of the car.

## Purchasing a Car

Before buying a car in Italy, become knowledgeable about the requirements. You must produce a certificate of residence, a *codice fiscale*, and you must have car insurance; it is mandatory that the insurance certificate be displayed in the windshield of the car. It is important to note that it is the car that is insured, not the driver, so you must purchase several types of policies to obtain comprehensive insurance coverage. Read the policies carefully: some obligate you for ten years, assuming that if you sell one car you'll buy another. Insurance companies cannot refuse to insure you if you have an Italian driver's license. If you intend to ship the car back home, make sure it adheres to your country's requirements. Not all manufacturers produce such cars. For

current information about manufacturers, addresses and telephone numbers, car models, and prices, look for the magazines **Gente Motori** and **Quattroruote** at newsstands. Call the manufacturers for current dealers in Rome or look in the Yellow Pages under *Automobile Vendita.*

Cars with European specifications cost less than those for export. When buying a car, inquire as to all the finance options. Leasing of cars is available, as is long term financing. Proof of income will be required. Take into account also the price of insurance; prices and coverage vary. Inquire about all the options, including bonus plans for safe drivers with no history of accidents.

If you intend to buy a car in another European country, consider some of the enticements offered by European car manufacturers. Saab of Sweden, Mercedes Benz and Volvo all offer incentives for European purchase of their cars. TDS has delivery points throughout Europe and will ship the car back home when you are ready (tel: [4631] 59-59-59). Call the local dealership of the car you are interested in purchasing to see whether there are any special packages offered for purchase and pickup in Europe. Last, Europe by Car, Inc. is a well-established American firm that offers rental, lease and purchase plans for a variety of new cars in Europe (US tels: East 800/223-1516; West 800/252-9401).

If you are knowledgeable about automobiles, you might also consider purchasing a used car and then selling it upon departure if your stay is not permanent (a small investment at the beginning of the sojourn and some money back at the end). The advertising supplement *Porta Portese* lists used cars for sale, but as in any like situation, the watchword is 'buyer beware.' It's probably better to go to a dealer, for most cars must be inspected before resale. It would be a good idea to ask an automobile mechanic to check over a car before you purchase it. To find an authorised dealer, see *Autoveicoli Usati* in the Yellow Pages. See the *English Yellow Pages* for mechanics who speak English.

## Bike and Moped Rental

The *moto* (motor scooter) is one of the most popular forms of transportation, as it is inexpensive and fast, and can wend its way through the traffic with an ease not possible for cars. Try renting one a few times before deciding to purchase one. Bikes are fun to rent on weekends. Ride through the parks and into the country on bicycle paths *(piste ciclabili)* such as the red-marked **Ottaviano**, which, starting at the corner of Viale delle Milizie and Viale Angelico, goes north of Rome for about five miles. It is obligatory to wear a *casco* (helmet). Make sure you know when the bike is due back, as each agency seems to have different hours. Rental areas can be found off the Corso at Largo Lombardi, in Via Principe Amedeo near Stazione Termini, Piazza Navona, and Piazza del Popolo. In addition consider these below. For bicycle purchase, see Chapter Fourteen.

- *Trastevere* — **Bicimania**: Piazza Sonnino. Bikes. Weekends only in Winter.
- *Campo de' Fiori* — **Collalti**: Via del Pellegrino 82 (tel: 65 41 084). Bikes.
- *Via Veneto* — **I Bike Rome**: Via Veneto 156 is in the underground parking garage of Villa Borghese (tel: 32 25 240). Bikes, tandems and *moto*.
- *Esquilino* — **Happy Rent**: Piazza Esquilino 8 (tel: 48 18 185). Rents bikes, *motos*, cars, audiovisual equipment, etc. Gives tourist information. English spoken.

183

- *Prati/Trastevere* — **St. Peter Moto**: Via di Porta Castello 43, near Castel Sant'Angelo (tel: 68 74 909). *Moto* and motorcycles.
- *Barberini* — **Scooters for Rent**: Via della Purificazione 84 (tel: 48 85 485). Bikes, mopeds, scooters and motorcycles.
- *Santa Maria Maggiore/Forum* — **Scoot-a-long**: Via Cavour 302 (tel: 67 80 206). Mopeds.

# PEOPLE WITH PHYSICAL DISABILITIES

Rome is not set up to accommodate people in wheelchairs or with other special needs. Many streets are cobblestoned, and sidewalks can be perilously narrow. Nonetheless, some efforts are being made, especially in such areas as Vatican City, the Pantheon, and the Forum, and at rail and air terminals. EPT offices should have *Roma Accessibile*, listing hotels, restaurants, shops, post offices and other facilities accessible for disabled persons; if not, contact the publisher: *CO.IN* in Via E. Giglioli 54/a (tel: 23 26 75 04). Book shops should carry Gengami's *Guida di Roma: Accessibilità, Barriere Architettoniche, Turismo, Cultura, Tempo Libero*.

- **Travel Information Service** at Moss Rehab Hospital, 1200 W. Tabor Road, Philadelphia PA 19141, offers telephone travel information and referrals for disabled people (U.S. tel: 215/456-9600).
- **Associazione Nazionale Handicappati** in Via Tommaso Fortifiocca 100, offers information and referrals (tel: 78 10 772); open weekdays.

- **Ufficio Handicap Comune di Roma** in Via Merulana 123 offers assistance to those who need help at home, taxis, or other services for the handicapped (tel: 67 10 53 45). Bus No. 590 for handicapped persons follows Line A of the metro. At Stazione Termini it meets Bus No. 157 which follows Line B. (Call ATAC for information, tel: 46 95 44 44). The Metropolitana is not equipped for wheelchairs.

If bringing a service dog, have a Health Certificate for the dog, issued the day before travel, including an up-to-date record of inoculations, especially rabies; the certificate should include the dog's breed, age and colour. There is no quarantine of animals; forms can be had from Italian government tourist offices, consulates and the embassy. Inquire of your airline about your dog riding with you in the cabin; if animals ride in the hold with cargo, they must undergo an immediate health examination. Dogs must be registered at the canine *anagrafe*. For information, call the **Veterinario Provinciale** in Via Giulio Romano 46 (tel: 85 23 31). In emergency, call the **Centro Veterinario Gregorio VII**, in Via Gregorio VII 518 (24-hour tel: 66 21 686), or **Ambulatorio Trastevere** in Via della Cisterna 15/b (tel: 58 96 650). See also *Veterinari* in the Yellow Pages. Inquire before departure about regulations for bringing animals back into your country.

## One Last Note: The Call of Nature

While you're out and about, you might need to find a bathroom. Large hotels have bathrooms, as does the department store **La Rinascente** in the Corso. Locations such as the Colosseum, Stazione Termini and Piazza San Pietro have attended public restrooms. Outside the tourist areas, it's best to find one of the fast food emporia or a bar, required by law to have bathrooms. Buy a cup of coffee and ask for the bathroom. Toilets are marked with a picture of a man or woman, with the letters WC, or with *Signori* for men and *Signore* for women. Women shouldn't be surprised if the toilets in bars — even the most elegant — are filthy and have no seats. Always carry your own tissues with you. Always.

185

# CHAPTER ELEVEN

# EATING ESTABLISHMENTS

## RISTORANTI – SPOILT FOR CHOICE

A taxi driver once pointed to a restaurant lauded by guidebooks and said to me *"Si paga bene ma si mangia male."* It is true that one often pays high prices in such restaurants and that the food may not be as good as in a neighbourhood trattoria. Nowadays, in fact, a 'moderate' meal is said by the guidebooks to cost as much as L65,000 per person, excluding wine. An 'expensive' meal, such as at the two-star **Relais le Jardin**, may run as high as L120,000, and even at more typical, yet well-publicised restaurants, meals can cost L85,000. It's better to go where the locals routinely go, where food is fresh, well prepared and reasonable in price. With some experimentation, it's easy to eat well in the range of L30,000-50,000. And pizza, of course, costs much less. Meal prices in guides generally cover a traditional four-course meal, but many people are eating lighter meals, ordering just one or two courses.

There are several good restaurant guides. *Roma*, published annually by Gambero Rosso, varies its offerings, and it also includes lists of food markets (L19,000). *Ristoranti a Roma*, published by Gangemi, lists restaurants by neighbourhood (L15,000). Both books are in Italian and are sold at bookstores. In English is *Eat Like the Romans: The Visitor's Food Guide* by Maureen B. Fant (L10,000). And, of course, tourist guides have lists of variously priced restaurants. Most include more than just the tourist establishments, describing some with particular specialties and some out of the city centre. But with 3500 restaurants of one sort or another in Rome, no guidebook can cover them all. Start by asking your friends, looking at the ads in the Yellow Pages under *Ristoranti*, or at the selections of *Roma C'è*.

There used to be a marked difference between types of restaurants, indicating not only the kind and quality of food served, but a cultural distinction as well. Although the names and categories now tend to overlap, the type of eating establishment still tells something about its clientele, as one will notice upon entering. A **ristorante** has refined dining and a carefully planned decor. A **trattoria** is less formal and has heartier, more simple cooking. An **osteria** is plainer yet, with simple yet substantial pastas. A **pizzeria** sells pizza, salads and antipasti, and a **rosticceria** has roasted chickens and pizza *al taglio* to take out, sometimes with tables or stools. Last, a **tavola calda** is a steam table.

Restaurants open from about 12:30 pm to mid-afternoon and from about 7:30 pm until 10:30 pm-12:00 midnight. They close one day a week *(riposo settimanale)*, often Sunday evening, many families having gone out for a leisurely lunch. Some restaurants close all of August for *ferie*; most are closed at least two weeks.

The traditional *coperto*, an automatic charge that included the bread, is no longer charged. Now you may be charged separately for bread, although some restaurants absorb it in the bill. A tip of about 10-15% is always included, although you can leave another

*Photo: Pomponi/Photoreporters*

*Tourists in Piazza Navona enjoying the Roman tradition of outdoor dining.*

few thousand lire, except in small family-run establishments. Check the bill to make sure it is accurate. You are required to take the receipt with you: take it home and throw it out, but take it. The receipt system is one way the tax authorities know that a cash-only restaurant is declaring its cash income; occasionally there are inspectors nearby making sure customers leaving the restaurant really do have their receipts. Legally, the burden is on the customer.

## CUCINA ROMANA

While emperors of ancient Rome were indulging in lavish banquets eating the most succulent parts of peacocks and flamingos, of wild pigs stuffed with live thrushes, of donkeys roasted on a spit, the ordinary citizens were eating what was left and what was growing nearby. Over the millennia, thus, Rome has developed a *cucina* of its own, simple and robust, using every part of the animal and the

188

freshest of regional produce, a tradition that has happily endured. In general, don't expect the cream sauces of the north, nor the tomato sauces of the south. Although meat is on every menu, other items generally take precedence, especially seasonal produce, interesting pasta combinations, and game. Restaurants that specialise in traditional Jewish recipes such as deep fried fillets of baccalà or fried artichokes have long been a part of the traditional Roman heritage. Look for signs saying *cucina romana* or *cucina casareccia* (home cooking).

- **abbacchio** — unweaned lamb roasted with herbs and oil
- **abbacchio brodettato** — lamb stew, egg yolks and lemon
- **abbacchio a scottadito** — grilled lamb cuts
- **bucatini all'amatriciana** — pasta with bacon, tomatoes, and grated pecorino cheese
- **cacciagione** — game, in season
- **coda alla vaccinara** — oxtail stew
- **carciofi** — artichokes cooked variously: *alla giudia* (flattened and fried); *alla romana* (braised with mint and garlic)
- **filetti di baccalà** — deep fried salt cod fillets
- **fritto misto** — fried meats and vegetables
- **fritto vegetale** — fried vegetables
- **gnocchi di patate** — small potato dumpling pasta generally served on Thursdays
- **involtini al sugo** — rolls of meat usually stewed in tomato sauce
- **ossobuco** — veal shanks with marrow stewed with vegetables
- **pagliata** — veal intestine, clotted milk, garlic, chilli, tomato & wine; also comes as *rigatoni alla pagliata.*
- **porchetta** — pig roasted on a spit, served by the slice
- **saltimbocca alla romana** — veal scallopine with ham and sage
- **seppiette ai carciofi** — small cuttlefish with artichokes
- **spaghetti alla carbonara** — pasta with bacon, cheese and eggs
- **spaghetti aglio e olio** — pasta with olive oil and garlic; also with **peperoncino**, red pepper flakes

- **spaghetti cacio e pepe** — spaghetti with grated pecorino cheese and pepper.
- **trippa alla romana** — tripe, tomato sauce, flavoured with mint.

There are others. If you are in Rome in March, try the sugared fritters called **bignè**, and any time try **supplì**, fried rice balls stuffed with mozzarella, eaten as appetisers or snacks. **Maritozzi**, small cakes with raisins, pine nuts and candied fruit and often with whipped cream are a breakfast alternative to the **cornetto**, a sweetish croissant. The restaurants below are well known for *cucina romana*, and some are described in detail in the restaurant guides; make sure to try those in Testaccio near the site of the old Roman *mattatoio* (slaughterhouse).

- *Campo de' Fiori* — **Filettaro Santa Barbara:** Largo dei Librari 88 (tel: 68 64 018). Only filetti di baccalà. Closed Sunday and August.
- *Cassia* – **Buccilli Hostavia:** Via due Ponti (tel: 33 40 048). Closed Monday
- *Ghetto* — **Al Pompiere**: Via Santa Maria de' Calderari 38 (tel: 68 68 377). Closed Sunday and August.
- *Ghetto* — **Giggetto al Portico**: Via del Portico d'Ottavia 21/a (tel: 68 61 105). Closed Monday and August.
- *Ghetto* — **Piperno**: Via Monte de' Cenci 9 (tel: 68 80 66 29). Closed Sunday evening and Monday; part of August.
- *Pantheon* — **San Eustachio**: Piazza dei Caprettari 63 (tel: 68 61 616). Closed Sunday.
- *San Lorenzo* — **Pommidoro**: Piazza dei Sanniti 44 (tel: 44 52 692). Closed Sunday; August.
- *Testaccio* — **Augustarello**: Via G. Branca 98 (tel: 57 46 585). Closed Sunday; latter part of August.
- *Testaccio* — **Checchino dal 1887**: Via di Monte Testaccio 30 (tel: 57 46 318). Closed Sunday evening, Monday; August.
- *Testaccio* — **Turiddu al Mattatoio**: Via Galvani 64 (tel: 57 50 447). Closed Thursday.

- *Trastevere* — **Checco er Carrettiere**: Via Benedetta 10 (tel: 58 00 985). Closed Sunday evening, Monday and August.
- *Trastevere* — **Comparone**: Piazza in Piscinula 47 (tel: 58 16 249). Closed Monday; August.
- *Trastevere* — **Paris**: Piazza San Calisto 7/a (tel: 58 15 378). Closed Sunday evening and Monday.

# FISH

Although Rome is close to the ocean, fish has been until recently a delicacy on the Roman menu. Nearby waters are often polluted, so fish in restaurants may not be local. This raises the price, so when ordering check whether the fish is priced by the plate or (more usually) by its weight (the *etto* or 100 gr). Fish on any menu will be fresh, but if not, the menu must indicate that it has been frozen. Some of the most popular seafoods, in addition to *baccalà*, are *pesce spada* (swordfish), *merluzzo* (cod), *sogliola* (sole) *calamari* (squid), *trota* (trout), *gamberi* (shrimp), *rombo* (turbot), *aragosta* (lobster), and *acciughe* (fresh anchovies).

- *Piazza Indipendenza* — **Da Vincenzo**: Via Castelfidardo 6 (tel: 48 45 96). Closed Sunday.
- *Ponte Marconi* — **La Dolce Vita**: Lungotevere Pietra Papa 49 (tel: 55 79 865). Closed Monday and August 15.
- *Prati* — **Benito & Gilberto**: Via del Falco 19 (tel: 68 30 80 86). Closed Sunday.
- *Laterano* — **Cannavota**: Piazza S. Giovanni in Laterano 20 (tel: 77 20 50 07). Closed Wednesday; August.
- *Testaccio* — **Da Bucatino**: Via Luca della Robbia 84 (tel: 57 46 886).
- *Trastevere* — **Sabatini**: Piazza S. Maria in Trastevere 13 (tel: 58 12 026) Closed Wednesday.
- *Via Tripoli* — **Baia Sardinia**: Via Benadir 20 (tel: 86 21 44 63). Closed Monday.
- *EUR* — **Pomodoro & Aragosta**: Via A.G. Resti 49 (tel: 50 36 464).

# PIZZA

**Pizzerie**, in which you can also get *suppli*, *bruschetta*, other *antipasti*, and salads, along with wine or beer, are popular with all Romans, from rich to poor, young to old. Typical Roman pizzas are **pizza alle patate** or **pizza alla rughetta**, with potatoes or raw greens. A pizza is usually for one person; it doesn't come in different sizes to be divided. Pizzerie are generally open evenings; most of those open all day are for tourists. For each of those listed below, there are Romans who insist it is the best pizzeria in town. True or not, they're all popular, so be prepared to wait.

- *Campo de' Fiori* — **Acchiappafantasmi**: Via dei Cappellari 66 (tel: 68 73 462). Closed Tuesday.
- *Cassia* – **Osvaldo:** Via Cassia 466 (tel: 33 12 422). Closed Monday. Also at Via Flaminia Vecchia 515 (tel: 33 32 528). Closed Wednesday.
- *Colosseo* — **Pizza Forum**: Via S. Giovanni in Laterano 34 (tel: 70 02 515). Naples-style pizza. Open daily.
- *Forum* — **Alle Carrette**: Vicolo delle Carrette 14 (tel: 67 92 770). Closed Monday and much of August.
- *Piazza di Trevi* — **Er Buco**: Via del Lavatore 91 (tel: 67 81 154). Closed Sunday.
- *Piazza del Popolo* — **Pizza Ré**: Via di Ripetta 14 (tel: 32 11 468). Naples-style. Open lunch, except Sunday.
- *Piazza Navona* — **Da Baffetto**: Via del Governo Vecchio 14 (tel: 68 61 617). Closed Sunday, end of August.
- *Prati* — **Giacomelli**: Via E. Faà di Bruno 25 (tel: 37 51 65 28). Closed Monday and August.
- *Prati* — **Antica Cucina**: Viale Giulio Cesare 91 (tel: 32 16 963). Closed Monday and part of August.
- *San Lorenzo* — **Formula 1**: Via degli Equi 13 (tel: 44 53 866). Closed Sunday and August.
- *San Lorenzo* — **Pizzeria Maratoneta** in Via dei Volsci 99 (tel: 49 00 27). Closed Tuesday and end of August.

- *San Lorenzo* — **Le Maschere**: Via degli Umbri 8 (tel: 68 79 444). Closed Monday.
- *Piramide* — **Gennargentu**: Via Ostiense 21 (tel: 57 59 817). Closed Monday; August.
- *Testaccio* — **Remo**: Piazza S. Maria Liberatrice 44 (tel: 57 46 270). Closed Sunday and August.
- *Trastevere* — **Da Gildo**: Via della Scala 31 (tel: 58 00 733). Closed Wednesday.
- *Trastevere* — **Da Vittorio**: Via di S. Cosimato 14a (tel: 58 00 353) Closed Monday. Reservations.
- *Trastevere* — **Ivo**: Via di San Francesco a Ripa 158 (tel: 58 17 082). Closed Tuesday and much of August.
- *Trastevere* — **Panattoni (L'Obitorio)**: Viale Trastevere 53 (tel: 58 00 919). Closed Wednesday and August.

During the daytime, try **pizza al taglio**, pizza by the slice or *etto* (100gm). Also known as **pizza rustica**, these small take-out establishments sometimes have tables or stools. *Pizzerie al taglio* are in every neighbourhood. Those below are known for their interesting variety of toppings.

193

- *Ghetto* — **Antico Forno Cordella**: Pizza Costaguti 31. Kosher pizza.
- *Montesacro* — **Angelo e simonetta**: Via Nomentana 58. Open evenings.
- *Parioli* — **Pippo**: Via E. Duse 1/d. Open evenings.
- *Piazza di Spagna*: **Fior Fiore**: Via della Croce 17. Also baked goods and fresh pasta.
- *Prati* — **Non Solo Pizza**: Via degli Scipioni 95. Also tavola calda. Open evenings.
- *Prati* — **Il Tempio del Buongustaio**: Piazza Risorgimento 50. Open evenings.
- *Talenti* — **Lo Zio d'America**: Via Ugo Ojetti 2. Large and varied emporium. Open evenings.
- *Trastevere* — **Frontoni**: Viale Trastevere 52. Pizza bianca prepared to your specifications. Open evenings.
- *Via del Corso* — **Defa**: Via del Corso 51. Also tavola calda. Open evenings.
- *Via Nazionale*: **Nadia e Davide**: Via Milano 33.

## VEGETARIAN

It's easy to be a vegetarian in Rome. Pastas with tomato sauces, pesto, mushrooms, or even just olive oil, garlic and red pepper flakes are menu regulars. The simplest Roman pasta is *cacio e pepe*, grated cheeses and pepper, with no oil. You can ask for meatless antipasti, and if *funghi porcini* are in season, ask for a selection to be grilled for your second course. Fresh vegetables and fruits are often displayed on tables at the front of restaurants. If you are interested in macrobiotic restaurants, there are several, some offering products other than food.

- *Centro Storico* — **Supernatural**: Via del Leoncino 38 (tel: 68 67 480). Vegetarian pizza, pastas, and hamburgers. Terrace.
- *Piazza del Popolo* — **Margutta Vegetariano**: Via Margutta 118 (tel: 36 00 18 05). Closed Sundays and August.

194

- *Piazza del Popolo* — **L'Antico Bottaro**: Passeggiata di Ripetta 15 (tel: 32 40 200). Closed Wednesdays.
- *Piazza di Spagna* — **Centro Macrobiotico Italiano**: Via della Vite 14, (tel: 67 92 509). Books, natural cosmetics. Hosts interesting speakers; offers classes in yoga and tai-chi.
- *Testaccio* — **Il Canestro**: Via Luca della Robbia 47/a (tel: 57 42 800). Restaurant and organic grocery. Closed Sundays.

## INTERNATIONAL RESTAURANTS

International dining is popular, especially in Asian restaurants, which — excepting the Japanese — are fairly inexpensive. French restaurants are rare and like **Relais La Piscine** in Via Mangili 6 (tel: 321.6126), expensive. See *Ristoranti* in the Yellow Pages, as well as *TrovaRoma* and *Roma C'è*.

- *African* — **Sahara**: Viale Ippocrate 43, near Piazza Bologna (tel: 44 24 25 83). Eritrean food, honey wine, desserts. Closed Wednesday, last half of August.
- *Chinese* — **Mandarin**: Via Emilia 85, near Via Veneto (tel: 48 25 577). Closed Monday; August.
- *Chinese* — **Golden Crown**: Via in Arcione 85 (tel: 67 89 831). Classic Cantonese with some Szechuan dishes. Open daily.
- *Egyptian* — **Shawerma**: Via Ostilia 24, near the Colosseum (tel: 70 08 101). Weekends there's also music. Closed Monday.
- *Ethiopian* — **Mar Rosso** in Via Conte Verde 62, off Piazza Vittorio Emanuele (tel: 44 64 495). Spicy Middle-Eastern specialties. Closed Tuesday.
- *French* — **L'Eau Vive**: Via Monterone 85, near Largo Argentina (tel: 68 80 10 95). Affordable French restaurant in a lovely setting.
- *German/Austrian* — **Birreria Viennese**: Via della Croce 21 (tel: 67 95 569). Hearty goulash, Wiener schnitzel, in an authentic beer house. Closed Wednesday.
- *Indian* — **India House**: Via di S. Cecilia 8, in Trastevere (tel: 58 18 508). In an Indian enclave; not cheap. Closed Monday.

- *Indian* — **Surya Mahal**: Piazza Trilussa 50, in Trastevere (tel: 58 94 554). Both vegetarian and meat specialties. Garden. Closed Sunday.
- *Japanese* — **Hamasei**: Via della Mercede 35, in the Centro Storico (tel: 67 92 134). Varied menu in selection and price. Fine sushi and sashimi. Closed Monday.
- *Japanese* — **Sogo Asahi**: Via di Propaganda 22 (tel: 67 86 093). Full range of Japanese specialties. Closed Sunday. Also try the informal **Caffè Sogo** Sushi Bar in Via di Ripetta 242 (tel: 36 12 272). Closed Monday.
- *Korean* — **Silla**: Borgo Angelico 26, near St. Peter's (tel: 68 30 75 51). Interesting selection. Closed Tuesday.
- *Kosher* — **Da Lisa**: Via Ugo Foscolo 16, near Via Merulana (tel: 70 49 54 56). Closed Saturday. Couscous, hummus, Roman specialties.
- *Malaysian* — **Oceano Chinese/Malay**: Viale Trastevere 132 (tel: 58 17 010). Spicy Malaysian and Chinese specialties. Closed Monday.
- *Mexican* — **La Piedra del Sol**: Vicolo Rosini 6, off the Corso (tel: 68 73 651). Good food, centrally located.
- *Mexican* — **Messico e Nuvole**: Via dei Magazzini Generali 8, in Ostiense (tel: 57 41 413). Closed Monday.
- *Middle Eastern* – **Kabab:** Via di Grottarossa 52, near the Cassia (tel: 30 31 02 31). Persian and other Middle Eastern specialties. Closed Monday.
- *Vietnamese* — **Thien Kim**: Via Giulia 201 (tel: 68 30 78 32). Closed Sunday; August.

## And Offbeat Favourites

One of Rome's pleasures is to discover the offbeat eateries often tucked into corners of the city that tourists and business travellers never see. Keep a list of your favourites and pass it on to friends; here are some of mine:

- *Borgo* — **Tre Pupazzi**: Borgo Pio 183, in a pedestrian zone, has a Roman and Abruzzan menu, with good antipasti, pizza and pastas (tel: 68 68 371). Outdoor tables at a *taverna tipica*. Closed Sunday.
- *Cassia* – **Primo Piano**: Via Cassia 999/b (tel: 30 31 07 11). Classic cooking, daily specials, good pizza. Closed Monday.
- *Gianicolo* — **Scarpone**: Vi S. Pancrazio 15 (tel: 58 14 094). Good food under a delightful pergola in summer, and in a grill room in winter.
- *Monteverde* — **Bruno ai Quattro Venti**: Viale Quattro Venti 172 (tel: 58 06 196). Popular with families and the young crowd, a lively trattoria with outdoor tables and fresh, hearty food. Closed Monday.
- *Piazza Navona* — **Fratelli Paladini**: Via del Governo Vecchio 28, an always-crowded sandwich shop, some say the best in Rome (tel: 68 61 237). Sandwiches are prepared per order on *focaccia* just out of the oven *(appena sfornata)* and your choice of fillings. Try a combination of prosciutto, brie cheese and rughetta, or prosciutto and fresh figs. Closed weekends; August.
- *Prati* — **Bibo Astoria**: Via Cola di Rienzo 60, a casual restaurant and bar (tel: 36 10 007). American breakfasts, including omelettes. Pizza, burgers, and other light foods. Covered veranda is open year round. Popular and crowded. Closed Sunday.
- *Prati* — **Osteria dell'Angelo**: Via Giovanni Bettolo 24, near Largo Trionfale (tel: 37 29 470). Indoor and outdoor seating, enormous portions of Roman fare at moderate prices. Closed Sunday and much of August.
- *San Lorenzo* — **Il Dito e la Luna**: Via dei Sabelli 51 (tel: 49 40 726). Charming locale with an imaginative menu, predominantly Sicilian. For dessert, the cannoli are special. Open evenings only; closed Sunday.

- *San Lorenzo* — **Pizzeria Economica Gallo Rosso**: Via Tiburtina 44 (tel: 44 56 669 ). Good pizza — cheap, as the name claims — with a friendly local atmosphere and outdoor tables.
- *Trastevere* — **Taverna del Moro**: Via del Moro 43, above Piazza S. Maria in Trastevere (tel: 58 09 165). Fresh fish, warm just-baked breads, draft beer and good, inexpensive pasta.
- *Trastevere* — **La Gensola**: Piazza della Gensola 15, near Isola Tiberina (tel: 58 16 312). Sicilian food in a relaxed atmosphere; try the pasta with sardines. Closed Saturday lunch, Sunday and August.
- *Via del Corso* — **Caffè Teichner**: Piazza S. Lorenzo in Lucina 15 (tel: 68 71 449). A bit of everything in a pleasant square. Coffee, sandwiches, take-out, desserts.

## COFFEE AND TEA

Many people seem to think of Italians as 'drinkers,' but if they are, the beverage is coffee. Coffee is consumed throughout the day, from the first gulp at the bar in the morning to leisurely cups in outdoor cafes in the afternoon, to the last jolt after dinner at a trattoria. There are many types:

- **caffè** — what foreigners call **espresso**. An inch of potent, dark coffee.
- **caffè lungo** — double caffè. You can also ask for a **caffè doppio.**
- **caffè latte** — coffee with milk.
- **caffè americano** — weaker, made for people who can't take regular caffè.
- **caffè ristretto** — stronger, made with even less water than caffè.
- **caffè macchiato** — coffee with a few drops of hot milk.
- **latte macchiato** — hot milk with a few drops of coffee.
- **cappuccino** — caffè with foamed milk. Sometimes topped with powdered chocolate. Not ordered after meals.

- **caffè corretto** — caffè with a few drops of liqueur, often cognac, or grappa.
- **caffè Hag** — decaffeinated coffee.
- **caffè freddo** — frozen coffee, chopped up, usually sugared. You can, however, ask for it **amaro**.
- **granita di caffè** — iced coffee, usually with whipped cream on top.

There are some five thousand **bars** in Rome. Romans head to their favourite bar first thing in the morning for a caffeine jolt and come back when they can. Here's the routine: after deciding what you want, pay at the *cassa* and bring the *scontrino* (receipt) to the *barista*, giving your order and — if you're so inclined — putting a L200 piece on the bar. Drink your morning coffee standing up; it's cheaper than table service, but tables are nice later in the day for lingering with a book. Bars generally serve light foods: **cornetti** for breakfast, **tramezzini** (prepared sandwiches) for lunch, and sweets, liquors, soft drinks and candies. See *Bar e Caffè* in the Yellow Pages.

- *Foro Italico* — **Bar del Tennis**: Viale dei Gladiatori 31 (tel: 32 07 422). Bar with outdoor tables by the sports centre. Closed Monday.
- *Via Merulana* — **Ornelli**: Via Merulana 224 between S. Maria Maggiore and the Lateran (tel: 48 72 788). A bar, enoteca, gelateria and tea room, open until midnight. Closed Sunday.
- *Monte Mario* — **Lo Zodiaco**: Viale del Parco Mellini 90 on the top of Monte Mario (tel: 35 45 10 32). Not near anything except the best view of the city. Closed Tuesday morning.
- *Pantheon* — **Caffè Sant'Eustachio**: Piazza di Sant'Eustachio 82 (tel: 68 61 309). An old and famous bar with outside tables, some say with the best coffee in Rome. Coffee beans in bulk. Try the 'special coffee.' Open late. Closed Monday and August.
- *Piazza del Popolo* — **Rosati**: Piazza del Popolo 5 (tel: 32 25 859). Now more famous for ice cream, this elegant old-time artists'

cafe still serves pastries baked in the original ovens. Closed Tuesday.

- *Piazza Navona* — **Antico Caffè della Pace**: Via della Pace 3 (tel: 6 86 12 16). This century-old caffè serves excellent coffee. Open late.
- *Piazza. di Spagna* — **Antico Caffè Greco**: Via Condotti 86 (tel: 67 82 554). Dating from 1760, it is Rome's most famous bar. The tables serve tourists, but it is still worth tossing off a coffee with the locals at the bar. Closed Sunday and much of August.
- *Prati* — **Antonini**: Via G. Sabotino 19 (tel: 37 51 78 45). Good bar, especially around lunch or snack time; try their famous canapés. Outdoor tables, bakery and take-out.
- *Prati* — **Dolci e Doni**: Via Marianna Dionigi 3 (tel: 32 14 918). Good light snacks and a pasticceria with excellent fruit tortes. Also in Via delle Carrozze 85/a (tel: 67 82 913).
- *Prati* — **Gran Caffè Esperia Ruschena**: Lungotevere dei Mellini 1 (tel: 32 04 652). This lovely old cafe/tea room serves light meals, ice cream and desserts, and **panettone romano,** a sweetish bread.
- *Prati* — **Vanni**: Via Col di Lana 10 (tel: 33 23 642). Light foods, with an indoor tea room as well. Also in Via Frattina 94, with outdoor tables (tel: 67 91 835).
- *Trastevere* — **Bar San Calisto**: Piazza S. Calisto 4 (tel: 58 35 869). Everyone comes here — young, old, students, professionals, and even tourists. Outdoor tables; open late.
- *Trastevere* — **Sacchetti**: Piazza S. Cosimato 61, on the market square (tel: 58 06 075). Good pastry shop, gelateria and bar, with a tea room on the second floor. Closed Monday.
- *Trastevere* — **Caffè Settimiano**: Via di Porta Settimiana 1 (tel: 58 10 468). Sandwiches, salads, hot dishes. Student hangout near John Cabot University. Closed Monday.
- *Via Veneto* — **Café de Paris**: Via V. Veneto 90 (tel: 48 85 284). A remnant of the days of *la dolce vita*. A good bar nonetheless with outdoor tables and a pleasant atmosphere.

- *Vigna Clara* — **Euclide**: Largo di Vigna Stelluti 1 (tel: 36 30 78 65). One of the most extensive bars in the city. Snacks, sandwiches, pastries and aperitifs. A larger branch with outdoor tables is in Via Flaminia (km 8.2), also offering pizza (tel: 33 30 695); and in Parioli: Via F. Civinini 119 (tel: 80 78 017).

You can get a cup of *tè* (also spelled *the*) at any bar, or a glass of *tè freddo*, lightly sugared cold lemon tea; ask for ice if you want it. The current rage is *tè freddo alla pesca*, which has a delightful aroma of peach.

- *Piazza di Spagna* — **Babington's Tea Room**: Piazza di Spagna 23 (tel: 67 86 027) An authentic and expensive English tea room that also serves traditional British food. Open nonstop; closed Tuesday.
- *Trastevere* — **Sala da Tè Trastè**: Via della Lungaretta 76 (tel: 58 94 430). Lively tea room/bar. Alcoholic drinks and food; popular into the late evening. Closed Monday.
- *Trastevere* — **Giardino dei Ciliegi**: Via dei Fienaroli 4 (tel: 58 03 423). Varied and popular tea room. Opens at 8:00 pm on weekdays, 5:00 pm weekends.

## WINE BARS

Although Italians don't usually drink outside of meal times *(fuori pasto)*, **enoteche** (wine bars) are popular for leisurely tasting of a selection of wines and the eating of light foods. In fact, sipping wines and eating in an enoteca is an inexpensive way to spend an evening out. Enoteche sell wine by the bottle, but see also Chapter Twelve for wine shops.

- *Campo de' Fiori* — **Vineria Reggio**: Campo de' Fiori 15 (tel: 68 80 32 68). Popular and crowded, with outdoor tables. Closed Sunday.
- *Campo de' Fiori* — **Il Goccetto**: Via dei Banchi Vecchi 14 (tel: 68 64 268). Charming, with beamed ceilings and intimate tables. Closed Sunday.

- *Forum* — **Cavour 313**: Via Cavour 313 (tel: 67 85 496). Relaxed atmosphere with beers, too, and light foods. Closed Sunday and August.
- *Piazza Indipendenza* — **Trimani**: Via Cernaia 37/b (tel: 44 69 630). Extensive wine bar, light meals and snacks, gourmet treats, etc. Around the corner from the wine shop in Via Goito 20 (tel: 44 69 661).
- *Piazza Mazzini* — **Enoteca Carso**: Viale Carso 37 (tel: 37 25 866). Outside tables, a good variety of wines and good prices. Closed Sunday.
- *Piazza Navona* — **Cul De Sac**: Piazza Pasquino 73 (tel: 68 80 10 94). One of the most famous, with an extensive menu along with the large selection of wines. Closed Monday.
- *Piazza del Parlamento* — **Vini e Buffet**: Piazza della Torretta 60 (tel: 68 71 445). Good light foods, lots of wines and grappa. Closed Sunday.
- *Piazza di Spagna* — **L'Enoteca Antica di Via della Croce**: Via della Croce 76/b (tel: 67 90 896). Good selection of wines, oils and snacks, including a *torta rustica*. Closed Sunday and end of August.
- *Salario* — **Enoteca Guerrini**: Viale Regina Margherita 205 (tel: 44 25 09 86). Serves lunches, sells wine.
- *Trastevere* — **Il Cantiniere di Santa Dorotea**: Via di S. Dorotea 9 (tel: 58 19 025). Soups, fondue and other light foods. Closed Tuesday; two weeks in August.

# BEER

**Birra** (beer) is extremely popular with young Romans, and especially for those who tend to drink it rather than wine, with pizza. Italy produces a few good light, lager beers, including **Moretti, Sans Souci, Nastro Azzurro** and **Peroni**, the most internationally known; ask for a **birra nazionale**. Imported beers are becoming increasingly available. You can order beer *in bottiglia* (bot-

tled), or *alla spina* (on tap), which comes in three sizes: *piccola/
media/grande*, and in two colours: *chiara* and *scura*. There are quite
a few Italian **birrerie**, Irish pubs and German beer houses. Look
in *Roma C'e* or *TrovaRoma* for recent additions.

- *Esquilino* — **Druid's Den**: Via San Martino ai Monti 28 (tel:
  48 80 258). Irish pub. Closed Monday.
- *Esquilino* — **Fiddler's Elbow**: Via dell'Olmata 43 (tel: 48 72
  110). Irish pub, one of the oldest in Rome. Closed Tuesday.
- *Laterano* — **Obelisk Pub**: Via M. Boardo 12 (tel: 70 49 46 78).
  Games, music, light foods. Good selection of beer. Closed
  Sunday and Monday.
- *Piazza Barberini* — **Albrecht**: Via Rasella 52 (tel: 48 80 457).
  One of Rome's oldest pubs, offering Austro- Hungarian foods.
  Closed Monday.
- *Piazza Navona* — **The Drunken Ship**: Campo de' Fiori 20 (tel:
  68 30 05 35). Variety of international beers.
- *Piazza del Popolo* — **Victoria House**: Via di Gesù e Maria 18
  (tel: 32 01 698). English pub. Full lunches, English teas. Closed
  Monday. Happy hour 6:00 pm-9:00 pm.
- *Piazza del Popolo* — **Green Rose Pub**: Passeggiata di Ripetta 33
  (tel: 32 15 548). Opens at 6:00 pm for tea and stays open until
  2:00 am.
- *Piazza. di Spagna* — **Birreria Viennese**: Via delle Croce 21 (tel:
  67 95 569). Hearty schnitzels and goulash, and a variety of
  beers on tap. Closed Wednesdays; mid-July to mid-August.
- *Prati* — **The Proud Lion**: Borgo Pio 36 (tel: 68 32 841). Scottish
  pub near St. Peter's. Open every evening.
- *Prati* — **Tiroler Keller**: Via G. Vitelleschi 23 (tel: 68 69 994).
  Authentic middle-European beer house.

# GELATO AND SUMMER TREATS

*Gelato* (ice cream), like coffee, is a staple of Roman life. What
makes *gelato* so delicious is that the flavours taste so true and that

the portions are not overwhelming. If a sign says *gelato artigianale*, it means that the ice cream was made according to a special process by a *gelato* artisan; if it says *produzione proprio*, it will have been made in-house.

You can have *gelato* with *panna* (whipped cream), in a *cono* (cone) or *coppetta* (cup). There are **gelaterie** in every neighbourhood, and some are starting to add frozen yoghurt to their repertoire. Many people don't bother to eat dessert in restaurants — unless there's a delicious *tiramisù* or in summer a mixed fruit *macedonia*; it's more fun to go to a nearby *gelateria*. A popular whipped fruit and milk drink, sometimes frozen, is **frullato**.

As with the pizzerie, for each of the gelaterie listed below there are Romans who swear that it is absolutely the best ice cream in Rome.

- *Appio* — **San Crispino**: Via Acaia 56 (tel: 70 45 04 12). Cups of exquisitely prepared gelato; fewer flavours but always the freshest ingredients. Closed Tuesday.
- *EUR* — **Casina dei Tre Laghi**: Viale Oceania 90, the second establishment of the famous Giolitti, described below (tel: 59 24 507).
- *Flaminia* — **Mondi**: Via Flaminia Vecchia 468/a, sells refrigerated pastries and tarts as well (tel: 33 36 466). Try the *torta di ricotta* and the *zabaione gelato*. Closed Monday.
- *Pantheon* — **Giolitti**: Via degli Uffici del Vicario 40 (tel: 69 91 243). Founded in 1900, this is the most famous of Rome's gelaterie. Closed Sunday afternoon and Monday.
- *Parioli* — **Bar San Filippo**: Via di Villa San Filippo 4-10, near Piazza Bligny; a popular neighbourhood bar (tel: 80 79 314). Closed Monday.

- *Parioli* — **Duse**: Via Eleanora Duse 1/e, near Piazza delle Muse (tel: 80 79 300). White chocolate a specialty. Closed Sunday.
- *Piazza Navona* — **Tre Scalini**: Piazza Navona 28, famous for *tartufo*, a rich, bitter chocolate ice cream (tel: 68 80 19 96). Closed Wednesday.
- *Piazza Vittorio* — **Palazzo del Freddo di Giovanni Fassi**: Via Principe Eugenio 65 (tel: 44 64 740). Try the hot chocolate in winter. Open late weekends. Closed Monday.
- *Prati* — **Pellacchia:** Via Cola di Rienzo 105 (tel: 32 10 807). Popular, on a busy shopping street.
- *San Lorenzo* — **Marani** in Via dei Volsci 57 (tel: 49 00 16). An extensive selection and an outdoor covered patio. Closed Monday and August.
- *Trastevere* — **La Fonte della Salute**: Via Cardinale Marmaggi 2 (tel: 58 97 471). Popular *gelateria*, open until 2:00 am.
- *Trastevere* — **Yogufruit**: Piazza G. Tavani Arquati 118, off Via della Lungaretta (tel: 58 79 72). Good frozen yoghurt blended with fresh fruit in season.

In summer, visit one of the **grattachecche**, portable bars specialising in flavoured shaved ice, mostly of fresh fruit flavour. Some, such as the stand at Largo Ravizza, have alcohol-flavoured ices. Many stay open late. The stand at Ponte Garibaldi in Trastevere is said to date back to near the turn of the century. And some people say that the *grattachecca* in Via Trionfale is the best in Rome; it too stays open late. Others rave about the kiosk in Trastevere at the intersection of Lungotevere Sanzio and Piazza G.G. Belli.

Also in summer, try to find one of the **cocomerari**, the occasional watermelon stands that sell by the slice. Watermelon has two names in Italian: *anguria* and *cocomero*.

205

— Chapter Twelve —

# THE FOOD MARKETS

## EATING IN

In a city where a Coca-Cola in a bar can cost US$2.00, it's worth considering how best to eat at home. Food shopping is an essential and pleasant part of Roman life. The outdoor daily markets sell foods of all kinds — not just produce — generally at low cost. There are small **alimentari** (groceries) in every neighbourhood, and although there are also convenient, well stocked **supermercati**, there is an official effort not to let them drive out the local shops. The **salumerie** offer smoked meats and cheeses, and some have prepared dishes to take home and reheat. People do most of their shopping in the outdoor markets, saving the indoor shops for staples, specialty items, breads and meat. Thus, instead of shopping rarely and stocking the freezer, shopping for small amounts more often ensures that the items will be fresh. This is important, for artificial *conservanti* (preservatives) are rarely used and food tends to spoil more quickly, although they are healthier and more flavourful than foods doctored with

206

chemicals. (Don't say *preservativi* in this regard; they're condoms.) The supermarkets and some other shops will deliver groceries *(a domicilio)*; look in *Roma C'è* for listings of establishments that deliver.

Food shops are often grouped: butchers and bakers are clustered around market squares, and even in the Centro Storico, for example, the narrow Via Laurina sees a greengrocer, a *salumeria* and a shop that sells chickens; in Via della Croce there are several *salumerie*, a fresh pasta emporium, a fruit shop, and a baker. Another central street, Via dei Serpenti, off Via Nazionale, holds a greengrocer, butcher, *alimentari* and coffee vendor. The best food shops, however, are out of the centre, in the neighbourhoods where the residents routinely shop. Although the small groceries may be somewhat more expensive than the supermarkets, they can have sales on items and special offers. See *Alimentari* and *Alimentari Dietetici* in the Yellow Pages.

The outdoor markets open early and close after lunch; they do not open on Sunday. Nor are *alimentari* open all day every day as are grocery shops at home. Generally they close Thursday afternoons, as well as all day Sunday; this may slowly change, for a new law now allows a Tuesday or Wednesday afternoon closing. A few stay closed Monday morning, like other shops. Daily hours are generally 8:00 am-1:00/1:30 pm and 4:30/5:00 pm-7:30 pm weekdays; in summer, the afternoon hours change to 5:30 pm-8:00 pm and shops are closed Saturday afternoon.

In summer you must plan ahead for grocery shopping. Shops may close for half of August, and from Saturday afternoon to Monday morning it's hard to find one open. Outdoor markets, too, will reduce in size toward the end of July, and some will close down for all of August. Stock up on staples, and check in advance to see which shops and markets in your area will be open.

Note that in small shops you may be asked to pay at the *cassa* after choosing your food, then to bring the receipt back to the counter to receive the packages.

207

# OUTDOOR MARKETS

All outdoor markets have fresh seasonal produce, most have meat and fish, many have shoes, clothes and household items. Some, such as **Campo de' Fiori**, are part of the historic fabric of the city. Others, such as **Piazza Vittorio Emanuele**, have an international selection, and most districts have small markets of their own. Try markets in different neighbourhoods. The **Mercati Generali** in Via Ostiense is Rome's wholesale market, open to the public from 10:00 am. Items are often sold in bulk; go with a friend and buy items together. A few food markets open only one day a week. The **Arab Market** in front of the Mosque in Viale della Moschea is open on Fridays, from noon until about 2:00 pm. The **Mercato Villaggio Olimpico** in Viale della XVII Olimpiade, with food and household items, is open Friday morning.

In the outdoor markets, as in the greengrocers listed further below, it is the vendors who select the produce, not the customer. Watch carefully and don't accept bad merchandise. As an alternative, some vendors sell vegetables such as artichokes already cleaned and trimmed (*carciofi capati*), and the quality will be higher.

- *Appia Nuova* — **Via Gino Capponi**. Small, daily neighbourhood market just off Via Appia Nuova.
- *l'Aventino* — **Piazza Gian Lorenzo Bernini**. Small daily market and a few food shops in an elegant residential area. It's easier to park a car in this area than in most others.
- *Campo de' Fiori* — **Piazza Campo de' Fiori**. Rome's most famous market, with fruits, vegetables, fish, cured meats, household goods.
- *Centro Storico* — **Piazza Monte d'Oro**. Lovely two-storey covered market in a small square in the heart of the Centro Storico. Permanent stands sell produce, cheeses, meats, fish, breads, and more.
- *Esquilino* — **Piazza Vittorio Emanuele**. Rome's international market. Seasonal produce, Indian lentils and grains, Arabian breads and spices. Good prices on meats, cheeses, game birds.

*Neighbourhood markets like this one are frequented by Romans for their daily supply of fresh produce.*

- *Flaminio/Farnesina* — **Piazzale Ponte Milvio**. Fresh fish, meats, eggs, seasonal produce, fresh pasta.
- *Parioli* — **Viale Parioli**, at Via Locchi. An interesting market that offers both food and household items.
- *Prati* — **Piazza dell'Unità** at Via Properzio and Via Cola di Rienzo. A large, lovely, covered market. Not the cheapest but high quality and ambience.
- *San Lorenzo* — **Largo degli Oschi** in San Lorenzo is a permanent outdoor market just past Via Tiburtina. Inexpensive clothing, shoes and other items.
- *Salario* — **Piazza Alessandria**, near Piazza Fiume. An old covered market, with a charming display of seasonal fruits and vegetables, meats and fish.
- *Testaccio* — **Piazza di Testaccio**. The freshest of fish and eggs, seasonal and imported fruits, salad greens, meats, including

209

the Roman *abbacchio*, and much more. Shoes are sold on Saturday mornings.

- *Trastevere* — **Piazza San Cosimato**. A famous market in the heart of Trastevere. Tasty cheeses and *salumerie* in addition to produce. For one-stop shopping, the square also has groceries and a bakery.
- *Trieste* — **Via Chiana**. A covered food market, with good quality produce.
- *Trionfale* — **Largo Trionfale**, at Via Andrea Doria. The most extensive and economical market in the area. Fruits, vegetables, and meats; fish on Tuesday and Friday. Some side streets also have stalls.

## *SALUMERIE*/TAKE-OUT FOODS

**Salumerie** (or **salsamenterie**) carry cured meats, cheeses, canned goods and some staple items. Some also sell already-prepared dishes, ready to reheat at home. In these you can buy a cooked chicken, roasted potatoes and a cooked vegetable; or you might find lasagna, already prepared, or rice-stuffed tomatoes and salmon mousse. Those noted below are especially well stocked.

- *Balduina* — **La Casa del Preparato**: Viale Medaglie d'Oro 368 (tel: 35 42 05 03). An interesting selection of ready-to-cook specialties, as well as already cooked dishes.
- *EUR* — **Delizie Alimentari**: Via Elio Vittorini 75 (tel: 50 02 617). An imaginative selection of take-out dishes, in addition to meats, cheese and other items of interest. Freshly baked pizza and focaccia.
- *Vigna Clara/Cassia* — **Ricci Salumiere in Roma**: Largo di Vigna Stelluti 9 (tel: 32 91 857). Cured meats, cheeses and a good selection of prepared foods. Excellent bakery/bar next door. Also at via Bragaglia 23/c (tel: 37 89 404).
- *Montesacro* — **Lo Zio d'America Stil Nuovo**: Via U. Ojetti 2 (tel: 82 72 741). Enormous shop with restaurant to eat in, or

food to take out. Grocery, coffees, cured meats, cheeses. *Pizzeria, gelateria*, etc.

- *Pantheon* — **Volpetti**: Via della Scrofa 32 (tel: 68 61 340). Salumeria, sandwich shop and *tavola calda*. Take-out dishes, salads, meats and more; bakery next door. Open nonstop; closed Sunday.
- *Prati* — **Franchi**: Via Cola di Rienzo 204 (tel: 68 64 576). Excellent salumeria. Elegant salads, meats, cooked chickens, seafood, full dinners and more: Open nonstop; credit cards accepted.
- *Piazza Mazzini* — **De Carolis**: Via Sabotino 28, north in Prati (tel: 37 24 050). Excellent salumeria, with fresh pasta, prepared meats and a nice selection of take-out dishes.
- *Salario* — **Cerasari**: Via Salaria 280 (tel: 84 16 998). Everything you need under one roof. Freshest of fruits and vegetables, cheeses and smoked meats, breads, fresh pasta, and a large selection of take-out dishes.
- *Testaccio* — **Emilio Volpetti**: Via Marmorata 47 (tel: 57 42 352). Long established, well-stocked salumeria, carrying caviar, paté, smoked fish, in addition to take-out dishes and excellent cheeses.
- *Trastevere* — **Frontoni**: Viale Trastevere 52 (tel: 58 12 436). An all-in-one experience: a wide variety of aromatic coffees, meats and cheeses, divine fresh baked pastries, sweets, and Rome's specialty, a *pizza bianca* called **scrocchiarella**. Pizza topped to order, and a take-home or eat-in *tavola calda*.
- *Trionfale* — **La Tradizione**: Via Cipro 8/e (tel: 39 72 03 49). A bit of everything, all at good prices. Prosciutto, domestic and imported cheeses, fancy olive oils, and prepared foods ready to reheat.
- *Via del Corso*: **Salumeria Focacci**: Via della Croce 43 (tel: 67 91 228). Conveniently located, selling cheeses, prosciutto and other cured meats, salads, pastas, and some canned staple goods.

- *Via Veneto* — **Carlo Gargani**: Via Lombardia 15 (tel: 47 40 865). Luxurious salumeria with the standard products, plus paté, caviar, smoked fishes, and take-out dishes either ready to eat or ready to cook.

# BAKERIES

Bakeries are in every neighbourhood, and each day they produce a dazzling display of fresh breads and desserts. Bakeries are of two types, but nowadays they tend to overlap. The **forno** generally specialises in breads, while the **pasticceria** offers desserts of all sorts. Small *alimentari* often carry a supply of fresh and packaged breads; sliced breads for toasting and international brands of biscuits are also available at the supermarkets and international stores. See *Pasticceria e Confetteria* in the Yellow Pages. Note that many bakeries are open on Sunday mornings and major holidays.

- *Africano* — **Romoli**: Viale Eritrea 140, near Piazza S. Emerenziana (tel: 86 32 50 77). A *pasticceria notturna*, selling hot *cornetti* and *maritozzi* late at night, to take home fresh for the next morning
- *Campo de' Fiori* — **Il Forno del Campo de' Fiori**: Piazza Campo de' Fiori 22 (tel: 68 80 66 62). Breads of all sorts and delicious apple cake. Try the *verdura*- stuffed *calzone*, to eat while roaming around the market.
- *Campo de' Fiori* — **IFA**: Via dei Baullari 5-7 (tel: 68 80 39 47). Breads in various shapes, *torte* and pizza.
- *Ghetto* — **Il Forno del Ghetto**: Via del Portico d'Ottavia 1 (tel: 68 78 637). A tiny, excellent Kosher-style bakery known for its fruitcake.
- *Ghetto* — **La Dolce Roma**: Via del Portico d'Ottavia 20/b (tel: 68 92 196). Austrian/American bakery selling cakes, strudels, Sacher torte and cheesecake. Chocolate chip cookies.
- *Piazza di Spagna* — **Krechel**: Via Frattina 134 (tel: 67 80 946). A small elegant European-style pasticceria specialising in apple strudel, Sacher torte, tiny doughnuts and more.

- *Parioli* — **Il Cigno**: Viale Parioli 16 (tel: 80 82 348). An elegant bakery. Delicious breads, *cornetti*, tortes, etc. Cafe with good, light foods. Closed Monday.
- *Prati* — **Cantiani**: Via Cola di Rienzo 234 (tel: 68 74 164). Breads, desserts, fresh pasta, gourmet items.
- *Piazza Mazzini* — **Antonini**: 1) Piazza Mazzini 9 (tel: 32 17 502). Known for *bomba*, a zabaione, cream and chocolate torte. Also a variety of *tartine* (small canapés) and other baked specialty products. Eat in or take out. 2) Nearby in Via Sabotino 21 (tel: 37 51 78 45).

*Photo: Lydia Predominato*

*A Trastevere baker displays her wares.*

- *Prati* — **Galligani:** Via Cola di Rienzo 245 (tel: 32 41 887). Fruit tarts, strudel and its *torta della nonna*.
- *San Lorenzo* — **Rodolfo Malatesta** Via degli Ausoni 46 (tel: 49 57 895). Small pasticceria and gelateria; known for its *zuccotti* and *semifreddi*. Closed Monday.
- *Santa Maria Maggiore* — **Panella**: Via Merulana 54 (tel: 48 72 344). An extensive, famous bakery with a variety of breads, rolls, desserts, take-out baked foods and dietetic products.
- *Testaccio* — **Passi**: Via Mastro Giorgio 87 (tel: 57 46 563). Large assortment of breads, pizza, and desserts.
- *Trastevere* — **Sacchetti**: Piazza S. Cosimato 62 (tel: 58 15 374). Bakery and cafe on the square. Gelato.
- *Trastevere* — **Valzani**: Via del Moro 37/b (tel: 58 03 792). Pasticceria. Traditional Roman specialties and European treats such as the Sacher torte.
- *Via Veneto* — **Palombi**: Via V. Veneto 114 (tel: 48 85 817). Pizza *al taglio*, breads, rolls — a good selection.

## COFFEE

For shops that sell coffee in bulk, look for signs that say **torrefazione**. Inside the shops you'll find sacks of all colours and aromas, and in some you can get *tostato americano* (American roast). Speciality shops such as **Castroni** sell fresh coffee as well. (See International Groceries, below.)

- *Esquilino/Forum* — **Antico Caffè do Brasil**: Via dei Serpenti 23 (tel: 48 82 319). It is said that the Pope's coffee comes from here. Ask for the 'miscela del Papa.'
- *Largo Argentina* — **Caffè Camerino**: Largo Arenula 30 (tel: 68 75 970). Coffee beans, a bar, gelato, packaged pasta, and some international packaged goods such as Old El Paso Mexican products.
- *Pantheon* — **La Casa del Caffè-Tazza d'Oro**: Via degli Orfani 84 (tel: 67 89 792). Some say it's the best coffee in the world.

- *Piazza Navona* — **Sant'Eustachio**: Piazza Sant'Eustachio 82 (tel: 68 61 309). Good coffee from a popular bar that opens early and stays open late.
- *Prati* — **Sciascia**: Via Fabio Massimo 80/a (tel: 32 11 580). An elegant old shop that also sells some candies and dietetic items.
- *Trieste* — **Giovanni de Sanctis**: Via Tagliamento 88 (tel: 85 52 287). Beans or ground coffees from around the world in a refined old coffee house.
- *Trastevere* — **Frontoni**: Viale Trastevere 52 (tel: 58 12 346). Coffees roasted on the premises and ground freshly in a shop that seemingly has everything.

## FISH MARKETS

Although some particular Romans drive to the seaport village of Fiumicino for fresh fish, you can find an excellent selection in the outdoor markets on Tuesday and Friday, and every day but Monday in the larger ones. Otherwise, if there is fish, it won't be as fresh. Make sure to find out when the **pescherie** (fish stores) are open; some, too, are open selected days and hours. Smoked fish can be found in many salumerie and a few shops specialise in it.

- *Colli Albani* — **Di Benedetto**: Via Mario Menghini 73 (tel: 78 57 846).
- *Corso Vittorio* — **La Corte**: Via della Gatta 1 (tel: 67 83 842). Smoked fishes, Häagen Dazs ice cream, New Zealand lamb.
- *Pinciano* — **Cestroni**: Via Flavia 30 (tel: 47 41 930).
- *Monteverde Nuovo* — **Anzio di Salvatore Cardoselli**: Via E. Jenner 76/a (tel: 58 20 95 81).
- *Monteverde Vecchio* — **Anzio di Guido & Casio Cardoselli**: Via G. Carini 37/a (tel: 58 03 124).
- *Via del Corso* — **La Stadera**: Via della Croce 71/a (tel: 67 92 683).
- *Via Nazionale* — **Antica Pescheria Galuzzi 1894**: Via Venezia 26 (tel: 47 44 444).
- *Vigna Clara* – **Frollanpesca:** Piazza Stefano Jacini 14 (tel: 36 30 38 87).

Photo: Pomponi/Photoreporters

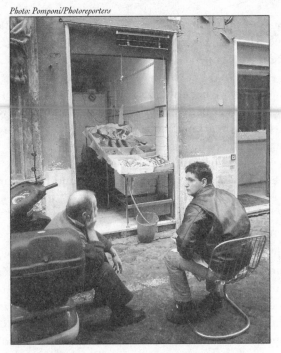

*A neighbourhood fish market*

# GREENGROCERS

In addition to the daily outdoor markets, the **fruttivendolo** in each
neighbourhood will have fruits and vegetables in season; most
also sell dried fruits, jams, mineral waters and some staple goods.
The shops are small, often without signage or show windows. It's
best to shop in the mornings, when the selection is largest. In general, the more elaborate the shop, the higher the prices. There are
also fruit stalls on some street corners; in the Centro these tend to
be expensive.

Remember that it is the salesperson — at the markets and in
the shops — who selects the fruit or vegetables, not the shopper.
It isn't taken kindly when a customer starts pawing the fruit.

Nonetheless, don't be intimidated and don't accept bad produce. Watch carefully while they choose, let it be known that you will be a regular, and you'll soon be treated like the locals.

- *Via del Corso* — **Delucchi**: Via della Croce 75 (tel: 67 91 630).
- *Ludovisi* — **Primizie di Luca Persiani**: Via Flavia 36 (tel: 47 43 726).
- *Monteverde Vecchio* — **Capone**: Via G. Carini 39 (tel: 58 09 166).
- *Parioli* — **Crescenzi**: Via Schiaparelli 21 (tel: 32 16 411).
- *Piazza del Popolo* — **Aureli**: Via Flaminia 50/a (tel: 32 03 456).
- *Salario* — **Quattro Stagioni di Danilo Grossi**: Via Sebino 9 (tel: 84 16 377).

## HEALTH FOOD SHOPS

Shopping at the outdoor markets generally ensures fresh, seasonal produce. In addition, the macrobiotic shops sell a variety of healthful items, including foods, cosmetics and vitamins. See also Chapter Eleven.

- **Il Canestro**: Via Luca della Robbia 47 (tel: 57 46 287). Macrobiotic food centre in Testaccio.
- **L'Albero del Pane**: macrobiotic food centre. 1) Via Santa Maria del Pianto 19 (tel: 68 65 016) specialises in oils, honey and baked goods; 2) Campo de'Fiori 22 (tel: 68 30 73 39), has organic fruits and vegetables.
- **La Strega**: a health food chain in several locations: Via dei Banchi Nuovi 21/b (tel: 6830.7567); Largo Trionfale 10 (tel: 3751.7536); Via dei Sardi 17 (tel: 445.4758); and Via Moncenisio 2 (tel: 8719.0909).
- **Sette Spighe**: Via Crescenzio 89/d, in Prati (tel: 68 80 55 66). Macrobiotic grocery with a large range of products including whole grain breads, seasonal fruits and vegetables, cheeses and packaged goods.

# INTERNATIONAL GROCERIES

If you crave some of your favourite packaged foods from home, look for them at the various **Castroni**, a diverse emporium in Via Cola di Rienzo 196 in Prati (tel: 68 74 383); in Via Ottaviano 55 (tel: 39 72 32 79) also in Prati; and in Via Flaminia 30 (tel: 36 11 029). For other international foods with known brand names, try below:

- *Campo de' Fiori* — **Ruggeri**: Campo de' Fiori 12 (tel: 68 80 10 91). International products such as V-8, Bisquick, etc. Authentic water buffalo mozzarella.

- *Esquilino* — **Korean Market**: Via Cavour 84 (tel: 48 85 060). Korean and other Asian food products, frozen dishes ready to cook, dumplings, pork bao, fish dishes.

- *Esquilino* — **Pacifico Trading**: Via Principe Eugenio 17 (tel: 44 68 406). Oriental supermarket with foods from the Middle East as well. Fresh vegetables and fish, and some cooking implements.

- *Prati* — **Danesi**: Via G. Ferrari 43 (tel: 37 20 858). Grocery and cafe with international products.

- *Piazza Vittorio Emanuele* — **China Foodstore**: Via Filippo Turati 130 (tel: 44 55 631). Asian grocery.

- *Piazza Vittorio Emanuele* — **Gombo**: Via Principe Amedeo 289, near Stazione Termini (tel: 44 62 322). African, South American and some Asian foods.

- *Piazza Vittorio Emanuele* — **Intermarket**: Via Napoleone III 95 (tel: 44 66 585). International products, macrobiotic products and confections for Christmas and Easter.

- *Piazza Vittorio Emanuele* — **Selli International Food Market**: Via dello Statuto 28 (tel: 47 45 777). International packaged goods, including Old El Paso Mexican products.

- *Trastevere* — **Innocenzi**: Piazza S. Cosimato 66 (tel: 58 12 725). Well known international grocery. Macrobiotic foods, Oriental specialties, coffees, and more.

When buying boxed products check the *scadenza* (expiration date) and note that the day, month and year are printed in that order.

## KOSHER PRODUCTS

To find out more about the Jewish community and shops, call the Synagogue (tel: 684.0061). Note that in Italian, Kosher is spelled *Kasher*. Most shops are closed on Saturday.

- *Campo de' Fiori* — **Marco Roscioli**: a bakery that doesn't use animal fat. Two locations: 1) Via dei Chiavari 34 (tel: 68 64 045); 2) Via dei Giubbonari 21 (tel: 68 75 287). Home delivery.
- *Ghetto* — **Sabra Kosher**: Via S. Ambrogio 7/a (tel: 68 77 966). Centre for Jewish information as well as a Kosher grocery and wine store. Notices of events and for minyans.
- *Ghetto* — **Diotallevi**: Via S. Maria del Pianto 69, off Via Arenula (tel: 68 80 29 44). Kosher and non- Kosher products: a well-stocked grocery.
- *Ghetto* — **Terracina**: Via Santa Maria del Pianto 64 (tel: 68 80 13 64). Kosher butcher.
- *Piazzale della Radio* — **Tornatora**: Via Oderisi da Gubbio 27 (tel: 55 93 658). Kosher pasticceria.
- *Monteverde Nuovo* — **Mario Spizzichino**: Via del Forte Bravetta 148 (tel: 66 15 77 96). Kosher butcher. Home delivery.
- *Ponte Marconi* — **Kosher Delight di Ouazana**: Via Silvestro Gherardi 44/a (tel: 55 65 231). Kosher salumeria. Home delivery.
- *Ponte Marconi* — **Pasta all'Uovo Kasher 1**: Via Federico Enriques 32 (tel: 55 65 760). Fresh pasta, plain or filled, including ravioli, lasagna, etc. All Kosher.

## MEAT MARKETS

In addition to the traditional *macellaio* (butchers) who make hamburgers, rolls roasts, and slices chicken breasts, etc., the specialty meat shops prepare *vitello tonnato*, meat-stuffed zucchini or egg-plant, and other imaginative ready-to-cook meat combinations. The **norcineria** specialises in pork products, both fresh and cured.

- *Campo de' Fiori* — **Il Fiorentino**: Piazza Campo de' Fiori 17 (tel: 68 80 12 96). Popular shop with many prepared meat dishes ready to cook, such as meat-stuffed zucchini, eggplant, etc.
- *Campo de' Fiori* — **Antica Norcineria Viola**: Piazza Campo de' Fiori 43 (tel: 68 80 61 14). Pork products, including sausages, prosciutto, bacons, as well as fresh pork chops and roasts.
- *Monteverde Nuovo* — **Mizzoni**: Piazza S. Giovanni di Dio 2 (tel: 58 23 07 14). Excellent butcher, with interesting specialty cuts.
- *Pantheon* — **Feroci**: Via della Maddalena 15 (tel: 68 80 10 16). Said to be one of the more imaginative butchers in Rome, with imported and domestic meats, well-cut steaks.
- *Parioli* — **Fratelli Giovannelli**: Via Antonelli 37/e (tel: 80 72 153). Traditional and ready-to-cook specialties.
- *Pinciano* — **De Angelis**: Via Flavia 74 (tel: 48 24 676). Traditional and ready-to-cook dishes.
- *Piazza del Popolo* — **La Macelleria di Sarandrea**: Via di Ripetta 30 (tel: 32 19 448). Ready-to-cook cotolette, involtini, meat-stuffed vegetables, preformed seasoned burgers of beef or veal, and seasoned chicken.
- *Prati* — **La Bottega della Carne**: Via G. Avezzana 17 (tel: 32 17 917). Traditional meat cuts and fancy prepared meats ready to cook at home.

# SUPERMARKETS

The **supermercati** (supermarkets) stock much the same types of foods as supermarkets anywhere: staples, produce, meats, dairy products, canned and frozen goods. In most you will be expected to bag your own foods; many will home-deliver groceries if a certain amount is spent. **Standa**, the large department store chain has supermarkets, including the Via Cola di Rienzo (Prati) and Viale Trastevere stores, and they are open daily. **UPIM** Department Store has some as well. **Panorama**, whose branches are mostly in the outlying districts, is also open on Sunday. **Metà** has simply-arranged stores with good prices and some unusual items. **PAM**, in Via Tiburtina and Piazzale della Radio, in addition to more outlying locations, also has a well-priced selection. Other supermarket chains are **GS**, **SIR**, and **SMA**. To find the supermarket most convenient to you, look in the phone books under *Supermercati*.

The large shopping malls all have extensive and varied supermarkets, with floor space large enough to be called *ipermercati*. Having parking lots, they are good for people with cars to stock up on staples. **Cinecittà Due** is accessible by Metro A, but the others, on the Grande Raccordo Anulare, need to be reached by car. For mall supermarkets, call Cinecittà Due: (tel: 72 20 600); **I Granai**: (tel: 51 95 58 90); or **La Romanina** (Tel: 72 33 552).

## PASTA FRESCA

Pasta means dough. **Pasta asciutta** is the dry noodle used for meals, rather than soup. Most people in Rome use dry pasta, and it is to the north, near Bologna, where making pasta at home is a daily event. But fresh pasta is easily obtained, and the pasta emporia sell a variety, including potato-based gnocchi, ready-made sauces, and often breads and other pastries.

- *Prati* — **L'Arte della Farina**: Via Candia 61/a (tel: 39 72 38 99).
- *Prati* — **Tascioni**: Via Cola di Rienzo 211 (tel: 32 43 152).
- *Salario* — **Marini**: Via Po 47/a, near Piazza Buenos Aires (tel: 85 54 134).
- *Via del Corso* — **Guerra Massimiliano Pasta all'Uovo**: Via della Croce 8 (tel: 67 93 102).
- *Via del Corso* — **Fior Fiore**: Via della Croce 17 (tel: 67 91 386). Pasta, packaged goods, pizza, bakery and **Häagen Dazs** ice cream.

221

# SPECIALTY SHOPS

Small, offbeat specialty shops sell just a few items, generally of high quality and sometimes of matching price.

- *Piazza Navona* — **Ai Monasteri**: Piazza delle Cinque Lune 76, near Piazza Navona (tel: 68 80 27 83). Outlet shop for monasteries selling oils, liqueurs, honey and other items. Good selection of wines.

- *Campo de' Fiori* — **Cisternino Cooperative fra Produttori di Latte di Lazio**: Dairy co-ops throughout the city selling a variety of fresh cheeses typical of Lazio. Two addresses: Vicolo del Gallo 20, off Piazza Farnese (tel: 68 72 875); Via del Pelligrino 53 (tel: 68 33 955).

- *Centro Storico* — **Azienda Agricola**: Vicolo della Torretta 3, near Piazza S. Lorenzo in Lucina (tel: 68 75 808). A tiny shop selling olive oils, honeys.

- *Laterano* — **Catena**: Via Appia Nuova 9 (tel: 70 49 16 64). Since 1928, selling interesting food items, tempting sweets such as caramels and pralines.

- *Piazza del Popolo* — **Cose Fritte**: Via di Ripetta 3 (tel: 36 19 257). Tiny shop selling already-fried foods such as supplì, meats, fish, and vegetables. Pizza al taglio. Ready to eat or to take home and reheat.

- *Prati* — **G. Giuliani**: Via Paolo Emilio 67 (tel: 32 43 548). Known for its marrons glacès, all the candies here are tempting; try the pralines and marzipan.

- *Piazza Venezia* — **Moriondo e Gariglio**: Via della Pilotta 2 (tel: 67 86 662). Fresh chocolates daily and marrons glacès are a specialty. Also in Via del Piè di Marmo 21 (tel: 69 90 856).

- *Parioli* — **Ricercatezze Alimentari**: Via Chelini 17 (tel: 80 78 569). Elegant gourmet shop, items of gift-giving quality, beautifully packaged.

# WINES

Wine production is graded on a two-tier system and is well regulated. A DOC label *(Denominazione di Origine Controllata)* means that the grapes are what the label claims and that the wine was produced where it says. In the past there was some laxity in enforcing these standards, so DOCG *(Denominazione di Origine Controllata e Garantita)* was developed to guarantee the certification of better wines. No matter, there are good locally produced wines in any area, many carrying no certification at all. When eating out in Rome, if you order the house wine, you'll probably get a decent regional wine at a good price. Experiment with the different bottled wines at home.

Lazio wines have improved somewhat in recent years, despite the continuing dominance of red Tuscan wines, and others from Veneto, Emilia Romagna, Trentino, Friuli and the Piedmont. The best regional wines are white, and they come from the Castelli Romani area, in the Alban hills south of Rome, around towns such as Albano, Grottaferrata, and Castel Gandolfo. Pleasant but rarely memorable, these are best when young. Two good red wines are **Cesanese del Piglio** and **Fiorano Rosso**. For the best regional wines, look for the small producers rather than those for the mass market. Some of the most popular whites are listed below.

- **Frascati**, the most famous, is fairly fruity and ranges in colour from clear to amber. It comes in dry, as well as demi-sec and sweet, which are served with dessert. When you order Frascati in a restaurant, you may get any one of a number of light white wines from the Castelli Romani area, all fairly alike.
- **Colli Albani** from near the Pope's summer residence of Castel Gandolfo. Generally fairly soft and fruity, and ranges from pale straw to amber, comes in dry or semi-dry. Often served both with fish and meat.
- **Est! Est! Est!**, refers to a bishop's wine taster who approved of the wine by writing "It is! It is! It is!" From Montefiascone,

223

to the north in Lazio, this is a smooth wine with a kind of stony taste. Comes in dry or semi-sweet. A little thin for those partial to sauvignon blanc.

- **Colli Lanuvini** is less fruity and drier than Frascati, generally served with fish dishes and antipasti. From an area slightly south, around Lago di Nemi.
- **Velletri**, from the same area, has both dry white and red varieties. The robust red is somewhat tannic like zinfandel. Red served with meats and pastas, and the white with fish.

The *enoteche* (See Chapter Eleven) offer wine tasting as well as wine sold by the bottle. Wine shops often have signage that says **vini & olii** and generally offer some tasting opportunities as well. The proprietors are usually willing to advise on purchases.

- *Cassia* – **Lucantoni:** Largo Vigna Stelluti 33 (tel: 32 93 743). Good selection of domestic and imported spirits.
- *Esquilino* — **Chirra:** Via Torino 133 (tel: 48 56 59). Good selection of wine and gourmet treats.
- *Piazza del Popolo* — **Buccone**: Via di Ripetta 19 (tel: 36 12 154). Wines for tasting and buying, and some gourmet snacks. Open Sunday.
- *Pinciano* — **Rocchi:** 1) Via Alessandro Scarlatti 7 (tel: 85 51 022). Also in Via della Balduina 120, north, near Loyola University (tel: 35 34 36 94). Long-established shop, domestic and imported wines.
- *Salario* — **Centrovini Arcioni**: Via Nemorense 57 (tel: 86 20 66 16). Wines from around Italy, plus gifts, candies, gourmet treats, etc. Also in Via della Giuliana 11 (tel: 39 73 32 05).
- *Stazione Termini* — **Trimani:** 1) Via Goito 20, off Piazza dell'Indipendenza (tel: 44 69 661); and Via Cernaia 37 has a wine bar with light meals and snacks (tel: 44 69 630). Well-established with a variety of wines, gourmet items and regional specialties.

# CHAPTER THIRTEEN

# SPORTS AND EXERCISE

## GOOD SPORTS

It is said that the Italian man loves three things: sex, food and football, and not always in that order. More women are admitting to being sports fans, but the passion still seems to be among the men. For daily news and schedules of sporting events, pick up the *Corriere dello Sport* at any newsstand, or the national *La Gazzetta dello Sport*. Look also in the weekly events guides.

The major public sports complex in Rome is the **Foro Italico**, toward the northern end of Via Flaminia. Begun by Mussolini in the early Thirties as an expression of his grandiose dreams for Rome, this vast example of Fascist architecture has been rebuilt periodically since World War II. The **Stadio Olimpico**, built for the 1960 Olympics, held 80,000 people during the finals of the 1990 World Cup soccer matches. Another stadium, the **Stadio dei Marmi**, boasts some sixty enormous marble statues of well-muscled athletes discreetly clothed in fig leaves. At present, the larger stadium hosts

225

weekly soccer matches; the swimming pools and tennis courts both host international competitions and are open to the public as noted below. The large **Tre Fontane Sports Centre** in EUR hosts rugby and hockey matches and other competitions as well.

**Calcio** (football) is the sport of Italy. Summer excepted, there are professional football matches Sunday afternoons at 3:00 pm and some Wednesday nights in the Stadio Olimpico, Viale dei Gladiatori (tel: 39 94 50). The two Roman teams, **AS Roma** and **SS Lazio**, play on alternate Sundays. Romans crowd the box office several hours before the matches, so if you can, buy tickets in advance. Tickets are available at some bars, at ticket agencies, plus such shops as the **Roma Shop** in Via Paolina 8, near Piazza dell'Esquilino (48 21 664); at **Lazio Point** in Via Farini 34 (tel: 48 26 768). Tickets can run up to L100,000 depending on the event and where you sit.

*Photo: Pomponi/Photoreporters*

*A street vendor selling football souvenirs. Soccer is the most popular sport in Italy.*

**Pallacanestro** (basketball) is another Roman sport passion. Known as 'basket,' professional games are played at the **Palazzo dello Sport** in EUR, in Viale dell' Umanesimo. Part of the construction for the 1960 Olympics, the complex hosts sporting events including boxing matches. Basketball games are usually held on Sunday at 5:30 pm, and tickets can be purchased at the box office. For information call the Basketball Federation in Via Fogliano 15 (tel: 88 63 071).

# FITNESS

The idea of fitness is taking hold. Parks are popular for jogging, well equipped gyms are cropping up throughout the city, and opportunities for all participatory sports are increasing. **Calcetto**, an intense version of football with five people on a side and a smaller playing field, is popular, as is tennis. Except for golf, the prices are reasonable. Finding athletic opportunities in your area should be fairly easy. Check out the public facilities listed below; they're less expensive than the private clubs, and depending on your neighbourhood, they may be just as convenient.

## Running

Running, of course, is the cheapest form of exercise, although not many of the traffic and fume burdened streets are appropriate. Pollution at times can be daunting. Some streets outside the centre are becoming popular, such as **Via Appia Antica**, beginning near the Lateran, and which further south is a sightseeing 'must' in guidebooks. **Viale delle Terme di Caracalla,** in much the same area, is a popular running street, as is the area near the Terme itself.

Parks, however, are popular, especially early mornings and weekends. Although there are many smaller parks, the five large parks listed below have special tracks or facilities for runners. Most parks are open from sunrise to sunset.

227

- **Villa Borghese**, the most central of Rome's parks. Walk from Parioli/Pinciano, from Via Veneto, or up from Piazza del Popolo. Designed in the 17th century for Cardinal Borghese, the modernised park extends over four miles, and it includes museums, a zoo, an aviary and an artificial lake with ducks and rental rowboats. There are two jogging tracks, the longer in Piazza di Siena (which hosts the Rome International Horse Show in Spring), and the winding paths throughout the park are used for running.
- **Villa Pamphili** on the Janiculum is Rome's largest park. Open sunrise to sunset. Built in the mid-17th century for a nephew of Pope Innocent X, Camillo Pamphili, it's now a popular place for runners and for meeting people under the beautiful parasol pines. The park has several running tracks and paths.
- **Villa Ada** can be entered from Via Salaria. There are jogging paths passing little ponds, flower-lined walks, a bicycle course and a riding stable. In addition there is also an exercise course.
- **Villa Glori** to the north, is a small park with a running track of about 1180 metres. The track is lit at night, so running is permitted after dark. Enter the park from Via dei Parioli into Viale di Villa Glori.
- **Villa Torlonia** off Via Nomentana, is centrally located in Salario. The track is set in a lovely little park with tropical trees and flower-lined paths. During World War II, the villa was Mussolini's residence in Rome.

## Multi-Sport Fitness Facilities

Many private multi-facility clubs offer racquet sports in addition to swimming and fully equipped gyms. They encourage membership, and if your sojourn is long enough, it would be worthwhile to consider joining rather than paying the daily non-member fee. Membership prices are reasonable. Notice how Romans are dressed in the gyms, on the tennis courts and on the golf courses.

*La bella figura* figures in sport as it does in the rest of Roman life. Some clubs insist its members wear spandex; ordinary shorts and sweats simply won't do. Bring attire appropriate to your sport.

- **Foro Italico**: the sports complex has tennis courts off the Largo de Martino in Viale delle Olimpiadi (tel: 36 19 021). The **Piscina Olimpica** in Lungotevere Maresciallo Cadorna is the larger of two Olympic-sized pools; both summer and winter pools are open to the public except during competitions (tel: 32 18 5 91).
- **Stadio Flaminio**: off Viale Maresciallo Pilsudski and Viale Tiziano in the Flaminio district (tel: 32 36 539). A public facility with a gym and an indoor swimming pool.
- **Associazione Sportiva Villa Flaminia**: in Via Donatello 20, at Villa Flaminia park (tel: 32 16 484). A pool, a large gym and lighted tennis courts.
- **YMCA Sporting Club**: Viale Libano 68, in EUR (tel: 59 23 595). Good facilities at reasonable prices. Indoor pool, tennis courts and fully equipped gym, as well as aerobics, karate and dance classes. Non-members may use the facilities for a reasonable fee, but must reserve courts in advance.
- **Roman Sport Centre**: Via del Galoppatoio 33, by the car park under Villa Borghese (tel 32 01 667). Well equipped, it includes two large swimming pools, sauna and steam, squash courts, two gyms and aerobics classes. Non-members pay a daily fee. A second facility is in Largo Somalia, near Villa Ada (tel: 86 21 24 11).
- **Lanciani Tennis Club**: Via Pietralata 139, to the northeast (tel: 45 01 202) Tennis and squash courts, gym and a pool.
- **Oasi di Pace**: Via degli Eugenii 2, south and east of the Lateran (tel: 71 84 550). Four tennis courts and outdoor/indoor swimming pools. Open June-September; non-members pay a daily court fee.

There are also a few hotels that offer multi-sport facilities. None are centrally located; almost all are expensive. All have pools, tennis courts and other athletic facilities open to non-guests.

- **Cavalieri Hilton**: Via Cadlolo 101 (tel: 35091). On Monte Mario, it runs a shuttle bus to the city centre, a half-hour ride. The hotel is set in 15 acres of gardens and there is a jogging path, outdoor pool, two clay tennis courts, steam room and sauna, and a playground. No indoor gym. Pool open daily from May to September.
- **Holiday Inn — St. Peter's**: Via Aurelia Antica 415, near Villa Pamphili (tel: 6642). Tennis courts, a gym and a pool. Small annual membership fee, plus low court fees for the tennis.
- **Holiday Inn — EUR Parco dei Medici**: Viale Castello della Magliana 65 (tel: 65581). Tennis court, a pool and other athletic facilities available to non-guests.
- **Sheraton Roma**: Viale del Pattinaggio in EUR on the ring-road (tel: 5453). Comfortable and well maintained. Outdoor heated pool, two squash courts, tennis courts, jogging track, and a sauna. Reserve courts in advance; low court fees.
- **Sheraton Golf Hotel Roma**: Viale Parco dei Medici 22, near the ring road (tel: 52 24 08). Fitness centre, indoor pool, tennis courts and an 18-hole golf course (Club house tel: 65 53 477).

## Gyms

Most of the smaller **palestre** (gymnasiums) are open to non-members for a daily fee. Most have aerobics classes in addition to the workout facilities. Listed below are a few that are centrally located. See *Associazioni Sportive* or *Palestre Ginnico Sportive* in the Yellow Pages.

- **Navona Health Centre**: Via dei Banchi Nuovi 39, near Piazza Navona (tel: 68 96 104). This small gym allows non-members to use its facilities, including the exercise classes. Open daily. Prices are reasonable.
- **Green Line**: Via Veio 27, near Metro A/San Giovanni (tel: 70 49 55 09). After a series of physical tests to determine fitness, a program will be suggested. Aerobics, body building, step training and cardio-fitness activities. Sauna, massage and solarium. Open nonstop.

- **Sporting Palace**: Via Carlo Sigonio 21, off Via Appia Nuova (tel: 78 56 391). An inviting and reasonably priced multi-facility gym, hi-tech, highly physical. Body building, aerobics, pool, boutique and restaurant. There is an initial physical evaluation, and the weight machines monitor heart rate. Closed Sunday.
- **Bodyshop**: Viale Parioli 162, in a courtyard off the major thoroughfare (80 85 835). Workout studio with a variety of exercise options. Closed Sunday.
- **Budokan**: Via Properzio 4 (tel: 68 92 543). Body building, gymnastics, aerobics, stretching, dance classes. Closed Sunday.
- **Fitness Studio**: Via Mocenigo 1/1a just off Via Candia (tel: 39 72 38 09). Aerobics, Kung Fu and body building programs. Closed Sunday.
- **Trastevere Sport**: Vicolo Moroni 2, near John Cabot University (tel: 58 18 473). Body building, aerobics, modern dance. Closed Sunday.
- **Phisicult**: Corso Trieste 86a, west of Salario (tel: 85 54 315). A variety of activities including aerobics of various types, body building and more. Solarium, sauna. Open daily.
- **Le Club 2001**: Via Igea 15, past Monte Mario, (tel: 30 71 024). An extensive complex with gyms, martial arts programs, sauna, organised sports, children's activities, etc.

## Tennis

Tennis is extremely popular, and most tennis clubs, although at a distance from the city centre, are accessible by public transportation. Book well in advance: there are few courts and many players, yet court fees remain reasonable. The courts below allow non-member access; see *Roma C'è*, which also sometimes has listings of courts accessible to non-members.

For tennis information, call the **Federazione Italiana Tennis** in Viale Tiziano 70 (tel: 32 33 807). You can get advance tickets here for the International Tennis Championships, which are held in May at the **Foro Italico** at Viale dei Gladiatori 31 (tel: 32 19 064). The championships are a major event and tickets to the later rounds are almost impossible to obtain. Information on tickets can be had from ticket agencies (see Chapter Fifteen) and from CONI (tel: 36851).

- **Tennis Club Belle Arti**: Via Flaminia 158, north of Piazzale Flaminio and one of the more accessible tennis clubs (tel: 32 33 555).
- **Circolo Canottieri e Tennis Lazio**: Lungotevere Flaminio 25, just north of the Risorgimento bridge (tel: 32 26 801). Tennis, gym, canoeing, sauna, Turkish baths, massage and a restaurant. Open daily.
- **Centro Sportivo Italiano**: Lungotevere Flaminio 55, along the river just north of Piazzale delle Belle Arti (tel: 32 24 842). Tennis lessons, gymnastics, aerobics and more.
- **Tennis Club Parioli**: Largo U. De Morpurgo 2 (tel: 86 20 08 83). Extensive, fashionable club in Parioli.
- **Circolo Tennis della Stampa**: Piazza Antonio Mancini 19, to the north (tel: 32 32 452). Journalists' tennis club.
- **Flaminio Andrea Doria**: Via del Baiardo 26, at Tor di Quinto (tel: 33 33 06 06). Seven clay courts, two synthetic.
- **Società Ginnastica Roma**: Via del Muro Torto 5, near Villa Borghese (tel 47 40 040). Five courts.
- **AS Pamphili**: Piazza S. Pancrazio 7 (tel: 58 09 341). Three clay courts at the western edge of the park.

- **Tennis Club Nomentana**: Via Nomentana 882, to the northeast (tel: 82 74 385).
- **Circolo Tennis EUR**: Via dell'Artigianato 35 (tel: 59 12 777).
- **Tre Fontane**: Via delle Tre Fontane, also in EUR (tel: 59 22 485).
- **Appio Claudio**: Viale Appio Claudio 115, near Cinecittà, has twelve clay courts (tel: 71 54 41 90).

## Golf

Golf is an expensive sport, and Rome is no exception. Greens fees can run upwards of L70,000 weekdays and to L100,000 weekends. There are no public golf courses and none convenient to the city centre; some clubs in the outlying areas will admit guests with a membership card and handicap from a home club. Otherwise, non-members can generally use the driving ranges *(campo pratica)*, which cost considerably less. There is one driving range, **Tevere Golf** in Via del Baiardo at Tor di Quinto; it also has a putting green, and lessons are available (tel: 33 30 609).

There are golf courses other than those listed. The **Federazione Italiana Golf** in Viale Tiziano 70, north of Piazza del Popolo, will give information about golfing around Rome and about the Spring Open Internazionale golf tournament (tel: 32 31 825).

- **Castelgandolfo Country Club**: Via di Santo Spirito 13, at Castelgandolfo to the southeast (tel: 93 12 301). An exclusive club with a 17th century villa-clubhouse, its course was designed by Robert Trent. Non-members may play a limited number of times per year. Driving range, swimming pool. Bar.
- **Circolo del Golf Roma/Acqua Santa**: Via dell'Acqua Santa 3 to the southeast of the city, was Rome's first golf club (tel: 78 03 407). With a membership card from a home club, non-members may play Tuesday through Friday; weekends with a member. Driving range, swimming pool. Closed Monday.
- **Golf Club Fioranello**: Viale della Repubblica off Via Appia Antica (tel: 71 38 058). 18-hole golf course about 16 km

233

southeast, past Ciampino Airport. Driving range, swimming pool. Closed Wednesday.

- **Olgiata Golf**: Largo Olgiata 15, about 9 km north of the city centre (tel: 30 88 91 41). Open to the public Tuesday-Friday, weekends with a member. Two challenging courses, one of nine holes and the other eighteen; driving range and swimming pool.
- **Golf Club Parco de Medici**: 10 km from downtown Rome in Viale Parco de Medici 20 (tel: 65 53 477). Eighteen-hole course, driving range, tennis, swimming pool, pro shop, restaurant and bar. Closed Tuesdays.

## Swimming Pools

As mentioned, large multi-sport clubs and hotels have swimming pools. There are others that allow non-members; **Comitato Regionale Lazio Federazione Italiana Nuoto** in Via Virgilio 8 should have a list (tel: 68 74 367). Note that many of the clubs will ask for a medical certificate before allowing you to swim. Some pools require membership, and some give lessons only.

- **Shangri-La Corsetti Hotel**: Viale Algeria 141 in EUR (tel: 59 16 441). Outdoor swimming pool.
- **Parco dei Principi Hotel**: Via M. Mercadante 15, at the edge of Villa Borghese (tel: 85 44 21). Open June-September.
- **Arca Swimming Club**: Via dei Monti Tiburtini 511 (45 10 552). A large covered pool, calcetto, two clay tennis courts. On Sundays from 10:00 am-1:00 pm the club opens its facilities, including the pool, to non-members.

- **Blue Eagles**: Via P. Matteucci 29, in Testaccio (tel: 57 58 008). Covered pool, open for lap swimming from 11:00 am-4:00 pm Closed Sunday.
- **Roma 70**: Piazza Zamorani 8, past Stazione Tiburtina (tel: 41 73 13 32). Open daily, but hours vary.
- **Piscina delle Rose**: Viale America 20 (EUR), one of the most popular public pools (59 26 717). An Olympic-sized outdoor pool, open summer from 9:00 am-7:00 pm daily.
- **Piscina Urbe Nuoto 90**: Via Tunisi 7/a, in Prati (tel: 39 72 08 56). Large indoor pool. Competitions, and swimming lessons available, for both children and adults.

## Bowling

There are several bowling alleys in Rome, offering games at reasonable prices. See *Sale Giochi* in the Yellow Pages.
- **Bowling Team Alley**: Viale Regina Margherita 181, is small but central (tel: 85 51 184). Open daily.
- **Bowling Brunswick**: Lungotevere dell'Acqua Acetosa 10 (tel: 80 86 147), north of Villa Glori. A large complex including mini-golf, a small bar, and *birreria*. Open daily.

## Oriental Arts

Oriental arts are popular, and you can find several multi-sport dojos in the Yellow Pages under *Palestre*. Look there also for yoga studios, offering a variety of yoga, meditation and relaxation techniques. Many of the facilities have gyms and aerobic programs, and many also have training sessions for children; regular gyms sometimes have yoga and martial arts programs, as well.
- **Takehaya Dojo**: Via Luigi Bodio 4, near Corso Francia (tel: 36 30 64 32). Karate, Tae Kwon Do, Jiu Jitsu, as well as yoga programs.
- **Mandala Yoga**: Via di Torre Argentina 47 (tels: 68 69 251; 68 79 258 ). Yoga, gymnastics, relaxation programs and cultural activities.

235

- **Arci Natura**: Viale Eritrea 91, near Piazza Emerenziana (tel: 86 32 64 45). Hatha yoga, meditation and shiatsu massage programs. School for teachers as well.
- **Body Action**: Via Turno 44, south of the Lateran (tel: 78 34 49 75). Martial arts programs, general gymnastics, and aerobics. Jiu Jitsu, Hapkido, Tae Kwon Do, etc.
- **Otzuka Club**: Via Baldo degli Ubaldi 147/a, west past the Vatican (tel: 66 37 670). Karate, Tai Chi, kickboxing, etc.).
- **Surya Chandra Yoga**: Via Pandosia 43, south of the Lateran (tel: 57 46 052). Traditional yoga programs.

# CHAPTER FOURTEEN

# SHOPPING AND SERVICES

Tourist guidebooks describe the 'best' shopping and services, focusing mostly on the Piazza di Spagna area, with its designer clothing and shoe shops, and famous beauty salons. But with some 40,000 stores of one sort or another in Rome, there are many more interesting possibilities further afield, shops undiscovered by tourists and perhaps even Romans from other parts of the city. In addition, the discount shop and shopping mall are increasingly making their imprint on the city.

This chapter does not pretend to be exhaustive in terms of the 'best' stores. There are so many shops for clothes and shoes, for example, that it would be folly to mention just a few. In addition to checking out the area around the Corso, head for Via Cola di Rienzo, Via Salaria, Via Nazionale, Viale Regina Margherita, Via dei Giubbonari, up along the Cassia, or down to Via Appia Nuova, also a good shopping street. The department stores have a varied selection, and the malls listed below house hundreds of shops under one roof. Be sure also to refer to the *English Yellow Pages* and to the Yellow Pages.

Note that most shops, even in the tourist areas of the city, close for several hours at midday. Hours are generally from 9:30 am to 1:00/1:30 pm and from 4:00/4:30 pm to 7:00/7:30 pm. Some shops have hours nonstop, meaning they are open all day; this includes the department stores and shopping malls. Many stores are closed on Monday morning, and in summer some close on Saturday afternoon. Some of the department stores are now open on Sunday, as are a few shops, and there have been experiments with allowing shops in two different areas to open each Sunday. It's best just to check with a store the first time you visit it to determine its particular schedule.

One exception to the above is the **Drugstore Termini** at Stazione Termini. A shop of small, practical boutiques, a bakery and a grocery store, it stays open 24-hours a day, seven days a week.

Prices in Rome are no more or less expensive than in any other major city: luxury shops and tourist areas charge more, neighbourhood shops charge less, although the merchandise may not be of the exact same make or style. Semi-annual sales take place in June and January.

# APPLIANCES

Rome uses 220 volt, 50 hertz electricity. If bringing large appliances, ascertain that they are appropriate, for you may need a transformer as well as an adapter plug; if they need repair, finding parts and service may be difficult. Note that transformers change the voltage, but not the hertz, so both must be appropriate; some 60 hertz appliances will function, others such as record players may run too slowly. Most small appliances such as hair dryers and irons come with dual voltage; otherwise, these are easy to buy in Rome. If you buy a television set in Rome, expect to receive a document from the Ministry of Finance requiring an additional tax to be paid for viewing the public channels; this can be paid at the post office.

You may find that voltage and outlet *(presa)* shapes vary. Hardware and electrical shops stock a wide variety of plugs *(spina)* and extension cords *(prolunga)*. Look in the Yellow Pages under *Elettrodomestici Commercio* and for hardware, see *Ferramenta Commercio*, or the listing below.

- **Cucciollo**: Via del Tempio 6, in the Ghetto, sells appliances and electrical goods, often at a discount. Internationally recognised brands (tel: 68 65 102).
- **Eldo**: is a chain that has a good selection of electronics, stereos, etc. Addresses include: Via del Corso 263 (tel: 67 91 370); Viale Furio Camillo 56 (tel: 78 00 971); Cinecittà Due (tel: 72 21 314).
- **F.E.R.**: Via Assisi 154, near Stazione Tuscolana (tel: 78 24 325). Appliances large and small, domestic and imported. TV, stereos, video cameras.
- **Ferramenta Castoro**: Via di Torre Argentina 16 (tel: 68 80 38 84). Small appliances, kitchen equipment.
- **Centro Giotto**: an appliance chain, with branches in I Granai (tel: 57 95 59 91); Via Appia 416 (tel: 782.7858); Piazza Pio XI 12, off Via Aurelia (tel: 63 69 91).
- **Gruppo Edom**: large chain of electronic stores offering small appliances, razors, faxes, stereos and more. Branches in Via Tiburtina 479 (tel: 43 58 70 61); Via della Croce 32 (tel: 67 91 645); Via Appia Nuova 430 (tel: 78 56 724); Largo Vigna Stelluti 14 (tel: 36 30 82 82); Via Piave 45 (tel: 42 87 34 18).
- **Petrolli**: Vi Grimaldi 15 (tel: 55 60 302). Large and small appliances, televisions, car radios. Good prices.
- **Radio Novelli** has several well stocked shops that sell a variety of electrical/electronic items. Via Tagliamento 29, in Salario (tel: 85 59 858); and Via del Corso 309 (tel: 67 91 432).
- **Radiovittoria**: Via Luisa di Savoia 12, near Piazzale Flaminio,

sells large and small appliances: televisions, refrigerators, freezers, stereos, portable phones, etc. (tel: 36 11 258).
* **Tonel**: Via di Porta Cavalleggeri 15, near St. Peter's (tel: 63 28 96); and Via delle Convertite 19, near Piazza San Silvestro (tel: 67 85 795). Photographic equipment, stereos, answering machines, and more.

Note that many of the larger electronic and television shops sell parabolas and other equipment needed to receive satellite TV transmissions, and there are also those that specialise in the selling and installation of the equipment.
* **Eurosat**: Via Sestio Calvino 121 (tel: 71 54 31 91).
* **Cosmosat**: Via N. Sauro 3 (tel: 39 73 33 56).
* **Video System**: Via Cornelia 183 (tel: 62 44 558).
* **Ennesat**: Via Piemonte 117 (tel: 48 83 749).

# BICYCLES AND MOTOS

Instead of renting a bicycle (see Chapter Ten), consider buying one and then selling it upon departure. See advertising in *Porta Portese* and *Wanted in Rome*, or the notice boards at churches. Spare bicycle parts can be found weekdays at the Porta Portese flea market. For bicycles, see *Biciclette Vendita* in the Yellow Pages. For motorcycles or scooters *(motorini)*, see *Motocicli & Motocarri Commercio* in the Yellow Pages.
* **AutoMotoMania**: Via del Serafico 108, in EUR (tel: 50 35 244). Bicycles, motos, motorcycles. Accessories.
* **Di Rocco Romeo**: Via Torino 5, near Stazione Termini (tel: 48 82 222). Bicycles, accessories, gear.
* **Emporio del Ciclo**: Viale Caduti nella Guerra di Liberazione 156, in EUR (tel: 50 71 470). Bicycles, etc.
* **Lazzaretti**: Via Bergamo 3/e, near Piazza Fiume (tel: 85 53 828). Bikes and accessories.
* **I Bike Rome**: Villa Borghese, at Via Veneto 156 (tel: 32 25 240). Rents and sells new and used bikes

- **MotoModa**: Via Portuense 756, in Trastevere (tel: 65 57 998). Sells motos and accessories.
- **Obiso**: Largo Gaetano La Loggia 24, in Trastevere (tel: 55 26 92 34). Bicycles.
- **St. Peter Moto**: Via di Porta Castello 43 (tel: 68 75 714). Rents and sells motos.

# BOOK SHOPS

There are several English-language book shops in Rome. Some also rent videos, and some have community bulletin boards. Many Italian book shops have sizeable English-language sections. There are also several open-air book markets, such as in Viale di Termini, near the train station, with stalls selling inexpensive books. A charming market in Largo della Fontanella di Borghese, off Via di Ripetta, sells old books, prints and posters; closed Sunday. Look also for the **bancarelle**, open air book stalls that crop up from time to time in various places; one permanent bancarella is in the arcade between Piazza del Popolo and Piazzale Flaminio. Note that English-language book imports cost considerably more than at home.

- **Al Tempo Ritrovato**: Via dei Fienaroli 31/a, in Trastevere (tel: 58 17 724). Rome's feminist book shop, it has some international books and books in English.
- **Anglo-American Book Shop**: Via della Vite 102, off the Corso (tel: 67 95 222). An English-language shop with a large selection of paperback fiction, guidebooks, dictionaries and books on Italian history. Branch in Via della Vite 27 sells technical and scientific books (tel: 68 79 657).
- **Bibli**: Via dei Fienaroli 28, in Trastevere (tel: 58 84 097). A bookstore that stays open until midnight, affords access to the Internet, and has a good selection of books.
- **Corner Book Shop**: Via del Moro 48, in Trastevere (tel: 58 36 942). There is a good selection of English-language writers, as

241

well as some that have been translated into English. Open Sunday at 11:00 am.

- **Economy Book and Video Centre**: Via Torino 136, off Piazza della Repubblica (tel: 47 46 877). English- language shop and cultural centre. Current books, new and used paperbacks, magazines, books on tape, and greeting cards. Video rental. Publishes a list of current events and happenings.
- **Fahrenheit 451**: Campo de' Fiori 44 (tel: 68 75 930). Some English-language books, and notices of events.
- **Feltrinelli**: chain of book shops of the publishing company. All are open on Sunday. Via del Babuino 41 (tel: 36 00 18 42); Largo Torre Argentina 5a (tel: 68 80 32 48); Via V. E. Orlando (tel: 47 46 880).
- **Libreria all'Orologio**: Via del Governo Vecchio 7, off Piazza Navona (tel: 68 80 66 59). An international shop featuring highly specialised books in several languages, plus a good selection of interesting maps.
- **Libreria del Viaggiatore**: Via del Pellegrino 78, off Corso Vittorio (tel: 68 80 10 48). A travellers' bookshop, with offerings in several languages. Guidebooks, travel literature, etc.
- **Libreria Herder**: Piazza Montecitorio 117, just off Piazza Colonna (tel: 67 94 628). Primarily German-language, it has a selection of books in English as well.
- **Libreria Remo Croce**: Corso Vittorio Emanuele 156 (tel: 68 80 22 69). A famous and well stocked shop near Largo Argentina. Open Sunday.
- **Libreria Mondadori**: Piazza Cola di Rienzo 81-93 in Prati (tel: 32 10 323). An international book store of the publishing company.
- **Mel Book Store**: Via Nazionale 254 (tel: 48 85 405). A large new book shop with an extensive selection.
- **Open Door Book Shop**: Via della Lungaretta 25, near Viale Trastevere (tel: 58 96 478). Paperbacks in several languages, videos, and a public fax machine.

- **Libreria Internazionale Rizzoli**: Largo Chigi 15, off the Corso (tel: 67 96 641); also in Via Tomacelli 156 (tel: 68 60 85 13). International chain with a selection of English-language books.
- **Remainders San Silvestro**: Piazza S. Silvestro 27 (tel: 67 92 824). Prices of up to 50% off original.

# CHILDREN'S CLOTHING

Children's clothes can be expensive: children are indoctrinated early into *la bella figura*. The fashionable shops are listed in tourist guides. For reasonably priced clothes, try **Standa, UPIM**, or the **Bimbus** chain, owned by the **COIN** Group. See *Abbigliamento per Bambini e Ragazzi* and *Abbigliamento Gestanti e Neonati* in the Yellow Pages.

Sizes are just about the same for British, American and Italian children's clothes. There is no 6x size, however, the next size up from six being seven. An American size seven, in consequence, would be an Italian size eight, and so on.

- **Baby Mania**: Via F. Grimaldi 68, near Viale Marconi (tel: 55 85 108). Shoes of all makes.
- **Baby Pace**: Via G. Vitelleschi 13, in Prati (tel: 68 80 64 02). Clothes for the young child to age 4.
- **Bimbo Shoes**: Via Appia Nuova 377, south of the Lateran (tel: 78 03 503). Brand-name shoes for children.
- **Bimbus**: A new chain of children's shops. Addresses in Rome include: Via Mantova 1/b in Trieste (tel: 88 42 312); Via Appia 101 in Appio (tel: 70 47 61 41); and nearby in Via Tuscolana.

243

- **Tablò**: Via della Croce 84 (tel: 67 94 468). High quality clothes and prices to match. For children over nine. Younger, try Via del Babuino 105.

# DISCOUNT CLOTHING

The discount shops may not seem really inexpensive, but given the original prices, some offer real bargains; visit these stores often, for merchandise turns over quickly. In addition, the summer and winter semi-annual sales all over the city bring reasonable prices on all merchandise. Not all shops take credit cards.

- **Balloon** is a chain of low cost women's clothing stores. Some addresses include: Piazza di Spagna 35 (tel: 67 89 806); Via Terenzio 14 in Prati (tel: 68 80 64 04); Via Flaminia Vecchia 495 near Ponte Milvio (tel: 33 33 352); and Via Duccio di Buoninsegna 105 in EUR (tel: 50 42 752). Sweaters, separates and dresses, much of it manufactured in China. Open nonstop.
- **Degli Effetti**: Men's shop in Piazza Capranica 79 (tel: 67 91 650). Women's shop in Piazza Capranica 93 (tel: 67 90 202). Discounts, up to 50% sometimes, on designer clothes.
- **Discount System**: Via Viminale 35, near Piazza Beniamino Gigli (tel: 47 46 545). For men and women, from top Italian designers. Discounts up to 50% off the original price.
- **Il Discount dell'Alta Moda**: Via di Gesù e Maria 16/a, off the Corso (tel: 36 13 796). Both men's and women's clothing and accessories. Prices 50% off the label. Closed Monday.
- **Il Discount Delle Firme**: Via dei Serviti 27 (tel: 48 27 790). 50% discount on Italian designer labels. Shoes, scarves, umbrellas, etc.
- **Leam Intimo**: Via Tomacelli 19, off the Corso (tel: 68 76 158). Not actually a discount shop, it sells lingerie at exceptionally good prices.
- **New Fashion**: Via Simone De Saint Bon 87, in Prati (tel: 37 51 39 47). Steep discounts on ready-to-wear and haute couture designer clothes.

**Clothing Size Conversions**
Basically, you have to try on clothes and shoes until you see what size fits; sizes vary from manufacturer to manufacturer and from store to store. In general, an American woman should add 30-32 to her dress size to find the comparable size; thus, a size 12 woman would look for a 42-44. British women should add 30. Sweaters are often sized by the centimetre, so a size 12 sweater might be about a 40. For men, a size 'small' shirt translates into about a 37-38, and a 'medium' is about 40; sizes are in centimetres of the collar, not inches.

In shoes, width differentials are rare, as are half sizes. Thus, both an American woman's size 6 to about 7 would be a size 38-39; a British woman's size 8 would be about 39-40. An American man's shoe size 9 would be about a size 43-44. It's approximately the same for the British man's shoe.

# SPORTS CLOTHING AND EQUIPMENT
Some of the gyms such as the Roman Sport Centre, in Via del Galappatoio 33, have pro shops (tel: 36 14 226). Some shops that sell athletic clothes also sell casual street clothes. International chains are making their appearance in Rome: **Foot Locker**, the athletic shoe chain, has two locations: Via del Corso 38 (tel: 36 00 18 77) and Via dei Condotti 88 (tel: 69 90 787). **Adidas** is in Via S. Claudio 85, at Piazza San Silvestro (tel: 67 95 768), and **Timberland**, the American chain for rugged outdoor clothing, is in Via del Babuino 73 (tel: 67 90 836). For athletic equipment and clothes, see *Articoli Sportivi* in the Yellow Pages.
- **Banchetti Sport**: Via Campo Marzio 38, in the Centro Storico, has sporting clothes (tel: 68 71 420).
- **Bartoni Tennis**: Via Masolino da Panicale 15, at Lungotevere Flaminio, specialises in tennis (tel: 36 10 093). Also in Via Monti di Creta 29, near Largo Boccea (tel: 66 32 555).
- **Cisalfa** has several locations, including Cinecittà Due (tel: 72 21 394). Other addresses include: Viale Libia 152, near Piazza

245

Photo: Pomponi/Photoreporters

*Window shopping in Rome – with over 40,000 stores in the city it can be a hectic pastime.*

S. Emerenziana (tel: 86 21 86 26); Via Colli Portuensi 8, south of Trastevere (tel: 58 20 19 65); and Largo Brindisi 3, at Piazzale Appio (tel: 70 08 062).

- **Fila Boutique**: Via Capo le Case 24, near Piazza di Spagna (tel: 67 88 973). Worldwide chain of sporting clothes.
- **Gaffi Sport**: has sports equipment and clothing of all sorts. Addresses in Nomentana include Viale Ippocrate 44 (tel: 44 29 0 845) and nearby Via Padova 68 (tel: 44 24 09 52).
- **Lacoste**: Via di Propaganda 1/a (tel: 67 88 445). Worldwide chain of sporting clothes.
- **Lineasport**, selling sports clothing and athletic shoes, plus jeans, has two locations on the Corso: Via del Corso 48 (tel: 36 12 230) and Via del Corso 35 (tel: 36 13 312).
- **Marango Sport**: Viale delle Provincie 168, near Piazza Bologna (tel: 44 23 20 39). A major sports shop selling equipment and clothes, at excellent prices.
- **Bottega del Campeggiatore Marchetti**: Piazza Firenze 25 (tel: 68 79 098). Supplies camping gear, as well as a selection of sports clothing and street wear.

## COMPUTERS, COMPUTER REPAIR AND TECH SUPPORT

Most laptop computers sense power voltage and convert automatically to local current, and most desktop models have a switch that converts the current. In this case you will need only an adapter plug, not a transformer; if you need a transformer, you may be able to buy one designed for your computer or printer directly from the company's accessory sales department. Note that many of the usual hair dryer/razor transformers now caution "not for use with electronic products." With larger, desktop computer/printers, you may need a step-up/step-down transformer, a small box that converts heavier-use appliances to different currents;

make sure you get the appropriate size. These are available at appliance shops and at **Appliances Overseas**, which also sells European-adapted computers and printers.

Not only are the voltage and hertz different, but the capacity in each apartment may not be the same. Some people in older apartments turn off other appliances when printing to avoid overload and blowing fuses. Others upgrade the kilowatts. Note also that power surges are frequent. Thus, some people unplug their computers (or turn off the fuse) when not using them. Buying a **para fulmine** (surge protector) would also be a good idea, not just for your computer but for stereos and other such equipment.

Computer shops are springing up everywhere, and you can now buy or rent just about any brand you want. Although prices have historically been high owing to duties and taxes, the advent of large shops and discount stores is making prices more competitive. Shop around for the best prices. In addition, make sure to get all the information available on models; they are changing quickly, and not all salespeople are knowledgeable about all the recent models. For **concessionari** (authorised sales outlets) see *Personal Computer* in the Yellow Pages. Note that many shops are closed weekends and not all take credit cards.

Technical support and repair are available for all computer makes. There are also some informational and technical support numbers for international companies: **IBM**'s help line is in Milan (tels: 02/59621; toll free info: 167/80 16 338; tech support: 167/82 00 94). **Apple**'s is 167/82 70 69. For further online information, see Chapter Nine.

- **Tecmatica**: Via S. Bargellini 4, off Via Tiburtina (tel: 43 95 264). Repair of IBM compatibles and printers.
- **Computer Age**: Via Silvestro Gherardi 46 (tel: 55 93 667). Well established firm carrying a wide assortment of hardware and software of all brands.

- **Computer Discount**: Via Anastasio II 340 (tel: 39 38 72 85); Via Merulana 245 (tel: 47 40 289); other locations. A full service computer shop with good prices. Sales of Compaq, HP, IBM, AST, Zenith. Software, accessories, CD ROM, etc.
- **DEDO Sistemi:** Via Postumia 2, near Viale Regina Margherita (tel: 84 12 438). Sells and rents IBM compatibles, plus software such as Microsoft and Lotus; repair shop. Training courses.
- **EMI (Enhanced Management Internet)**: Corso di Francia 216 (tel: 36 30 63 93). Access and training courses in the Internet, DOS, Windows, etc. Sales of hardware and software.
- **HTS Informatica**: Via Valsugana 58 (tel: 86 02 346). Personal computers, technical support. Good prices.
- **Sivet**: Via della Scrofa 73 (tel: 68 80 53 82). IBM, Toshiba, Epson and Hewlett Packard.
- **Sparta Informatica**: Via delle Sette Chiese 142, south off Via Appia Antica (tel: 59 29 231). Large, well known shop selling all the major brands.
- **Unidata**: Via San Damaso 20, to the west (tel: 39 38 73 18). Sells hardware and Microsoft software, and IBM compatibles. Toll-free number for technical assistance (167/86 02 87).
- **Vobis**: an extensive chain of shops, selling IBM compatibles, software, accessories, etc. Tech support. The largest shop is in Largo de Dominicis 4 (tel: 43 82 872); Stazione Termini (tel: 40 90 39 15; Piazza Mancini 3, in Flaminio (tel: 36 00 10 04).

# COSMETICS AND PERFUMES

The **profumeria** sells cosmetics, perfumes and hair and body products; generally they do not carry health products. *Profumeria* are in every neighbourhood, but the smaller shops may not sell exactly the international products you are accustomed to. In that case, try one of those listed below, any in the Centro Storico, or a department store. *Farmacie* and *eboristerie* (see Chapter Six) often carry hpyo-allergenic products and healthful body supplies.

- **Bertozzini** in Via Cola di Rienzo 192 (tel: 68 74 662). Large emporium selling a variety of international beauty products.
- **Body Shop**: a worldwide chain of body product shops. Via del Corso 168 (tel: 67 98 887); Centro La Romanina (tel: 72 33 371); Centro I Granai (tel: 51 95 60 15); Via Cola di Rienzo 238 (tel: 68 32 849).
- **Farmacia Trinità de' Monti**: Piazza di Spagna 63 (tel: 69 94 10 96). A pharmacy that carries internationally known beauty products.
- **Materozzoli**: Piazza S. Lorenzo in Lucina 5, off the Corso (tel: 68 71 456): Good international products.
- **Il Mercantissimo:** Via Prati della Farnesina 59-61 (tel: 33 32 914). Almost a supermarket for beauty and hygiene products.
- **New Look**: A chain of profumerie, including I Granai (tel: 51 95 56 60); Via Bragadin 100, past the Vatican (tel: 39 72 06 68); Via Casetta Mattei 171, to the southwest (tel: 65 52 101).
- **Sun Shop**: Via del Corso 132 (tel: 67 92 537). Lotions, shampoos, conditioners and cosmetics.
- **Wisa Profumerie**: Via Tirso 15 (tel: 85 53 433). American and British brands for both men and women.

## DEPARTMENT STORES

The four large **grandi magazzini** (department stores) vary in quality and price. **La Rinascente** in the Corso and in Piazza Fiume, is upscale, although conservative. The Piazza Fiume store is larger and has housewares in addition to clothing and personal goods. **COIN** is the most modern, with moderate prices and a varied selection of clothing and housewares; it has now opened three of its **Bimbus** children's shops in Rome. **Standa**, with two important branches in Prati and Trastevere, is less expensive, and the supermarkets in the basements are generally well stocked. **UPIM**, at the lowest rung of the ladder has basic, inexpensive goods. Some of the department stores are now open on Sunday, including La

Rinascente, UPIM and Standa's supermarkets. See *Supermercati, Grandi Magazzini & Centri Commerciali* in the Yellow Pages.

- **La Rinascente**: 1) Piazza Fiume (tel: 88 41 231); 2) Via del Corso 189 (tel: 67 97 691).
- **COIN**: Piazzale Appio 15 (tel: 70 80 020); Cinecittà Due (tel: 72 20 931); Via Mantova 1/b (tel: 84 15 875); Viale Libia 61 (tel: 86 21 46 60).
- **Standa**: Viale Trastevere 60 (tel: 58 95 342); Via Cola di Rienzo 173 (tel: 32 43 283); Viale Regina Margherita 123 (tel: 85 57 427); Corso Francia 124 (tel: 33 38 719).
- **UPIM**: Piazza S. Maria Maggiore (tel: 44 65 579); Via Nazionale 211 (tel: 48 45 02); Via del Tritone 172 (tel: 67 83 336).

# HAIR SERVICES

Before finding the hairdresser that's right for you, try one of these below. Some are internationally known and are more expensive; generally there are English speakers. Others are neighbourhood shops or chains that are long established and well recommended. If you use hair dye, bring a few bottles with you until you find a comparable colour, as brands and colours are not the same as at home. Note that most hairdressers are closed on Monday. See *Parrucchiere Per Donne* (for women) and *Parrucchiere Per Uomo* (for men) in the Yellow Pages.

- **Alberto & Tony**: Via V. Veneto 155, near the United States Embassy (tel: 48 21 793). An international clientele and a variety of beauty services.
- **Biancaneve e i 7 Nani**: Via Metastasio 17, in the Centro (tel: 68 65 409). Long time salon for children.
- **Capelli Verdi**: Via della Cisterna 15, in Trastevere (tel: 58 18 691). A unisex hair stylist using natural, ecological products. Open nonstop.
- **Dino**: Via Lucrezio Caro 46/b, off Piazza Cavour (tel: 36 11 775). Man's emporium, with massage, Turkish bath, manicures and pedicures.

251

- **La Meluccia**: Via dei Cosmati 9/a, near Ponte Cavour (tel: 32 04 651). For all members of the family.
- **Monticelli 31**: Via T. Monticelli 31, in Parioli. (tel: 32 03 847). Barber, offering tanning, massage, steam, manicures, etc.
- **Rolando Elisei**: La Rinascente Department Store in Piazza Fiume (tel: 85 54 669). Branch of a country-wide chain. Open Sunday.
- **I Sargassi**: Women's salons, reliable and affordable. Addresses include: *Piazza di Spagna* - Via Frattina 48 (tel: 67 90 637); *Lateran* - Piazzale Appio 1 (tel: 70 47 42 59); *Tiburtina* - Via De Ritis 8 (tel: 43 92 052); *Prati* - Via Cola di Rienzo 163 (tel: 32 43 157); *Porta Pia* - Via Nomentana 65 (tel: 44 25 03 22).
- **Sandra Kennedy Coiffure**: Via di Santa Cecilia 10, in Trastevere (tel: 58 95 793). Unisex salon run by an Australian woman.
- **Sergio Russo**: Piazza Mignanelli 25, off Piazza di Spagna (tel: 67 81 110). One of the top hair stylists.
- **Sergio Valente**: Via Condotti 11 (tel: 67 94 515). One of the top hairstylists. Unisex, including massage and sauna. In an interesting palazzo. First come, first served. Hours nonstop.
- **Studio 3**: Piazza di Spagna 51 (tel: 67 86 223). Slightly less expensive than others in this tourist area. Friendly people, some of whom speak English.
- **Studio 13**: Piazza Cavour 13, in Prati (tel: 68 80 39 77). Unisex hairdresser, profumeria, makeup centre.
- **Vergottini**: Via del Lavatore 44, near Fontana di Trevi, is a branch of a country-wide chain (tel: 67 80 784). A woman's beauty centre, with tanning, makeup, etc.

# HARDWARE

**Ferramenta** (hardware stores) are generally well stocked. You can find hidden treasures of all helpful sorts, have keys made, find appropriate tools, and sometimes even indulge your favourite hobby. Most are small and crowded. Look for *Ferramenta* in the Yellow Pages.

- **Ferramenta Candia**: a chain that carries hardware, household, and kitchen equipment. All near Prati. Via Candia (tel: 39 74 21 59); Viale degli Ammiragli 29 (tel: 63 80 845); Viale Anastasio II 434 (tel: 63 84 253).

- **Ferramenta Cavour**: Via Cavour 281-291, in Esquilino (tel: 48 80 821). Large selection of hardware items.

- **Ferramenta Regina**: Piazza Regina Margherita 30 (tel: 85 35 43 79). Small but well stocked store in Salario. Open Saturday morning.

- **Ferramenta Toresi**: Via di Ripetta 26, near Piazza del Popolo (tel: 32 19 268). Closed Saturday afternoon; last half of August.

- **Ruberto Ferramenta**: Via dei Baullari 135, near Campo de' Fiori (tel: 68 61 372). Tools and electrical equipment.

- **Sinistri & Pepe**: two hardware/paint shops that have some hobby items. Via Ostiense 75 (tel: 57 50 751); Via Marmorata 95 (tel: 57 46 184).

# HOME FURNISHINGS

Even if your apartment comes fully equipped, you may need to buy some incidental items such as lamps, towels or kitchen equipment. The department stores carry household items at reasonable prices. **Rocco Casa** is a chain of well-stocked discount stores that specialises in household items (see below for addresses). For furniture stores, see *Mobili Vendita* in the Yellow Pages. See also Kitchen Items, below.

- *Furniture* — **Habitat**: Via Cristoforo Colombo 88 (tel: 51 27 552). A multi-storey furniture centre in EUR, off Via Cristoforo Colombo and near Fiera di Roma. Parking provided

- *Furniture* — **Gallerie Grilli**: Piazza Vittorio 127 (tel: 44 67 188). Large furniture store in the city centre. Good prices.

- *Home Equipment* — **Habitat** is a chain of reasonably priced stores, carrying furniture, kitchen equipment, dishes, etc. Addresses

include: Via Cola di Rienzo 197 (tel: 32 3013 67); Viale Regina
Margherita 18 (tel: 85 58 641); Viale Marconi 259 (tel: 55 82
701). No connection with the Habitat showroom in EUR.

- *Home Equipment* — **Leone Limentani**: Via Portico d'Ottavia
47, in the Ghetto area (tel: 68 80 66 86). Many known brand
names of fine china and crystal, sometimes at substantial
discounts. **Limentani Argenti** at Via Portico d'Ottavia 63
specialises in fine silver (tel: 68 92 862).

- *Home Equipment* — **Magazzini Forma & Memoria**: Vicolo di
San Onofrio 24 (tel: 68 32 915). A large assortment of kitchen
and houseware items.

- *Home Equipment* — **Studio Due Pi Arreda**: Piazza Nicosia 30,
off Via della Scrofa (tel: 68 30 73 84). Elegant shop selling
china, glassware, trays, kitchen equipment, other household
items and some furniture.

- *Home Equipment* — **Rocco Casa**: Good discounts on a large
selection of products. Addresses include: Via Raffaele de Cesare
16 (tel: 71 35 80 41); Viale dei Colli Portuensi 14 (tel: 71 35 80
40); Via de Viti de Marco 44; Viale Oceano Pacifico 249 (tel:
71 35 80) with free parking.

- *Lamps/Telephones* — **VP Technolight**: Via Marianna Dionigi
11/c, in Prati (tel: 36 11 662). Lamps, bulbs and telephone
equipment.

- *Lamps* — **Tuttaluce**: Via della Palombella 32, near the Pantheon
(tel: 68 75 660). A wide variety of lamps.

- *Table Linens* — **Frette**: a chain of table linen shops: Piazza di
Spagna 11 (tel: 67 90 673); Via Nazionale 84 (tel: 48 82 641);
Viale Libia 192 (tel: 86 20 39 91); Via del Corso 381 (tel: 67 86
862).

- *Table Linens* — **Non Solo Bianco**: Via della Fontanella di
Borghese 38 (tel: 68 76 657). A selection of table linens in
various sizes and colours. Sheets, towels. Fair prices.

# KITCHEN EQUIPMENT

The department stores have the most reasonable prices for basic kitchen equipment. For more interesting and varied fare, try these below. Some hardware stores carry kitchen implements, as do the home furnishing shops such as Habitat and Studio Due Pi.

- **Casa del Cellophan**: Via Labicana 37 (tel: 77 20 62 97). Disposable dining items of all sorts and sizes. Glasses, dishes, platters, etc. all of paper, plastic and aluminium.
- **C.U.C.I.N.A.**: Via del Babuino 118/a (tel: 67 91 275). Upscale store, featuring out-of-the-ordinary implements.
- **Oscar Zucchi**: Via Sant'Antonio all'Esquilino 15 (tel: 44 65 871). Pots, pans, interesting kitchen items.
- **La Maison Blanche**: Via Mario de' Fiori 62 (tel: 67 89 642). White oven-proof casseroles, trays, etc.
- **Pepe Bianco**: Via Tagliamento 5/b (tel: 85 49 715). Basic white dishes ready to be decorated.
- **Stock Market**: Via dei Banchi Vecchi 51 (tel: 68 64 238). Household items, imported and domestic. Grills, quality pots and pans, tablecloths in a variety of styles and colours. Good prices and some bargains.

# LAUNDRIES AND DRY CLEANING

Laundries and dry cleaners are generally small shops in which women carefully press each piece by hand, which is why cleaning tends to be expensive. Rush orders are rare; the time frame is longer than you'd expect at home. Some of the more modern dry cleaners offer one price for all standard items *(monoprezzo)*, and prices are around L4000-5000. Some are good, some aren't, as with any dry cleaner. Self-service laundromats are beginning to appear, but in general, be prepared to take your sheets to the laundry and to wait about a week. Many furnished apartments come with washing machines, but few have dryers. Many of the establishments are open weekdays only, and many close in August. For dry cleaners, see *Lavanderie a secco* in the Yellow Pages; for laundries, see *Lavanderie*; and for coin laundries see *Lavanderie a gettone*.

- **Lavasecco Pony Sec**: Via Basilio Bricci 25, in Monteverde (tel: 58 17 758). Monoprezzo for usual laundry items. Free pick up and delivery for residents of the area.
- **Lavasecco Monoprezzo**: Via Tiburtina 11 in San Lorenzo, near Piazzale Tiburtina. Monoprezzo for all standard pieces of clothing. Larger and unusual items cost more. Open nonstop; open Saturday morning.
- **Lavaservice**: Via Montebello 44 is a laundromat north of Stazione Termini. Hours: nonstop weekdays.
- **Lavanderia Acqua Secco**: Via Castelfidardo 20, near Piazza Indipendenza. Open Saturday mornings.
- **Zampa**: Campo de' Fiori 38 (tel: 68 79 096). Good dry cleaner. Open weekdays.
- **Onda Blu:** Via Principe Amedeo 70/b (tel: 47 44 647); Via La Marmora 10 (tel: 44 64 172). Self-service laundromats.
- **Lavanderia Americana**: Via A. Venturi 27, north of Piazza Bologna. (tel: 44 23 84 41). Self-service.
- **Greensec/Lavasecco Ecologico**: Via Napoleone III (tel: 49 17 22). Dry cleaner/laundry with 24-hour service. Open weekdays.
- **Tintoria Elensec**: Via S. Cosimato 4 (tel: 58 81 523). A wide range of cleaning and laundry services. Open Saturday until 2:00 pm, closed August.
- **Tintoria Gilmas**: Piazza della Cancelleria 88, near Campo de' Fiori (tel: 68 67 907). Dry cleaning and laundry. Specialises in furs, carpets. Open Saturday mornings.

# LUGGAGE

For luggage shops, look under *Valigerie ed Articoli da Viaggio Vendita* in the Yellow Pages.

- **Casini**: Piazza San Silvestro 25 (tel: 67 90 129). Well stocked, with a variety of brands and sizes.

- **Piero Pellicceria**: Viale Eritrea 107, near Piazza S. Emerenziana (tel: 86 21 48 15). A large assortment of brands. Free parking nearby.
- **Pratesi**: Piazza Firenze 22 (tel: 68 80 37 20). Luggage sales and repair. Leather bags of all sizes and styles.
- **Tedeschi**: Via Nazionale 166, at Via XXIV Maggio (tel: 67 95 575). All major brands of luggage.
- **Valigeria Romana**: sells and repairs luggage, especially Samsonite. Locations: Via Silla 51, in Prati (tel: 39 73 28 45); and I Granai (tel: 51 95 59 38).

## MUSIC: RECORDS/CD/TAPES

Many of the music shops carry books, videos, and musical equipment as well as records, tapes, and CDs. Most will have notices of current events, concerts, rock happenings, etc. See *Audio, Videocassette, Compact Disc Commercio* in the Yellow Pages.

- **Disfunzioni Musicali**: Via degli Etruschi 14, in San Lorenzo (tel: 44 61 984). New releases, underground music, second-hand records and CDs. Notice board lists upcoming musical events. Open until 11:00 pm Friday and Saturday; open Sunday.
- **Messaggerie Musicali**: Via del Corso 123 (tel: 67 98 197). Multi-storey music shop, with a large variety of musical offerings on tape and CD. Electronic musical equipment.
- **Metropoli Rock**: Via Cavour 72, in Esquilino (tel: 48 80 443). Thousands of CDs, and records of all musical styles and generations.
- **Ricordi**: a chain of large, well stocked music stores, offering records, tapes and CDs of all types of music, from classical to heavy metal. Videos and books. Via del Corso 506 (tel: 36 12 331); Via C. Battisti 120/c (tel: 67 98 022); Piazza Indipendenza 24 (tel: 44 40 706); Viale Giulio Cesare 88 (tel: 37 35 15 89).

- **Rinascita**: Via delle Botteghe Oscure 3, near Piazza Venezia (tel: 67 97 637). Large selection of discs, tapes and CDs, and books. Ticket service, maps and guidebooks. Open Sunday.

## OPTICAL SERVICES

Rome doesn't have inexpensive international optical chains like For Eyes or LensCrafters. Glasses are a fashion statement, like anything worn. Most optical stores will make new glasses or contact lenses from your prescription from home. See *Ottica Apparecchi* in the Yellow Pages.

- **Berti Optometria**: Viale Giulio Cesare 71, in Prati (tel: 32 43 457). Contact lenses and glasses. Eye exams by a Fellow of the American Academy of Optometry. English spoken.
- **Fios**: Via del Viminale 41, in Esquilino, specialises in contact lenses (tel: 48 19 051) and eyeglasses (tel: 48 27 019). Member of National Academy of Sports Vision. English spoken.
- **La Barbera**: Via Barberini 74, in Ludovisi, in business since 1837 (tel: 48 36 28). Reproduces prescriptions. Sunglasses, cameras, binoculars and other optical equipment. Some product repair.
- **Lucchesi**: Via del Corso 146 (tel: 67 90 298). Glasses, contact lenses, sunglasses. Foreign prescriptions accepted. Takes all credit cards. English spoken.
- **Ottica Lord**: Via Sistina 142, off Piazza Barberini (tel: 48 19 242). Contact lenses.
- **Ottica Scientifica Tonel**: Via delle Convertite 19, near San Silvestro (tel: 67 92 579). Eye exams. Glasses, contact lenses. Optical equipment; good brand name cameras; other electronics.
- **Ottica Romani** has several addresses for eyeglasses, including: Via Flavia 122, off Via XX Settembre (tel: 47 41 818); Via Frattina 39 (tel: 67 97 638); Viale Europa 81 in EUR (tel: 59 19 551). For

contact lenses: Via Piave 8, near Piazza Fiume (tel: 48 14 415). Other locations are in the Yellow Pages.
- **Vision Optika Group**: Via di S. Claudio 87 near San Silvestro (tel: 67 85 983). Eyeglasses from your prescriptions. Specialises in contact lenses and carries all the major brands.

# OUTDOOR MARKETS

In addition to the outdoor food markets described in Chapter Twelve, there are several interesting markets that sell clothing, shoes or other items of interest, all at low prices, and often of matching quality, although there are sometimes good bargains to be found.
- **Porta Portese** is Rome's famous Sunday morning flea market. At Via Portuense and Via Ippolito Nievo. A mile of aisles crowded with stalls selling everything from furniture and appliances to leather goods, from fake Louis Vuitton bags to authentic old clothes. Russians sell icons, Italians old war medals; some may even be real. Records, cameras, kitchenware. Everyone comes to Porta Portese, including pickpockets.
- **Underground**: Twice-monthly flea market selling antiques, jewellery, furniture. Space for children to participate as well. Every second Saturday at the Ludovisi underground parking garage in Via Crispi 96.
- **Mercato dei Fiori** in Via Trionfale 47, is Rome's largest flower market, in a two-storey hall off Via Andrea Doria. Open to the public only on Tuesdays from 10:30 am-1:00 pm.
- **Mercati Generali** in Via Ostiense, is off Piazzale Ostiense. Rome's large wholesale food market. This is the market that has a famous fish festival in the winter (see Chapter Fifteen). Open from 10:00 am; closed Sunday.
- **Mercato di Fontanella Borghese**, between the Corso and Via di Ripetta, features old books and prints. Hours: 8:00 am-4:00 pm; closed Sunday.

- **Mercato Via Sannio** in the Lateran off Piazzale Appio sells both new and used clothes, shoes, camping gear and more. Metro A/S. Giovanni or Tram #13. Great bargains and worthless junk; shop selectively. Hours: 10:00 am-1:30 pm weekdays; Closed Sunday, when the stalls move to Porta Portese.

# PHOTOGRAPHY

As you'd expect in a tourist city, photo developing shops are everywhere. You can get your film developed in one hour in just about any street in the Centro Storico, and in most camera shops out of the centre as well. For cameras, see *Fotografia — Apparecchi e Materiali* in the Yellow Pages; note also that many of the optical shops also carry photographic equipment.

*Photo: Lydia Predominato*

*Household items such as linen can often be bought cheaply from the outdoor markets.*

- **De Bernardis**: Piazza della Cancelleria 63, off Corso Vittorio Emanuele (tel: 68 64 143). Sells and repairs cameras, develops photos. Closed Saturday afternoon.
- **Centro Riparazioni Fratelli Rossi**: Via Aurelia 190, near the Vatican (tel: 39 36 63 57). Repairs a variety of camera brands. Closed weekends.
- **Eidos**: Via Appia Nuova, 258, in the Lateran (tel: 70 11 961). International brands of cameras, such as Nikon, Canon, Hasselblad, Pentax.
- **Fotottica Randazzo**: Piazza SS. Apostoli 80, off the Corso (tel: 67 958 82). Cameras, videos, glasses and contact lenses.
- **Metroimport**: Via Anastasio II 438, to the west of the Vatican (tel: 63 00 06). A large store with a good selection of cameras and photographic equipment.
- **Pennetta**: Via Dandolo 2, in Trastevere (tel: 58 96 648). Sells both new and used cameras and accessories.

## SHOPPING MALLS

The shopping mall has found Rome. Multi-storey and high-tech, the malls house many of the top Roman shops — clothing, household items and more — all under one roof. With large parking lots, these are generally out of the city centre and best reached by car, except for **Cinecittà Due**, which is near Metro A/Cinecittà or Subaugusta.

- **Centro Commerciale Cinecittà Due**: Viale Palmiro Togliatti 2 at Via Tuscolana, near Cinecittà (tel: 72 20 910). Opened in 1989, there are 110 shops in a modern glass two-storey structure. The top Roman stores are represented, and there are casual eateries and a bank with a cash machine. Large supermarket. Underground parking. Open nonstop.
- **La Romanina**: Exit 20 of the Grande Raccordo Anulare (tel: 72 67 00 01). Built in 1992, a modern, four-level mall with 130 upscale shops, boutiques, a supermarket, bank, restaurants and bars.

261

- **I Granai** Via Granai di Nerva (tel: 51 95 58 90). Large modern mall near EUR/Laurentina. I Granai has more than a hundred shops, bars, restaurants, banks and other services. It also has a large supermarket for stocking up on groceries and offers underground parking for its customers.

## STATIONERY/ART SUPPLIES

For stationery stores, see *Cartolerie* in the Yellow Pages. For artists' supplies, look under *Disegno, Grafica, Belle Arti — Articoli*. For writing implements, see *Penne Stilografiche*.

- **L'Artistica Roma**: Via del Babuino 24 (tel: 36 00 09 63). Well stocked shop for artists' supplies.
- **Ditta G. Poggi**: Via del Gesù sells art supplies (tel: 67 84 477); branch around the corner in Via Piè di Marmo 40 (67 93 674). Open Saturday mornings.
- **Nuovo Artecnica**: Via dei Savorelli 37, near Piazza Pio XI (tel: 63 81 441). Large, well stocked graphic art and office supply store.
- **Pineider**: Via Due Macelli 69 (tel: 67 95 884); Via delle Fontanella di Borghese 22 (tel: 68 30 80 14). Elegant stationery and paper store.
- **Vertecchi**: Via della Croce 70/a (tel: 67 83 110). An extensive selection of stationery, lovely papers and writing supplies. Also good for presents. Open nonstop.
- **Stilo Fetti**: Via degli Orfani 82, near the Pantheon (tel: 68 99 662). Pens, from the expensive and elegant to the everyday. Desk sets and other items of interest. A repair service is also available.
- **Stilograph**: Via Ottaviano 79, in Prati (tel: 39 72 32 84). Pens of all sorts on sale. Repair service.

# TELEPHONES

Telephone shops may display signs that say **Telecom Italia Mobile Autorizzato Dealer** or **insip Telecom**, indicating that they are authorised dealers of Telecom Italia. There are also some **AT&T** authorised dealers. Cellular phones are extremely popular, and there are many outlets for sales, rental and technical support. See also Home Furnishings above.

- **Asotec**: Via della Scrofa 40 (tel: 68 80 83 20). Telephones, cellular phones, answering machines, security systems. Sales, assistance, repairs.
- **Easy Line**: Via Tagliamento 55 (tel: 84 13 273; toll free: 167/ 01 06 00). Rental of cellular phones.
- **Gruppo de Benedetti** has several locations and names: Via Frattina 65 (tel: 67 92 825); RDB Telefonia: Via dei Serpenti 118 (tel: 47 41 944); RDB Telefonia Cinecittà Due: Via P. Togliatti 2 (tel: 72 21 790).
- **Omnitel**: Via del Corso 417 (68 72 872; toll-free tel: 167/19 01 90). Sales of cellular phones.
- **Pick Up A Phone**: Via Palumbo 22, in Prati (tel: 37 21 562). Rental of cellular phones.
- **Rentel**: Via Angelico 77 (tel: 32 51 75). Rental of cellular phones.
- **Telefonissimo**: Piazzale Clodio 15 (tel: 39 73 37 90). Telephones, cellular phones, faxes, answering machines. Tech support. Good prices offered on international brands.

# TOYS

All the international brands of toys and games are available, including Fisher-Price, Lego, and Nintendo. See *Giocattoli e Giocchi Vendita* in the Yellow Pages.

- **Città del Sole**: Via della Scrofa 65, northeast of the Pantheon (tel: 68 75 404). Excellent educational games, puzzles, books, and toys. Also in Piazza della Chiesa Nuova 20 (tel: 68 72 922).
- **Enfant Prodige**: via Marco Aurelio 27 (tel: 70 04 630). Toys, accessories and shoes for babies. Fisher-Price and Playskool.
- **Galleria San Carlo**: Via del Corso 114 (tel: 67 90 571). A large shop with games, Fisher-Price toys, stuffed animals, dolls, Nintendo, and model kits.
- **La Chioccia**: Viale Marconi 277, off Piazzale della Radio (tel: 55 79 993). Video and electronic games.
- **Al Sogno**: Piazza Navona 53 (tel: 68 64 198). A rather expensive but interesting toy shop that has stuffed animals, dolls, etc. Games also for adults.

# VIDEO RENTAL

**Videofilm noleggio** (video rental) is popular, and in addition to regular shops, there are some outlets with *videobancomats*, machines that take credit cards and dispense the cassette. Check the Economy Book and Video Centre for English-language videos. See *Audiovisivi* in the Yellow Pages; sometimes *TrovaRoma* publishes a list of outlets by city region.

Note that Italy uses the PAL video system. PAL is used in England, but not in France, which uses SECAM, or in the United States, which uses NTSC. Video recorders using different systems are not interchangeable, and videos must be played on compatible televisions. Some rental facilities, including **Videoteca Navona** in Piazza Navona 103 (tel: 68 69 823) and **Filmania 4** in Viale del Vignola 51 (tel: 32 24 992) rent films in *versione originale*.

- *Campo de' Fiori* — **Hollywood Tutto sul Cinema**: Via di Monserrato 107 (tel: 68 69 197)
- *Esquilino* — **Video Immagine**: Via Merulana 217 (tel: 70 45 39 34)
- *Ludovisi* — **Slim**: Via Sicilia 233 (tel: 48 80 589)
- *Monte Mario* — **Happy Video**: Via Trionfale 8310 (tel: 30 53 044)
- *Parioli* — **Hole Club**: Viale Parioli 170 (tel: 80 78 866)
- *Piazza di Spagna* — **Video House**: Via Frattina 50 (tel: 67 91 493)
- *Prati* — **Mambo Video**: Viale Giulio Cesare 86 (tel: 37 29 318)
- *EUR* — **EUR Video**: Viale dell' Aeronautica 97 (tel: 59 18 918)

# CHAPTER FIFTEEN

# ENTERTAINMENT, EVENTS, AND HOLIDAYS

## WHAT'S ON IN ROME

Cultural events and activities in Rome are well publicised. To find out the upcoming events, get each Thursday at your newsstand *Roma C'è*, a comprehensive weekly events listing with an insert in English. Also on Thursday *La Repubblica* publishes a special tabloid section called *TrovaRoma* and *Il Messaggero* publishes *Metro*. These are in Italian, but even with no Italian language knowledge, the names of music groups, plays, and concerts should be easy to pick out, as well as days and times. *Un Ospite a Roma*, and *Where: Rome,* published monthly in English, can be found for free in hotel lobbies; they list the month's events. Look also at *Metropolitan* and *Wanted in Rome* as well as posters plastered on walls around the city.

The summer especially sees an exuberant season of public events — many held outdoors in parks, courtyards and squares. Classical music concerts are held outdoors in various venues, and classical dramas are staged in the amphitheatre at Ostia Antica, the ancient city about fifteen miles to the west. Park concerts are often free; on Sunday mornings around 10:30 am, for example, groups such as the ATAC band play in the Pincio while kids ride bikes nearby. And more formal concerts are held in July in parks such as Villa Pamphili. **Estate Romana** is a summer-long festival of films, jazz, dance and rock concerts, much of it outdoors. At the end of July, the Festa de Noantri transforms Trastevere, where everyone browses through stalls, eats in outdoor cafes and watches fireworks. And there's always something interesting at Castel Sant'Angelo. It's fortunate that there are so many public events in summer, for otherwise entertainment may be sparse: even the most popular nightclubs and discos tend to close down in August or move to the beach, as Roman entertainment continues under the stars.

## Ticket Agencies

Except for opera, which must be booked in advance, theatre and concert tickets may often be bought at the box office. Yet ticket agencies, despite the commission charged, are the easiest way to buy tickets to events, avoiding crowds and ensuring seats.

- **Box Office**: Viale Giulio Cesare 88, in Prati (tel: 37 20 216; credit card order tel: 44 54 351). Tickets for theatre, musical concerts and some sporting events. Closed weekends and Monday afternoon. Branch: Via del Corso 506 (tel: 36 12 682).
- **Gesman 92**: Via A. Emo 65, near the Vatican (tel: 39 74 07 89; fax: 39 37 83 31). Theatre tickets, classical music, rock/jazz concerts. Open Saturday mornings.
- **Orbis**: Piazza dell' Esquilino 37 (tels: 47 44 776; 48 27 403). Tickets for rock/jazz/pop concerts, theatre and sporting events. Open Saturday mornings. No credit cards.

267

- **Preno Ticket** (tel: 52 20 03 42) offers tickets to concerts, theatre, ballet and sporting events. Book by credit card over the telephone only.
- **Rinascita**: Via delle Botteghe Oscure 1, off Via Arenula (tels: 67 97 460; 69 92 24 86). A large book, record and video shop that sells tickets for rock and jazz events. Open daily.
- **Romacomoda**: Via G. Bettolo 4 (tel: 37 23 956). Tickets for theatre, classical concerts, opera. Open Saturday mornings.

# THEATRE

Rome has an extensive theatre season, and there are some international offerings at the theatres listed below; be sure to check the weekly events listings. In summer, watch for events at **Ostia Antica** (tel: 68 77 390) and at the **Anfiteatro Quercia del Tasso**, near the poet Tasso's home on the Gianicolo (tel: 57 50 827).

- **Teatro** Nazionale: Via del Viminale 51 (tel: 48 70 614). Inexpensive and a varied repertoire.
- **Teatro Argentina**: Largo Argentina 52 (tel: 68 80 46 01). At the 1816 premiere of the *Barber of Seville*, Rossini hurled insults back at the audience after it roundly expressed its dislike.
- **Teatro Agorà 80**: Via della Penitenza 33 in Trastevere presents professionally produced English-language productions, as well as productions in other languages (tel: 68 80 71 07).

- **Teatro Quirino**: Via Marco Minghetti 1 (tel: 67 94 585). Major works of all theatrical types.
- **Teatro Valle**: Via del Teatro Valle 23/a (tel: 68 80 37 94). Classics and a varied repertoire.
- **Teatro Ghione**: Via delle Fornaci 37, near Trastevere, offers theatrical and musical events (tel: 63 72 294).
- **Teatro Sistina**: Via Sistina 129, said to be Rome's most lively cabaret (tel: 48 26 841).

# CLASSICAL MUSIC

The regular **opera** season at the **Teatro dell'Opera** in Piazza Beniamino Gigli 8, is January–May (tel: 48 16 01; toll free: 167/ 01 66 65). Check the weekly and monthly events listings, for opera is occasionally presented in other theatrical venues. Tickets may be ordered from a ticket agency or bought at the box office two days in advance (closed Monday). Information can also be had there about the **Roma Opera Ballet**, which also has its home in the Teatro dell'Opera. Note that *esaurito* means 'sold out.'

There's also excellent professional **orchestral** and **chamber music**. Churches such as the Anglican St. Paul's Within the Walls often sponsor concerts, and there are many small chamber concerts around the city, and outdoors during the summer.

- **Accademia Nazionale di Santa Cecilia** puts on orchestral and chamber concerts in its auditorium in Via della Conciliazione 4, near the Vatican (tel: 68 80 10 44; credit card reservations: 39 38 72 97). In summer, performances are held in Villa Giulia.
- **Accademia Filarmonica Romana**: Via Flaminia 118, offers symphonic and chamber music from October-May (tel: 32 01 752; box office: 32 34 890). Summer festivals. Dance troupes. Closed most of August.
- **La Sapienza**: Piazzale Aldo Moro 5, at Rome University (info. tel: 36 10 051). A wide range of classical concerts, evenings or afternoons, at the Aula Magna of the University. Tickets may

be reserved through Instituzione Universitario dei Concerti (IUC): Lungotevere Flaminio 50 (tel: 36 10 052). Reduced prices for students and children.

- **Oratorio del Gonfalone**: Via del Gonfalone 32, off Via Giulia, offers baroque, medieval and choral music (tels: 68 75 952; 47 70 46 64).
- **Concerti del Tempietto**: Piazza Campitelli 9 (tel: 48 14 800). Summer season has outdoor concerts starting at 9:00 pm. Tickets may be purchased two hours before the performance. In case of rain, concerts are held at S. Nicola in Carcere.

# MODERN MUSIC

For music events, look in the weekly publications, as well as checking the ticket agencies, which also have up-to-date information. Rock concerts are most often held at the Foro Italico, at the Stadio Flaminio in the Villaggio Olimpico, or in EUR at the Palazzo dello Sport.

Although rock music is popular, Italian groups generally incorporate their own distinctive Mediterranean rhythm. If Rome itself doesn't seem on the cutting edge of modern music, many international groups come through for concerts, and there are night spots that showcase live jazz, blues, rock, Caribbean and Brazilian. There are quiet piano bars, noisy discos, nightclubs, and dance clubs, and there are some nightspots that call themselves clubs, but which only charge a nominal fee to avoid the bureaucracy of liquor licenses. Generally the night spots charge an **ingresso più consumazione** (cover charge, including the first drink), that varies with the establishment, the event and the day of the week. The 'in' spots change, of course, but those below were popular at the time of writing.

- **Alexanderplatz**: Via Ostia 9, in Prati (tel: 39 74 21 71). Live music. Traditional jazz hangout. Bands change frequently. Moderately priced restaurant. Closed Sunday.

- **Alien**: Via Velletri 17, near Nomentana (tel: 84 12 212). Raucous rock disco. Alien-style high tech strobe lighting and a raised catwalk in one room; another has a dance floor for more mellow music. Closed Monday.
- **Alpheus**: Via del Commercio 36 (tel: 57 47 826). A variety of live music in three venues, a cabaret, a restaurant and a garden. Rock, funk, rhythm 'n' blues. From Thursday to Sunday, there's also salsa.
- **Big Mama**: Via S. Francesco a Ripa 18, in Trastevere (tel: 58 12 551). Live music; home of the blues in Rome.
- **Gilda**: Via Mario de' Fiori 97, near Piazza di Spagna (tel: 67 84 838). Disco and nightclub with live music and guest performances. Piano bar. Moderately expensive restaurant. Closed Sunday, Monday and summer.
- **Il Locale**: Vicolo del Fico 3, near Piazza Navona (tel: 68 79 075). Live music in a hot jazz club.
- **Jive**: Via Giuseppe Libetta 7, near Ostiense (tel: 57 45 989). Live and disco jazz, Italian music, famous singers. Fusion, blues.
- **Joy**: Via Massaciuccoli 35, off Viale Eritrea (tel: 86 21 02 25). Tiny establishment but the music is hot. Revivals, Latin music.

- **New Open Gate**: Via San Nicolò da Tolentino 4, off Via Barberini (tel: 48 24 464). Popular disco and cocktail bar. Closed Sunday and July–September.
- **Piper:** Via Tagliamento 9, near Parioli (85 55 398). First Roman disco. Concerts, videos and on Wednesday nights a roller disco. A younger crowd. Sunday afternoons there's music for children.
- **St. Louis Music City**: Via del Cardello 13, off Via Cavour (tel: 47 45 076). Live music, from traditional to jazz to rock; frequent visiting groups. Moderately priced restaurant. Closed Monday and summer.
- **Radio Londra**: Via di Monte Testaccio 67 (tel: 57 50 04). A disco and bar with something for everybody, gays or straight. Several levels, outdoor terrace.
- **Yes Brasil**: Via San Francesco a Ripa 103, in Trastevere (tel: 58 16 267). Live Latin music in a club that stays open late. Closed Sunday.

## Cocktail Bars

For more quiet entertainment — such as conversation — try **Mediterraneo** in Vicolo del Cinque 15 (tel: 58 03 630). **Hemingway** in Piazza delle Coppelle 10, near the Pantheon, is a popular, attractive bar/restaurant that offers deep, comfortable seats and an intimate atmosphere (tel: 68 64 490). **Le Cornacchie** in Piazza Rondanini 53 is a good cocktail bar, also serving light foods such as sandwiches, salads and ice cream (tel: 68 64 485). And many of the popular daytime bars such as **Caffè della Pace**, mentioned previously, become fashionable in the evenings.

## Social Centres

A new phenomenon are the **centri sociali**: impromptu, almost underground, groups that organise various evening activities, from showing films and putting on plays, to classical and dance music, rock and reggae, to exercise classes, lectures, courses in Italian for foreigners, or even drug counselling sessions. Most of the venues are slightly outside the city centre, such as in Ostiense, Monte Sacro or Testaccio, and sites change. See *Roma C'è*, daily newspapers and posters around the city for the most up-to-date-listings.

# FILMS

Foreign films in Italy are dubbed, not subtitled, so don't expect to hear dialogue in English, unless there's a *versione originale*. Theatres listed below regularly schedule English-language films, as do the cineclubs **Il Labirinto** in Via Pompeo Magno 27 (tel: 32 16 283), **Azzurro Scipioni** in Via degli Scipioni 8 (tel: 39 73 71 61), both in Prati, and **Grauco Cineclub** in Via Perugia 34 (tel: 70 30 01 99), which charge a small membership fee. The **British Council** has a schedule of English films. **Palazzo delle Esposizioni** in Via Nazionale 194 is a multimedia arts centre (tel: 48 85 465); it hosts exhibitions and international films. There is also a new multi-screen complex near Cinecittà in Via dei Narcisi, with access for the disabled.

Film tickets currently cost L12,000; there is a **tariffa ridotta** for disabled persons and senior citizens, and in some theatres the price is reduced on Wednesdays. Note that cinemas open around 4:00 pm, and that there are usually three screenings per evening. In the summer there are often film festivals, with both classic and recent films shown outdoors. The newspapers have daily listings, as do the weekly events guides, and posters display current venues.

- **Alcazar**: Via Cardinal Merry del Val 14, in Trastevere (tel: 58 80 099). English-language films Monday.
- **Augustus**: Corso Vittorio Emanuele 203 (tel: 68 75 455). *Versione originale* films on Tuesday.
- **Greenwich 1, 2 & 3**: Via Giovanni Battista Bodoni 59, in Testaccio (tel: 57 45 825). Multi-screen cinema showing a variety of international films.

- **Majestic**: Via SS. Apostoli 20, just off the Corso (tel: 67 94 908). First-run English language films on Monday.
- **Nuovo Sacher**: Largo Ascianghi 1, in Trastevere (tel: 58 18 116). *Versione originale* films on Monday and Tuesday.
- **Pasquino**: Vicolo del Piede 19, in Trastevere (tel: 58 03 622). English-language cinema. Closed August. In early summer the roof rolls back.
- **Rouge et Noir**: Via Salaria 31, east of Villa Borghese (tel: 85 54 305). Weekly *versione originale* films.

# GAY AND LESBIAN ROME

Although there is a flourishing gay and lesbian community in Rome, it's not as visible as in Bologna, the most open of Italy's cities. In Rome, the headquarters for the national **ARCI-Gay** and **ARCI-Lesbica**, an activist group, is in Via Acciaresi 7 (tel: 41 73 07 52). **Circolo Mario Mieli** in Via Corinto 5 is a multi-service social centre for gays and lesbians (tel: 54 13 985; fax: 54 13 971). Inquire about *Pianta Gay di Roma*, a map and listing for gays in Rome, the annual *Guida Gai* and the monthly magazine *Babilonia*, that has a small section for lesbians.

Lesbians can also contact **Coordinamento Lesbiche Italiano** in Via San Francesco di Sales 1/a, in Trastevere (tel: 68 64 201).

- **L'Alibi**: Via Monte di Testaccio 44 in Testaccio, is one of the most fashionable clubs in Rome (tel: 57 43 448). This three-storey club with an outdoor terrace boasts a mixture of different kinds of music, dancing, and a generally energetic scene. Videos, art and fashion shows, etc. Closed Monday and Tuesday.
- **L'Angelo Azzurro**: Via Cardinal Merry del Val 13, for men and women, is a large centre in Trastevere (tel: 58 00 472). Hours: 10:00 pm-3:30 am; weekends. Friday, women only. Sunday night has added attractions such as shopping and other services.

- **Hangar**: Via in Selci 69, is a long-established gay club, popular, noisy and crowded (tel: 48 81 397). Closed Tuesday. Videos on Monday.
- **New Joli Coeur:** Via Sirte 5, off Viale Eritrea and near Villa Ada, is a disco; for women only Saturday night after 11:00 pm (tel: 86 21 58 27).

# ANNUAL EVENTS AND LEGAL HOLIDAYS

Below is a list of annual festivals, holidays and events in Rome. The dates and venues of many festivals vary from year to year, of course; both *TrovaRoma* and *Roma C'è* will have current information. Legal holidays when the banks are closed are noted. The tourist office will have a booklet detailing the festivals in Lazio.

## January
- **1st – New Year's Day:** *Legal holiday*. Light candles at the Catacombs of Saint Priscilla.
- **6th – Epiphany:** *Legal holiday*. The last day of the festival of Befana in Piazza Navona. The night before is the climax of the fair.
- **17th – Feast of Sant'Antonio Abate:** People bring their pets to be blessed at Sant'Eusebio all'Esquilino, in Piazza Vittorio.
- **21st – Festa di Sant'Agnese:** Blessing and shearing of two lambs to make a woollen cloak for the Pope. In Piazza Navona.
- **All month:** semi-annual sales of clothing, shoes, etc.

## February
As Lent begins, **Carnevale** celebrates Mardi Gras with parades, colourful masks and outrageous costumes. Celebrated wildly in Venice and Viareggio, Rome also hosts street processions, but is mostly noted for its private parties. Traditional pastries served are **bignè, frappe** and **castagnole**.

275

## March

- **9th – Festa di Santa Francesca Romana:** The patron saint of motorists. Blessing of cars, trams, buses, and cars in Piazzale del Colosseo, near the Forum.
- **19th – Festa di San Giuseppe and Father's day:** In Via Andrea Doria, in the Trionfale area. Street stalls, food, music and some sporting events. **Bignè** and **frittelle** are specialties eaten during this time.

## April

**Maundy Thursday:** Pope traditionally washes feet of the poor at the Lateran. There's also a papal mass. English language list of Holy Week events available at the Vatican Tourist Office.

- **Palm Sunday:** Open-air mass at St. Peter's. Palm fronds distributed.
- **Good Friday:** Pope leads 9:00 pm procession of the Cross from the Colosseum to the Palatine. Pope's blessing in many languages.
- **Easter Sunday**: Pope blesses and addresses the crowd at St. Peter's.
- **Easter Monday:** *Legal Holiday*. **Pasquetta** (Little Easter), people take to the hills *(fuori porta)* for picnics.
- **April 21st – Rome's birthday celebration in Piazza del Campidoglio:** Roman candles on the rooftops of the Capitoline and in other areas of the city celebrate the founding of Rome on April 21, 753 BC.
- **Rome Masters:** Golf tournament.
- **April 25th – Liberation Day:** *Legal Holiday*. The day the Allies liberated Italy in World War II. In Rome, there is a ceremony at the Fosse Ardeatine, site of a Nazi massacre of 335 Romans.
- **Festa della Primavera at Piazza di Spagna:** With azaleas blooming in thousands of vases arranged on the steps.

- **International Horse Show at Piazza di Siena in Villa Borghese:** The 'Nations Cup' is the most important event.
- **From April to July:** free concerts by bands in Pincio Park.

## May
- **1st – May Day:** *Legal Holiday*. A workers' holiday, there's usually a loud union-sponsored rock concert in the Lateran district that goes on at length. A special dish served is pecorino cheese and fava beans.
- **Mid-month:** Two-week semi-annual antique fair in Via dei Coronari near Piazza Navona. Lighted torches line streets that have been carpeted; shops stay open late.
- **Fiera di Via Margutta:** An art exhibition in the ateliers of artists in Via Margutta, near Piazza di Spagna.
- **Tennis Championships at the Foro Italico.**
- **25th – Rome International Trade Fair:** At the EUR Fiera di Roma in Via Cristoforo Colombo. A week-long display of Italian products.
- **26th – Rome Motor Show:** Modern and antique cars and motorcycles are displayed in the Pincio.
- **Late May and early June:** Rose Show in the Rose Garden in l'Aventino, in front of the Circo Massimo. Opens when the roses bloom.

## June
- **First Sunday:** Festa della Repubblica: there is a military parade along Via dei Fori Imperiali.
- **Mid month:** Estate Romana begins and runs through August. Outdoor films, rock concerts, classical music.
- **Mid-June – mid-July:** Tevere Expo, a month-long exhibition of Italian products, regional foods and wines, arts and crafts. Stalls are set up on both sides of the river between the

Sant'Angelo and Cavour bridges. Good food and music, entertainment, fireworks and a generally festive atmosphere.

- **23rd-24th – Festa di San Giovanni:** Held in the Lateran district. Midsummer evening festivities, with outdoor restaurants serving snails and porchetta. Dancing, fireworks. The Pope leads a procession into the basilica.
- **29 – Festa di San Pietro e Paolo:** *Legal Holiday*. In Rome only, honouring the city's patron saints. Celebrations at St. Peter's and a street fair near Saint Paul's, in Via Ostiense.

## July

- **Semi-annual sales in the clothing and shoe shops.**
- **Estate Romana:** The annual arts festival continues, with films, concerts, dance, and more.
- **Roma Europa:** The midsummer international modern arts festival including dance performances by European troupes, theatre, films, electronic arts. Look in the media for events and sites which include Villa Medici, The British Council, Palazzo Farnese, Palazzo Falconieri and others.
- **16th – Festa de Noantri:** Starts in Trastevere, and lasts until the end of the month. A famous folk festival, Viale Trastevere is lined with stalls. Processions and entertainment, good food specialties, music, tables outside of restaurants in every piazza.

## August

- **5th – Festa della Madonna della Neve at S. Maria Maggiore:** A 4th-century miraculous snowfall is re-enacted with white flower petals.
- **15th – Ferragosto:** *Legal Holiday*. The Feast of the Assumption, when all of Italy celebrates and everything is closed if it hasn't already for August.

## September

- **Sagra dell'Uva:** Grape festival in the Basilica of Maxentius, in the Forum. A harvest festival with grapes and lots of entertainment, and musicians in period costumes.
- **Crafts fair on Via dell'Orso, off Via della Scrofa:** Selling various gifts, leather products and fashion jewellery.

## October

- **4th – Celebration and religious ceremonies:** Commemorating San Francesco, the patron saint of Italy.
- **The year's second antique fair in Via dei Coronari:** Usually held at the end of September or early October.
- **Film Fest Italia:** An international cinema and TV festival, held in several venues.
- **National golf championship tournament.**
- **Second art exhibition in Via Margutta.**
- **Late October – early November:** Concert and opera season begins.

## November

- **1 – All Saints Day:** *Legal Holiday*. All Saints Day is followed on November 2nd by All Souls Day, with prayers for the dead offered in churches and cemeteries.
- **Late November – Vino Novello:** Wine tasting in Campo de' Fiori.

## December

- **6th-18th – Natale nel Mondo:** International Christmas Today exhibition at the Fiera di Roma, in Via Cristoforo Colombo. Gift items of all sorts, from clothes and jewels to food.
- **8 – Feast of the Immaculate Conception:** *Legal Holiday*. Flowers are brought to the statue of the Virgin Mary in Piazza

di Spagna, and the Pope prays there and at Santa Maria Maggiore.

- **Mid-month–January 6th: – La Befana:** A children's fair in Piazza Navona. Bright lights, lots of excitement. La Befana is a witch who, like **Babbo Natale**, brings presents to children; she occasionally turns up at the fair.
- **22nd – Cottìo del Pesce:** The Mercati Generali in Via Ostiense holds sort of a fish fair, with fish cooked in enormous vats and free samples given all around.
- **24th – Stores and restaurants close early.**
- **24th – Midnight Mass:** St. Peter's, Santa Maria Maggiore and most other churches.
- **25th – Christmas:** *Legal Holiday*. High Mass in St. Peter's. Blessings by the Pope from his balcony at noon. St. Peter's Square decorated for Christmas with a large tree and handsome **presepe** (crèche). Beautifully crafted *presepi* of various sorts are displayed in many churches around the city, one of the most famous and beautiful of the nativity scenes is in S. Maria d'Aracoeli.
- **26th – Feast of St. Stephen:** *Legal Holiday*
- **31st – Feast of San Silvestro:** Around 5:00 pm there is the singing of the *Te Deum* at the Chiesa del Gesù, with the Pope in attendance, along with the Mayor of Rome and other dignitaries.
- **31st – New Year's Eve (*Capodanno*):** An occasion for wild parties all over town, firecrackers, and objects such as old pots and pans tossed out of windows. People drink **spumante italiano** or champagne, and eat **zampone con le lenticche** (pig's feet with lentils), the lentils signifying financial success in the new year.

# CHAPTER SIXTEEN

# RELIGION

## THE CATHOLIC CHURCH

A person could go to a different Catholic church in Rome each day and at the end of the year still need at least another year to have seen them all. With more than 700 churches — famous and unknown, grandiose and humble — it is clear in every street how much the Catholic Church dominates in Rome. Yet although it is said that fewer than 10% of Romans attend mass regularly, some 99% of the population affirms itself to be Catholic. **The Vatican**, an independent state created in 1929 by the Lateran Treaty between the Church and Mussolini's Italy, is a vital part of the everyday workings of the city, whether it is Romans themselves or tourists using the Vatican's post office and pharmacy, the Pope coming to San Giovanni in Laterano, his cathedral in Rome, or whether it is the number of clergy one sees throughout the city, here on training, business, or other matters pertaining to their religious vocation.

Vatican City itself occupies 108 acres, less than half a square mile. Like any state, however, it has its own army, police force, and laws. It has its own radio and television stations, and its newspaper, *L'Osservatore Romano*, contains the official word from the Holy See. The **Information Office for Pilgrims and Tourists** is in St. Peter's Square (tel: 69 88 48 66). Hours are 8:30 am-7:00 pm, daily. It publishes a calendar of events for Holy Week, as well as offering free informational brochures and pamphlets and handouts concerning Vatican and papal activities.

Every Sunday that the Pope is in residence he appears at a window at noon to address the crowd in St. Peter's. There is also a general Papal audience on Wednesdays at 11:00 am in St. Peter's Square; in inclement weather, it moves inside into the Aula Paolo VI (Sala Nervi). Free tickets for the indoor blessings may be obtained from the **Prefettura della Casa Pontifica**, by the Portone di Bronzo in the colonnade on the right side of St. Peter's Square (tel: 6982). Inquire also at the English-language Catholic churches listed below. For a private audience with the Pope, apply to your local bishop well in advance of departure.

The **North American College**, a seminary and graduate school for priests, has a **Bishops' Office for U.S. Visitors to the Vatican** in Via dell'Umiltà 30 (tel: 69 00 11; fax: 67 91 448). This 'Audience Office' is a free service that distributes papal audience tickets; inquire weekday mornings or Tuesday afternoon.

## Rome's Historic Churches

Churches of every era and architectural style can be found throughout the city, sometimes built layer upon layer over those that came before. Some, such as the 5th-century **Santa Sabina** in l'Aventino, although restored, still contain parts of the ancient church. Others are built over the original homes of the earliest and secret Christian worshippers, who were allowed to build churches openly only upon the 4th-century conversion of the Emperor Constantine to Christianity. On the side of **Santi Giovanni e Paolo**, for example, one can still distinguish three Roman houses, incorporated in the 4th century into a basilica, and built over the tombs of early Christian martyrs. In the heart of the Centro Storico, **San Lorenzo in Lucina**, constructed 800 years ago to replace an even more ancient Christian church, is said itself to sit atop a spot sacred to Romans who worshipped the goddess Juno. Even **St. Peter's** began as a small shrine for Christian pilgrims just a few decades after the martyrdom of Saint Peter, then became a monument and was finally built into an official basilica after Constantine's conversion. By the Middle Ages, however, having fallen into disrepair, it was rebuilt and consecrated in 1626, more than a thousand years after the building begun by Constantine. Now, some 400 years further on, this historical site of St. Peter's remains the worldwide focal point of the Church. Other churches throughout Rome are of varying histories, ages, and styles, and are worth exploring to understand the intricate braid of history that binds the Catholic Church and Rome.

Because the Church serves all nationalities, both mass and confession can be heard in many languages. Look for the language indicated outside the confessional. The five major basilicas marked with an asterisk below are open all day, unlike other churches that are closed sometime during the afternoons. Confession in English can be heard at the churches listed below.

283

- **\*San Pietro**, in Piazza San Pietro (tel: 69 88 37 12). Although tourists wander around, the Chapel of the Holy Sacrament is reserved for those who want to reflect or pray and is guarded at the entrance to make sure it remains so. Masses are said in many languages, including Latin. The Basilica opens at 7:00 am.

- **\*Santa Maria Maggiore**, on the Esquiline Hill, between Piazza S. Maria Maggiore and Piazza dell' Esquilino (tel: 48 31 95). On the site of a temple to the goddess Juno, the original church — since rebuilt and restored — was constructed in the 5th century, and mass has been said here every day since.

- **\*San Giovanni in Laterano**, in Piazza San Giovanni in Laterano (tel: 69 88 64 33). Begun in the 4th century by the Emperor Constantine, it is the seat of the Pope as Bishop of Rome, and is the official cathedral of Rome. The church has seen much damage over the centuries, the most recent caused by a bomb in 1993, but has been restored.

- **\*San Paolo fuori le Mura**, in Via Ostiense 186 at Piazzale San Paolo (tel: 54 10 341). The basilica was begun by Constantine in AD 314. Enlarged and embellished for centuries, it was elegantly restored after a fire in 1823.

- **\*San Lorenzo fuori le Mura** in Piazzale del Verano 3 (tel: 49 15 11). Named after a Christian martyr who was burned at the stake in AD 258, the original church was begun by Constantine and rebuilt and added to, and in the 8th century incorporated a smaller church nearby. It was damaged by bombs in World War II, but has since been restored.

- **Santa Maria sopra Minerva** in Piazza della Minerva 42 dominates this square near the Pantheon (tel: 67 91 217). The church itself dates from the 13th century and was built on the site of already ancient ruins of a temple dedicated to Minerva, the goddess of wisdom.

- **San Silvestro**: Piazza San Silvestro 1 (tel: 67 97 775). Convenient to all parts of the city centre. Masses are said in English for a multicultural community.

- **San Patrizio**: Via Boncompagni 31 (tel: 48 85 716). The 'Irish' Catholic church.
- **Santi Martiri Canadesi** in Via Giovanni Battista de Rossi 46, between Via Nomentana and Piazza Bologna (tel: 44 23 79 87). The 'Canadian' Catholic church.
- **American Church of Santa Susanna**, in Via XX Settembre 14 at Piazza San Bernardo (tels: 48 82 748; 48 27 510). The 'American' Catholic church.

## JUDAISM

The recent wave of Muslim immigration has displaced Judaism from its traditional position as the second religion in Rome. Said to be the oldest Jewish community in Europe, signs of Jewish presence in ancient Rome are extensive, including ruins at nearby Ostia Antica of a 3rd century synagogue constructed over the ruins of one from hundreds of years before. There is also a depiction of Jewish slaves carrying artifacts on the Arch of Titus in the Forum; the arch was built by Domitian in AD 81 after the Judean campaigns culminated in the fall of Jerusalem in AD 70. For centuries, Jews were prohibited to walk under the arch, but after the establishment of the State of Israel, they danced under it instead.

Jews came to Rome as early as 140 BC as emissaries and as merchants. At the fall of Jerusalem they also came as slaves, but already well-established Jews helped buy their freedom. Many settled in Trastevere, which today still sees an active Jewish community. From the time of the Caesars until the 4th-century conversion of Constantine to Christianity, Roman Jews flourished, and although after that their fortunes varied according to the edicts of particular popes, they managed to maintain their community amidst periodic anti-Semitic rumblings and strictures. In 1492, some Jews expelled from Spain by the Inquisition came to Rome, to a then thriving community. In 1555, however, Pope Paul IV, formerly Grand Inquisitor of the Kingdom of Naples, established the Ghetto and forced all Jews to live in what was an unhealthy, low-lying embankment on the other side of the river. There they stayed through constant persecution until 1848 when the walls came down and the 1870 unification of Italy allowed Jews full civil rights. In World War II, to accommodate Hitler, Mussolini pressed forward with racial laws that had previously been enforced only sporadically. During the German occupation some 8000 Italian Jews disappeared, including some 2000 from Rome. Now there are 15,000 Jews in Rome, although the minority live in the newly-chic Ghetto area. Nonetheless, dominated by the **Chief Synagogue** and maintained by Jewish services and shops, the Ghetto remains the heart of the Jewish community.

There are more than a dozen synagogues, schools of all levels, health organisations and other associations. For information about the Jewish community, call the **Comunità Ebraica** at the synagogue in Lungotevere Cenci 9 (tel: 68 40 061). Also ask at the synagogue for the annually published *Lunario*, which has information on all aspects of Jewish life in Rome.

- **Sinagoga Ebraica**: Lungotevere Cenci 9, near the river at Via Catalana and Via Portico d'Ottavia (tel: 68 40 061). An Italianate synagogue built shortly after the Ghetto walls were torn down after 1870. Women are separated from the men during services, and the service is entirely in Hebrew. Sephardic services are held in the basement. Services are Sunday-Friday at 7:45 am and Saturday at 8:30 am. Plaques on the outside walls of the synagogue commemorate Jews who perished during World War II and the 1982 bombing that is the cause of the constant security that surrounds the synagogue.

- **The Jewish Museum** in the synagogue contains memorabilia and sacred objects from the Roman Jewish community, including a plan of the 1555 ghetto (tel: 68 40 061). Small book shop. Call for opening hours.

- **Sinagoga Ashkenazita** holds Orthodox Ashkenazi services in Via Balbo 33 near Piazza dell'Esquilino (tel: 47 59 881). This is also the centre for the **Oratorio Di Castro**, with Italian services.

## OTHER RELIGIONS

There is a wide variety of religious worship in Rome, perhaps more than one would expect. The Anglican community is becoming quite substantial, and Islam has recently become the second religion in Rome, owing to the new wave of immigration from Africa and the Middle East. In fact, there is a recent and impressive addition to Rome's religious community — an exotic and modern Islamic mosque, focal point for the still-growing Islamic community. Worship times change, especially in summer; check before you go.

Note that the **Joint Planning Committee of the English Language Churches of Rome** meets monthly. Nine English language churches are currently involved, and both pastors and lay people serve on the committee. Contact any of the English language churches for information.

- **Anglican**: All Saints Anglican in Via del Babuino 153 (tel: 36 00 18 81). Entrance in Via Gesù e Maria. Saturday Holy Communion. Sunday Communion and sung Eucharist. First Sunday of the month, sung Matins at 10:30 am, Eucharist at 11:30 am. Sung Evensong on the second and last Sundays.
- **Baptist**: Rome Baptist Church in Piazza di San Lorenzo in Lucina 35, off the Corso (tel: 68 76 652). Sunday morning service and Bible study afterwards.
- **Episcopalian**: St. Paul's in Via Napoli 58, at Via Nazionale (tel: 48 83 339). Weekday and Sunday services and a sung Eucharist.
- **Greek Orthodox**: Via Sardegna 153 (tel: 48 18 820), in Ludovisi. Services are held on Sundays at 10:30 am.

- **International Christian Fellowship**: at St. Paul's, listed above (tel: 86 89 08 82). Sunday afternoon worship.
- **Islam**: Viale della Moschea, north of Parioli (80 82 167). Prayers are held Friday afternoons.
- **Jesus Christ of Latter Day Saints**: the Mormon church. Main office in via Cimone 103 near Monte Sacra (tel: 82 72 708). Services Sunday morning and afternoon. One chapel is in Piazza Canaro 20; call the office for other locations.
- **Lutheran**: Via Toscana 7, off Via V. Veneto (tel: 48 17 519). Services are on Sundays at 10:00 am
- **Methodist**: Ponte Sant'Angelo Methodist Church, in Piazza Ponte Sant'Angelo, Via del Banco di Santo Spirito 3 (tel: 68 68 314). Sunday morning service; communion first Sunday of the month.
- **Presbyterian**: St. Andrew's Church, on Via XX Settembre 7 (tel: 48 27 627). Services are held on Sundays at 11:00 am
- **Russian Orthodox**: Via Palestro 71, off Via XX Settembre (tel: 44 50 729). Services are on Saturday evening and Sunday morning.
- **Seventh Day Adventists**: Lungotevere Michelangelo 7 (tel: 32 12 808). Worship Friday evening and Saturday morning. There are several other locations throughout Rome.

# USEFUL TELEPHONE NUMBERS

## EMERGENCIES AT HOME (Chapter Two)

- Emergency: 113
- Carabinieri (English-speakers): 112
- Fire Emergency: 115
- General Health Emergency: 118
- Electricity Emergency (ENEL): 32 12 200; 16441
- Electricity Emergency (ACEA): 57 51 61
- Water Emergency (ACEA): 57 51 71
- Gas Emergency: 1678/03 020
- Telephone Out of Order: 182
- Telephone Customer Service: 187

## HEALTH EMERGENCIES (Chapter Six)

- General Emergencies (Police): 113
- Pronto Intervento Cittadino (Emergency calls) 118
- Anti-Poison Centers: 49 06 63; 30 54 343
- Croce Rossa (Red Cross) ambulance: 5510
- Guardia Medica (House Calls/Telephone Assistance): 48 26 741
- Soccorso Medico Domiciliare (House Calls): 57 46 265

## TELEPHONE ACCESS NUMBERS (Chapter Nine)
- Italy Country Code: 39
- Rome City Code: 06
- European Directory: 176
- Worldwide Directory: 1790
- Rome Operator/Directory: 12
- Intercontinental Operator: 170
- European Calls Operator: 15
- Toll-free Number Prefix: 167
- General Information: 110
- International Dialing Prefix: 00

## AUTOMOBILE EMERGENCIES (Chapter Ten)
- Traffic Police: 67691
- Highway Patrol: 55441
- Emergency Car Breakdown: 116
- Police Emergency (in English): 112
- Towed Cars: 67 69 838

# THE AUTHOR

Frances Gendlin has held leadership positions in both magazine and book publishing. Formerly she was editor and Publisher of *Sierra*, the magazine of the Sierra Club, a worldwide environmental organisation, and she was the association's Director of Public affairs. As Executive Director of the Association of American University Presses, she represented the 100-member publishing houses to the public, and fostered scholarly publishing interests.

While she was growing up, her family moved several times to different areas of the United States, each with its own characteristics and culture, climate and cuisine. This has led her to appreciate and enjoy new cultures, to wonder about their differences and similarities to her own, and to try and understand them. All her life she has looked forward to travels and new adventures, and to meeting interesting people and making new friends.

Frances Gendlin now lives in San Francisco and owns a free-lance editorial business, *The Right Word*. She evaluates manuscripts, guides and helps writers with their projects, and teaches English and business writing to foreign professionals, both in the United States and abroad. Thanks to the advent of the modem and fax, she can work anywhere in the world she can plug in a computer and use a telephone. She has thus been able to arrange her professional life to accommodate her love of travel. Currently, she feels fortunate to be able to spend part of each year in Rome and Paris.

# INDEX